# THE FAITHFULNESS OF GOD

## DEVOTIONAL STUDIES IN II CHRONICLES

by

## CYRIL J. BARBER

Promise Publishing Co.    Santa Ana CA 92711

# TABLE OF CONTENTS

# Dedicated to

## DAVID AND SHARON CAHN

**"Twin Pillars" of Plymouth Church**

**Whittier, California**

# INTRODUCTION

Soon after I became a Christian, I began reading the Bible. I realized that the church I attended, though it had had a long and enviable history, was in a state of spiritual decline. I did not know why, but I sensed inwardly that I would have to take responsibility for my own spiritual growth. After reading through the New Testament several times, I began to work through the Old Testament. When I came to the Books of Chronicles, I found that it contained similar material to what I had just finished reading in I and II Samuel and I and II Kings.

I asked my pastor about this unexpected repetition, and received the following answer: "Chronicles contains *things added* (i.e., brought together in one place) that could not be comfortably included in the earlier historical books." And with this response, I read through these books once and did not return to them until I began my seminary training. Only then did I find that this approach to the Book(s) of Chronicles had a long and misleading history, and I had deprived myself of much blessing as a result of my neglect of this portion of God's inspired revelation.

In writing this history of the kingdom of Judah, the writer of Chronicles had a special purpose in mind. His emphasis was different from the compiler of the Book(s) of Kings. He used the history of his people to illustrate the *faithfulness of God to His word* (note Psalm 132:11-12), and because He is true to His word, He is trustworthy. And so in interpreting this portion of Scripture, we need to keep in mind the first recipients of this material and the need to continuously remind ourselves of the faithfulness of God.

i

Those to whom this book was read had returned from captivity in Babylonia. Life for them was hard. Their cities lay in ruins, the wall of Jerusalem had been broken down, Solomon's Temple had been destroyed, their houses were in a state of disrepair, and their fields (that had lain fallow for more than half a century) were overgrown with thorns and thistles. They were in desperate need of assurance that God still cared for them. The Chronicler was aware of this and wrote to illustrate the fact that *God is indeed faithful to His spoken and written word, and He rewards faithfulness on the part of His people.*

Some Bible scholars, however, reject the idea that the *theme* of Chronicles is the faithfulness of God. They believe that the purpose of II Chronicles differs from I Chronicles in that its primary focus is the Temple. In support of their thesis, they are quick to point out that II Chronicles begins with the building of the Temple and ends with the decree of Cyrus to rebuild it. They also affirm that the criterion by which the kings of Judah were deemed to have succeeded or failed is to be found in their attitude toward the Temple and their support of its ministry.

At first glance this seems to be a very reasonable hypothesis. It is difficult to maintain, however, for a careful reading of the biblical text reveals that it is David who is repeatedly referred to as the standard by which the reigns of other kings are measured (cf. 11:17; 17:3-4; 20:32; 21:6, 12-13; 22:3; 28:2; 34:2).[1] Furthermore prayer is so prominent in the dedication of the Temple, and indeed throughout the book, that the Temple is overshadowed. And let us not forget the words of the Lord Jesus that

---

[1] It seems preferable to see the Temple as a subordinate theme.

underscore the importance of prayer (Matthew 21:13; cf. Mark 11:17; Luke 19:46).

Chapter 7 is central to the message of Chronicles, and verses 12-16 contain one of the best-known portions in the entire Old Testament. When these verses are read in light of the experience of the exiles who knew that the Temple had been destroyed, it was only prayer that had kept their hope alive (cf. Daniel 9:3ff.).

It is the better part of wisdom, therefore, to see the theme of II Chronicles as a continuation of the theme of I Chronicles, *viz.*, the faithfulness of God to His word, and the assurance that God both hears and answers prayer.

But is there incontrovertible evidence that the theme of I Chronicles is continued in II Chronicles? An incidental bit of evidence that is often overlooked comes from the first word of the Hebrew text of II Chronicles. It is *waw*, "And," and it points unmistakably to the fact that II Chronicles continues I Chronicles. Second Chronicles develops a selective history of the southern kingdom from the death of David to the Babylonian Captivity. Dr. Charles C. Ryrie writes:

> We know that Ezra led a group of exiles back to Palestine in 458 [B.C.] and was concerned about building a true spiritual foundation for the people. To further that purpose the author evidently compiled the Chronicles in order to emphasize the importance of racial and religious purity, the proper place of the law, the Temple, and the priesthood. Thus he omits detailed activities of the kings and prophets, stressing

instead the rich heritage of the people *and* the
blessings of their covenant relationship to God.[2]

We often fail to realize the significance of the
unconditional, unilateral covenants God entered into with
His people. He made different covenants with different
people. The most important of these covenants are the
Abrahamic, Palestinian, Davidic, and the New Covenant.[3]
The unique importance of these covenants becomes
apparent as we construct a rough timeline beginning with
the covenant God entered into with Abraham prior to 2090
B.C. (see Genesis 12:1-3).[4] This covenant was reaffirmed
and enlarged, but never cancelled. Then, nearly seven
centuries later, in 1407 B.C., He instituted the Palestinian
Covenant with the people of Israel in which He reassured
the descendants of the patriarchs that He was giving them
the land of Palestine (Deuteronomy 30:1-10).[5] Again time
passed. Then around 1000 B.C., He made His covenant
with David[6] in which He promised David an enduring
dynasty. David's heirs, however, would only enjoy the
benefits of this covenant if they obeyed His revealed will.

---

[2] C. C. Ryrie, *Ryrie Study Bible, Expanded Edition* (Chicago:
Moody, 1995), 625 (emphasis added). See also *Nelson's New
Illustrated Bible Commentary*, ed. E. Rademacher, R. B. Allen, and H.
Wayne House (Nashville: Nelson, 1999), 532.

[3] For a discussion of the New Covenant (Jeremiah 31:31-34),
see J. D. Pentecost, *Thy Kingdom Come* (Wheaton, IL: Victor, 1990),
164-77. See also Luke 22:20; Hebrews 8:8-12; 10:16-17.

[4] Pentecost, *Thy Kingdom Come*, 51-100.

[5] Pentecost, *Thy Kingdom Come*, 101-23.

[6] Pentecost, *Thy Kingdom Come*, 137-56.

Speaking specifically of Solomon (though His words applied to all of David's descendants), God said to David:

> *"When your days are complete and you lie down with your fathers, I will raise up your descendant after you, who will come forth from you, and I will establish his kingdom. He shall build a house for My name, and I will establish the throne of his kingdom forever. I will be a father to him and he will be a son to Me; when he commits iniquity, I will correct him with the rod of men and the strokes of the sons of men, but My loving-kindness shall not depart from him, as I took it away from Saul, whom I removed from before you. Your house and your kingdom shall endure before Me forever; your throne shall be established forever"* *(II Samuel 7:12-16).*

Though God had said that David's throne would continue *"forever,"* the exiles that had recently resettled in Judah had good cause to question whether the Lord would still honor His word. Hence there was a need for a book like Chronicles.[7] All of this highlights the fact that each king of Judah stood in the line of the theocracy and was responsible to rule over God's people as His chosen representative. The supreme example of such loyal service was King David. That is why, in reading through the Book of Chronicles, we frequently encounter statements like, "He walked in the ways of David" or, "He did not walk in the ways of David."

---

[7] Sometime between 610-578 B.C., Jeremiah assured them that the Lord's covenant with David would never be cancelled (Jeremiah 33:17-21).

# AUTHORSHIP

A question often debated is, "Who wrote Chronicles?" In the Introduction to volume I, we advanced the belief that Ezra was the compiler of Chronicles and, though we will refer to the biblical writer as "the Chronicler," we see no reason to question the long-standing tradition that Ezra wrote this important summary of the history of the people of Judah.

Ezra had been born in Babylonia. He had received his secular schooling as well as his biblical training in that pagan land and after founding an academy for the preservation and propagation of the Scriptures among the Jews scattered throughout the land, he led a group of expatriates back to Judah. By training as well as experience (cf. Ezra 7:10) Ezra was well equipped to compile a work such as the Book of Chronicles. In addition, when he arrived in Judah he had access to Nehemiah's large private library (see the Apocrypha, II Maccabees 2:13. This library included, among other volumes, the Book of the Kings of Israel and Judah [27:7; 35:27; 36:8]; the Book of the Kings of Judah and Israel [16:11; 2:26; 28:26; 32:32]; the Book of the Kings of Israel [20:34; 33:18]; the Annals of the Book of Kings [24:27]; the Book of Nathan; the prophecy of Ahijah; and the visions of Iddo [9:29]; the writings of the prophet Isaiah [26:22]; the sayings of Hozai [33:19)] and Jeremiah's lament for Josiah [35:25]). If Ezra was not the author, who else had the requisite training and resources to trace Judah's history in such fine detail?

In spite of this, the majority of modern scholars have repudiated the idea that Ezra was the author. They have advanced several alternate theories, even asserting that some of the words used in the Book(s) of Chronicles differ from Ezra's vocabulary in the book of Ezra/ Nehemiah. However, they are not agreed as to which words supposedly lie outside Ezra's literary grasp. Others have shown that inasmuch as Ezra had been born in Babylonia, the words that are not found in Ezra/Nehemiah can be accounted for on the basis of different subject matter.

In this connection, we do well to consider Abraham Lincoln's Gettysburg Address. When President Lincoln's Gettysburg Address is compared with his Second Inaugural Address (both speeches discussed the war and were delivered only two years apart), the new words found in the Gettysburg Address account for 51 per cent of the content. Are those who reject Ezra's authorship of the Book of Chronicles prepared to apply the same criteria to Lincoln's Gettysburg Address? If so, then who delivered it?

Obviously such a view is ludicrous. It does reveal, however, the tenuous nature of the position adopted by Bible critics, and there seems to be no valid reason why we should not accept Ezra's authorship.

# OUTLINE

In broad outline, II Chronicles continues the history of the United Kingdom under Solomon (chs. 1-9). It ignores the Northern Kingdom and provides what some regard as a "divine editorial" on the lives and deeds of succeeding kings who sat on David's throne (chs. 10-36). The emphasis is clear. Only those monarchs who subordinated themselves to the revealed will of God received His blessing.

Originally the Book of Chronicles comprised a single scroll. The division of the single scroll into two scrolls took place in the second century B.C. when certain Jewish rabbis translated the Hebrew Old Testament into Greek. Hebrew is a consonantal language. Greek, however, contains vowels and this added significantly to the length of the manuscript. It became necessary, therefore, for the Book of Chronicles to be divided into two parts. Ideally, the life of Solomon should have been included on the same scroll with the life of David, for they were both rulers of the United Kingdom of Israel and Judah. This was not done, for the Chronicler's history was divided roughly at the midpoint, and so the first part of II Chronicles deals with the United Kingdom under Solomon. Only after that do we have information on the Divided Kingdom and a summary of the successive reigns of those who ruled over the Southern Kingdom of Judah.

Here is a brief outline of II Chronicles that continues I Chronicles:

## OF SPECIAL IMPORTANCE

Certain statements give us hints about the things the Chronicler thought important. For example, there is repeated emphasis on the word *"all"* (e.g., *"all the people," "all Israel")*, and there is also frequent mention of words like *"forever"*(e.g., *"I will establish his throne forever"*), the warning not to forsake the Lord or be unfaithful to Him, and the repeated reference to *"seeking God."* Also of significance is the fact that the Chronicler sought to show the relevance of the Word of the Lord (no matter how long ago it was given) to the needs of the remnant that had returned to Judah. This was done with a view to strengthening their faith. His intent was to develop an intrinsic spirituality as opposed to a formal adherence to the ritualistic observance of rites and ceremonies (cf. Isaiah 1:11-17; Mark 7:6-8).

However, a question is often asked, "Of what value is II Chronicles to us?" The Apostle Paul answered that question for us in Romans 15:4, *"For whatever was written in earlier times was written for our instruction, so that through perseverance and the encouragement of the Scriptures we might have hope."* Though the Chronicler's material was written for the people of Judah, the events of their lives were instructive for they grappled with the same kinds of tensions we face today. A rich and rewarding experience awaits us therefore as we seek to master the truths taught in this greatly neglected book.

In the Introduction to I Chronicles I mentioned that having documented matters of history and grammar, et cetera, in my works on I and II Samuel and I and II Kings, my documentation in the Book(s) of Chronicles would avoid unnecessary duplication. I remind my readers of this just in case they wonder why my use of notes is less copious in these books than I have used previously.

It is with regret that I must end on a personal note. In my previous commentaries of Judges, Ruth, I and II Samuel, I and II Kings, and I Chronicles, I provided my own translation of the Hebrew text. I intended to do the same for II Chronicles. My eyesight had been failing for several years and, though I was aware of my growing limitations, I presumed that with perseverance I could still furnish a translation of the Masoretic Text. However, part way through chapter 3, I realized that this would be impossible. Fortunately, before I even began writing this commentary, I read everything I could lay my hands on. This included commentaries, histories and journal articles. I shall to the best of my ability continue to provide a fresh translation of special verses, but I have had to lay aside the painstaking work of translating the entire text. In its place, I have included the text of the New American Standard Bible.

# CHAPTER ONE

# A GOOD BEGINNING

## II CHRONICLES 1:1-17

My wife and I have had a longstanding interest in the history and culture of the people of antiquity. Whether studying the religion and practices of American Indians or visiting religious sites in the Caribbean, we have been fascinated by their conceptions of a "supreme being" (or beings) and the worship ceremonies associated with them. And no less interesting to us has been the Polynesian culture.

On a recent visit to Tahiti, we noticed a large idol-statue in the foyer of the hotel where we were staying. It was quite unlike any we had seen on the different islands for it wore a smile on its face. All the other representations of the gods that at one time had been worshiped by the people invariably had facial expressions that were horrific and reminded us of the cruel and rapacious representations of deities on the island of Hawaii.

One day after returning from a tour, I asked our guide about the Tahitian gods. "Do you know of any that were benign or smiled?" I asked. "No," was his response, "these gods were designed to instill dread in their enemies and compel submission on the part of their followers." I then asked him about the larger-than-life idol in the foyer of the hotel. "Oh that," he said with a broad smile on his face, "that was made recently for the benefit of tourists. It looks old, but it isn't."

As we study the Bible, we find that the God of biblical revelation is totally unlike the deities worshipped by people living in the ancient Near East. His true character is reflected in the passage before us.

## OUTLINE

The biblical writer's outline is easy to follow. We have:

## SOLOMON'S GOOD BEGINNING (1:1-17)

    A. Introduction (1:1)

    B. Solomon's Worship (1:2-6)

    C. Solomon's Wisdom (1:7-13)

    D. Solomon's Wealth (1:14-17)

## SOLOMON'S GOOD BEGINNING

### *Introduction (1:1)*

When David's son, Solomon, was crowned king[1] his brothers and all of the officials of David's court pledged their allegiance to him (I:29:23-35). Even though Solomon's parents had given him the name *"Shelemoh"* (from *shalom*, "peace") at the time of his birth, there was smoldering resentment over the fact that one of David's youngest sons had been chosen to succeed his father. And

---

[1] Solomon reigned from 971-931 B.C. (excluding the year or two he was co-regent with his father).

forgotten by those who opposed his elevation to the throne
of a united Israel (*viz.*, Adonijah, Joab) was the fact that
about two decades earlier, the Lord (speaking through
Nathan the prophet) had given Solomon another name,
"Jedediah" ("Beloved of God"). If anyone remembered
this incident they probably discounted it as the pious
musing of an old man who wanted to encourage the royal
couple with the prospect of God's blessing. And so, as
time passed, less and less attention was paid to what the
Lord had revealed. Now, however, Solomon sat on the
throne of his father.

> *And Solomon the son of David made
> himself strong over his kingdom, and Yahweh his
> God was with him and made him great (1:1).*

Dr. Martin J. Selman, in his excellent study of the
Books of Chronicles, has established a valid connection
between God's blessing of David and the favor He now
showed David's son.

Every phrase in this verse illustrates that David's
blessings continued under Solomon, as indicated by the
addition of *son of David* to the original text (I Kings 2:46*b*).
David had also been *"strengthened"* at the beginning of his
reign (cf. I Ch. 11:10), *God was with him*, had made him
great (I Ch. 11:9), and *made him exceedingly great* (also I
Ch. 29:25). This continuity is not just the result of
instituting a dynasty, but of God keeping His promises
about establishing David's house (cf. vv. 8-9; 2 Ch. 6:3, 10;
I Ch. 17:23-27).[2]

---

[2] M. J. Selman, *2 Chronicles, an Introduction and
Commentary* (Downers Grove, IL: InterVarsity, 1994), 290.

This brief introductory statement covers the early trials of the young king's[3] reign before he began to build the Temple.  During this time Adonijah attempted a coup (I Kings 2:13-46), and Joab and Abiathar were removed from their positions of leadership.  In spite of the opposition Solomon encountered, his kingdom was established with the help of the Lord; and, according to the Oxford historian, Professor George Rawlinson, Solomon's kingdom rivaled the splendor of the courts of Egypt and Assyria.[4]

### Solomon's Worship (1:2-6)

Readers of the parallel record in I Kings 3:4ff. will readily notice a difference in emphasis.  Here the Chronicler emphasizes (1) Solomon's personal relationship with the Lord, as well as (2) his involvement of *"all Israel"* and *"the whole assembly"* in the activities that take place.  Long before leadership styles were divided into *authoritarian*, *permissive*, and *authoritative* categories, Solomon set an example of *proactive inclusion* by taking the initiative and inviting all the leaders of Israel to

---

[3] How old was Solomon at the time of his ascension?  Some writers, following Eusebius, believe that he was not yet twelve years old when he came to the throne.  Josephus believes he was about fourteen (cf. *Antiquities of the Jews*, VIII:7:8).  Most modern writers believe he was born when his father was about fifty, making him twenty at the time he ascended the throne.  This seems reasonable, for he had a son at the time of his coronation (cf. I Kings 11:42 and 14:21.  Solomon ruled for 40 years, and Rehoboam was 41 at the time he succeeded his father).

[4] G. Rawlinson, *The Five Great Monarchies of the Ancient Eastern World* (London:  Murray, 1871), II:235; III:207, 313.

participate with him in the events that were to take place at Gibeon.

> *And Solomon spoke to all Israel, to the heads of thousands, and [to the heads of] hundreds, and to the judges, and to every leader in all Israel, the chiefs of the fathers' [households]. And Solomon and all the assembly with him went to the high place that [was] at Gibeon; for God's tent of meeting was there, that Moses the servant of Yahweh had made in the wilderness. But David had brought up the Ark of God from Kiriath-jearim to the place he had prepared for it, for he had pitched a tent for it in Jerusalem. And the bronze altar, that Bezalel the son of Uri, the son of Hur, had made, was there before the Tabernacle of Yahweh, and Solomon and the assembly sought it out. And Solomon went up to the bronze altar before Yahweh that was at the tent of meeting, and offered on it a thousand burnt offerings (1:2-6).*

Though there had been a deliberate move away from any form of worship on the "high places" (i.e., mountaintops) because of heathen connotations, the high place in Gibeon was an exception. Thomas Kirk, a well-known Scottish preacher of a former generation, wrote:

> Gibeon, which was chosen as the place of thanksgiving, was invested with a particular sacredness on account of its having the Tabernacle that Moses had erected on the wilderness, and the brazen altar that Bazalel the grandson of Hur had made. The Ark, which had belonged to that old Tabernacle till its capture by the Philistines in the closing days of Eli, was now in the Tabernacle which David had erected for it on Mount Zion in

the City of David.... Hence Gibeon and Mount
Zion were then the two grand centres of national
worship. The reason why Solomon gave the
preference to Gibeon may have been to avoid
giving offense to those with whom it was the
favourite place of worship, which was probably
the case with all the tribes other than Judah, and
perhaps because, on account of the preparations
going on at Jerusalem for building the Temple....[5]

The celebrations lasted several days during which
time Solomon offered up a thousand burnt offerings. Some
writers have disputed this number, claiming that such an act
on such a large scale is highly improbable, and that the
figure of one thousand animal sacrifices is in all likelihood
an exaggeration. These critics are either ignorant of or
ignore the fact that Croesus, king of Lydia, sacrificed 3,000
animals at one time, and that Xerxes, king of the Persians,
offered up 1,000 animals at Troy.[6] There is no reason to
doubt the Bible's essential accuracy.

### Solomon's Wisdom (1:7-13)

The Lord was obviously pleased with Solomon's
devotion and his desire to unite *"all Israel"* in following
Him, for He came to Solomon in a dream at night and said

---

[5] T. Kirk and G. Rawlinson, *Studies in the Books of Kings.* 2
Vols. in 1 (Minneapolis: Klock and Klock, 1983), I:62.

[6] Herodotus, *Histories.* Trans. A. D. Godley. Loeb Classical
Library (Cambridge, MA: Harvard University Press, 1963), I:50;
VII:43.

to him, *"Ask what I shall give to you."* And Solomon replied,

> *"You have dealt with my father David with great kindness, and have made me king in his place. Now, O Yahweh God, Your word (i.e., promise) to my father David is fulfilled, for You have made me king over a people as numerous as the dust of the earth. Now give me wisdom and knowledge, that I may go out and come in before this people, for who can rule this great people of Yours?" (1:7-10).*

Verse 7 is unique. There is nothing like it anywhere in the Old Testament. It does, however, set a precedent for Christ's promise in the New Testament when He said,

> *"Ask whatever you wish, and it will be done for you" (John 15:7. Cf. John 14:13-14; 15:16, 23; 16:23, 26; I John 5:14-15; etc.).*

Of importance as we study this passage in II Chronicles is the fact that Solomon first acknowledged God's faithfulness to the promise He had made to David. He had fulfilled His word by making him king over Israel (something that, during the intervening years, may have seemed impossible in light of the fact that others had different ideas of what would be best for the nation). Then Solomon bore testimony to God's faithfulness to the patriarchs by making their descendents as numerous as the dust of the earth, for as he looked out over those assembled at Gibeon, their number could not be counted (cf. Genesis 13:16; 28:14).

Second, Solomon asked the Lord to give him wisdom and knowledge. "Wisdom," *hokma,* looks at a manner of thinking about life's experiences. It covers the whole spectrum of human knowledge, including matters of basic morality, a sagacious approach to secular affairs, moral sensitivity and an understanding of the ways of the Lord.[7] "Knowledge," *madda'*, is frequently found in connection with "wisdom" and denotes the practical application of knowledge gained by experience.

All wisdom begins and ends in the reverential awe of God (Proverbs 1:7; 9:10; 15:33), and is expressed in a submission to His will (Job 28:28; Ecclesiastes 12:13). According to II Kings 4:29-34 Solomon's wisdom included great discernment and breadth of understanding, so that he became wiser than all the learned men of his time. His fame also spread, for his accomplishments embraced botany, literature, biology, ornithology and other branches of science. In time, he came to the attention of learned people in other lands, and they came to discuss their problems with him (I Kings 4:29-34; Ecclesiastes 2:4-9; 12:9-10).

The Lord was evidently pleased with Solomon's desire to lead the people of Israel wisely,[8] for he said:

> *"Because this has been in your heart, and you have not asked [for yourself] riches, wealth, or honor, or the life of those who hate you, nor*

---

[7] *Theological Wordbook of the Old Testament*, eds. R. L. Harris, G. L. Archer, Jr., and B. K. Waltke. 2 vols. (Chicago: Moody, 1980), I:282-84 (#647*a*).

[8] Because a king's judicial functions placed him in the role of being both judge and jury, many successors to the throne were trained for the task (cf. Xenophon, *Cyropaedia*, 7 vols. in 2. Trans. W. Miller. Loeb Classical Library (Cambridge: Harvard University Press, 1968), I:3:16-18.

*have you even asked for long life, but you have*
*asked for yourself wisdom and knowledge that you*
*may judge My people over whom I have made you*
*king, wisdom and knowledge have been given to*
*you, and I will give you riches and wealth and*
*honor, such as none of the kings who [were]*
*before you [possessed] nor those who will come*
*after you" (1:11-12).*

These verses serve as an Old Testament illustration of two truths taught in the New Testament: (1) Christ's statement that we should *"seek first the kingdom of God and His righteousness, and then all these things will be added to us"* (Matthew 6:33); and (2) Paul's promise that *"God is able to do exceeding abundantly beyond all that we ask or think, according to the power that works in us"* (Ephesians 3:20).

In response to Solomon's request, the Lord gave him immeasurably more than he asked for, and a brief look ahead at the closing verses of this chapter gives some indication of the extent to which the Lord fulfilled His word.

The Chronicler does not tell us how the Lord communicated with Solomon. There were three ways in which God spoke to people in Old Testament times: dreams, visions and face to face. The text of I Kings 3 informs us that *"Solomon awoke"* and so we conclude that all of this came in the form of a dream. But how do we know that this wasn't the wishful thinking on the part of the young king or the effects of too much rich food the night before? Perhaps some indication of what took place is to be found in Acts 7:2. There, Stephen informs us that *"the God of glory"* appeared to Abraham and told him to leave Ur and journey to Canaan. And when the Lord Jesus appeared to Saul (later called Paul) on the road to Damascus, Saul saw a light brighter than the sun (Acts 9:3) and knew instinctively that it was God who spoke to him (Acts 22:6-7). It is possible that when the Lord appeared to Solomon he was not only conscious of the words spoken to him but also of an intense bright light attesting to the presence of the Lord.

Solomon was profoundly influenced by all that the Lord had said to him, and as soon as it was possible for him to leave Gibeon, he did so. He went to the Tabernacle in Jerusalem where, in a far more private ceremony, he offered up burnt offerings and thank offerings. He also made a great feast for his "servants" (i.e., court officials. I Kings 3:15).

### Solomon's Wealth (1:14-17)

This paragraph shows us that God made good His promise to Solomon.

Solomon amassed chariots and horsemen. He had 1,400 chariots and 12,000 horsemen, and he stationed them in the chariot cities and with the king at Jerusalem. The king made silver and gold as plentiful in Jerusalem as stones, and he made cedars as plentiful as sycamores in the lowland. Solomon's horses were imported from Egypt and from Kue; the king's traders procured them from Kue for a price. They imported chariots from Egypt for 600 shekels of silver apiece and horses for 150 apiece, and by the same means they exported them to all the kings of the Hittites and the kings of Syria.

First, Solomon realized that a powerful standing army was his nation's best defense. To maintain the peace of his people, he amassed chariots and horsemen and stationed them in strategic places throughout the land. Other nations would think twice before making war with Israel, for any kind of hostile action could only be undertaken at great cost to themselves.

Second, by controlling the trade routes[9] and imposing tariffs on goods being conveyed through the land of Israel via caravans from the east or the west, north or south, Solomon brought considerable wealth to his people.

Third, Solomon also assessed the need to maintain the balance of power among the other countries of the Near East. If their military strength was comparable, wars could be avoided, for their outcome was unpredictable. He saw that Israel was strategically situated to meet the needs of these countries, and that by strengthening these nations Israel could benefit economically. To further improve his nation's economy he imported horses and chariots from Egypt and Kue (possibly Cilicia) to the south and exported them to the Hittites and Syrians (Arameans) to the north. Thus strengthened, these nations could keep at bay their hostile neighbors (while also forming a buffer for Israel.)

The result of Solomon's wise administration was that *"silver and gold become as plentiful in Jerusalem as stones,"* and the people were able to panel their houses with wood.[10] The Chronicler's use of hyperbole in verse

---

[9] See *The Macmillan Bible Atlas*, eds. Y. Aharoni and M. Avi-Yonah, revised by A. F. Rainey and Z. Safrai (3d ed., New York: Macmillan, 1993), #s 9-12, and especially 115. See text on p. 88 of the atlas.

[10] See M. Zohary, *Plants of the Bible* (Cambridge: Cambridge University Press, 1982), 68-69.

15 paints a vivid pen-picture for us and illustrates the extent to which Solomon's wise administration brought wealth to his people.[11]

## THE IMPORTANCE OF A STRONG GODWARD RELATIONSHIP

*Reflection on the contents of this chapter reveals several important facts. David had trained Solomon to be his successor, and Solomon shared many of the positive traits his father had possessed. Of paramount importance was a strong, internal Godward relationship. The Chronicler was aware of this and began his treatment of the young king's reign with his worship of the Lord at Gibeah. And such was Solomon's desire to continue the godly leadership begun by his father that he involved "all Israel" in the event.*

Sometime during the festivities, God appeared to him and offered him whatever he wished. In Solomon's response, we have his spontaneous prayer. And while it is brief, it is also significant. It illustrates an important aspect of his Godward relationship (cf. Psalm 34:11-22). He wanted to do what was right and needed wisdom to know how to act righteously and dispense justice with equity.

In the events that took place at Gibeon, we have an *example* of the way in which we should pray for our needs. Solomon was aware of his lack of experience. He spoke of himself as a *"little child."* This is a Hebraism that we are

---

[11] Solomon is not universally praised. As capable a Bible scholar as H. F. Vos indicts him for his lack of wisdom in a variety of different areas, see *Nelson's New Illustrated Bible Manner and Customs* (Nashville: Nelson, 1999), 167.

to understand metaphorically, not literally. He already possessed great gifts, but instead of being animated by a proud spirit of self-sufficiency, he was humble before the Lord and spoke of his inadequacies (e.g., youthfulness, inexperience). Then, when the Lord gave him what amounted to a "blank check," all Solomon asked for was for a wise and understanding heart so that he might judge God's people righteously. And the Lord responded by giving him far more than he expected. He not only gave him wisdom so that he became the wisest of all men of all time, but He gave to him in abundant measure the things he did not ask for.

We frequently experience difficulty in prayer. Solomon's example reminds us that the Lord is able to do exceeding abundantly above all that we ask or think (Ephesians 3:20). It also puts us in mind of God's impartiality. When He revealed His will through James, Christ's brother, He said that if any of us lack wisdom we should ask God for it, for He gives to all liberally and does not withhold His blessings. Then He added a word of assurance: *"And it shall be given him"* (James 1:5).

God also promised Solomon length of days if he continued faithful to all that He commanded him. Scripture affirms that, in his youth, Solomon was devoted to the Lord, loved Him with all his heart and walked in His statutes (I Kings 3:3). Sadly, as Solomon grew older, his ardor cooled. He made some tragic mistakes, and eventually died at about age 60. However, before he departed this life, he apparently repented of his waywardness and penned the Book of Ecclesiastes. This great testament to Solomon's quest for happiness ends with a wise admonition to *"fear God"* and serve Him (Ecclesiastes 12:13-14).

In conclusion, let us observe that in answering Solomon's prayer for wisdom, God did so in a way that permitted Solomon's sagacity to be seen in every department of life. It pervaded his thoughts and actions, his judicial decisions and his writings. It enabled him to raise his country to a height of wellbeing and prosperity never again equaled by any of his successors, and he did so by peaceful means. He knew the value of a powerful standing army, and he acted decisively so as to insure his people's safety. Then he established trade policies so that Israel used its strategic position to its advantage. He also insured that all goods exported brought a profit, and that goods and materials imported never exceeded what the nation exported.

Solomon began well. The primary thrust of his reign was the building of the Temple, and this will be the focus of our next chapter.

# CHAPTER TWO

# FULFILLMENT OF A DREAM

II CHRONICLES 2:1-5:1

A devout Christian couple, James and Amelia Taylor, wanted to have children. One cold winter's night they sat by the fire in a room behind the pharmacy in which they worked and prayed, "Dear God, if You should give us a son, grant that he may work for You." They firmly believed the teaching of the Old Testament that the firstborn child in a family belonged to the Lord (Exodus 13:2), and they were concerned that their son (if they should have one) early yield his heart to the Lord and serve Him devotedly all the days of his life.

God heard their prayer, and in mid-spring the following year their son was born. They named him James after his father and also gave him his mother's maiden name, Hudson. From young James' earliest years, his parents impressed upon him the importance of dedicating his life to Christ and serving Him in some special way. And years later, he would recall his father's admonition to him to "Learn to love your Bible."

Young James, having been dedicated to the service of the Lord even before he was born, grew to adulthood with a strong desire to fulfill some special mission. His father was an avid student of history, and he had read all he could find on the ancient civilizations of Persia, Greece and Rome. It was the history of China, however, that fascinated him most of all. Whereas the great civilizations of Persia, Greece and Rome had arisen, peaked and gone into decline, the Chinese Empire had remained. And to him it was a shameful thing that during his lifetime no Protestant missionary had gone to that land.

With an atmosphere of true godliness pervading the home, and with James' father and friends talking "theology, sermons, politics, [and] the Lord's work at home and abroad" after dinner, we are not surprised that a deep impression was made on the young lad. In the course of time, James Hudson Taylor committed himself to starting a mission in China. By the time he set sail for the Far East, he had married a young woman who was also dedicated to the cause of missions, and together they brought many Chinese people to know Jesus Christ as their Savior.

This is only one story, and if time and space permitted it could be multiplied many times over. It does serve to underscore the fact that parents exert a remarkable influence on their children. Elkanah and Hannah molded the life of their son, Samuel, whom the Lord gave them in answer to Hannah's prayer. From his earliest years, he had a sense of mission that did not desert him through his many years of ministry to the nation of Israel. And David and Bathsheba did likewise. They impressed upon Solomon God's choosing him to build the Temple and, as soon as Solomon had been crowned king, he began this important work. Though the actual erection of the Temple did not begin for four years, we may be sure that Solomon was busy preparing for its construction. Then, when the time came, he could build the Temple without time-consuming delays.

Some will ask, "How may we impress on our children a similar sense of their calling?" The process is three-fold and involves *involvement, modeling* and *instruction*—all three. David and Bathsheba spent time with their children (note carefully David's instructions contained in Psalm 34:11-22). They also would have impressed on Solomon the honor of God's selection of him for this special task. Initially it would have been natural for him to wonder how he could ever orchestrate such a difficult assignment. But as his parents gave him the opportunity to express his misgivings and reassured him of the Lord's help, his confidence grew. And over the years his commitment to the project increased.

In like manner, parents today can, and indeed should, spend time with their children. Children are special (I Corinthians 7:14b; Ephesians 1:4; I Peter 2:4), and it is a parent's responsibility to mold each young life.

As Solomon grew toward young manhood his sense of identity and mission increased. His prayers (II Chronicles 1 and 6) show that he had accepted the task of building the Temple as having been given him by God, and though he was aware of his youthfulness and the difficulties he faced, he carried out the work with humility and an absence of pride.

## OUTLINE

Chapters 2:1 to 7:22 form a unit and may be outlined as follows:

## THE TEMPLE OF THE LORD (2:11-7:22)

1. The Construction of the Temple (2:1-5:1)

2. The Dedication of the Temple (5:2-7:22).

We will deal with the building of the Temple in this chapter and treat its dedication in our next chapter.

### CONSTRUCTION OF THE TEMPLE (2:1-5:1)

For several years prior to his death, David had been preoccupied with making provision for building a Temple in honor of the Lord his God. He had set aside a vast amount of material from his spoils of war, and when the sun began to set on his long and eventful life, he gave an official charge to Solomon:

> *"Now behold, in my affliction I have prepared for the house of the Yahweh: of gold 100,000 talents, and of silver1,000,000 talents, and of the bronze and the iron there is no weighing, for it is in great quantity; also timber and stone I have prepared, and you may add to them. And, there are many workmen (lit. 'doers of work') with you-stonecutters and masons of stone and wood, and all [men] who are skillful in every kind of work" (I Chronicles 22:14-15).*

Then, shortly before his death, David spoke to the leaders of the nation. He challenged them to give liberally to the adornment of the Temple, and set an example by adding to what he had already set aside.

> *"Moreover (lit. 'and also'), because I delighted in the house of my God, the treasure I have of gold and silver, I give to the house of my*

*God, even more than all that I have already
provided for the house of the sanctuary (i.e., the
holy temple), [namely] 3,000 talents of gold, of the
gold of Ophir, and 7,000 talents of refined silver,
to overlay the walls of the buildings. Of gold for
the things of gold and of silver for the things of
silver, [and] for all the work done by the hand of
skilled workers. Who then is willing to consecrate
himself (lit. 'his hand') this day to the [Temple of]
Yahweh?" (I Chronicles 29:3-5).*

When David died and Solomon sat on his throne, he
immediately made preparations to build the Temple.
Because the noise of hammer and axe and chisel was not to
be heard during its construction, everything was prepared at
specific places some distance from Jerusalem (I Kings 6:7).
A visitor to these sites would have observed literally
thousands of people working at different tasks.  Overseers,
with the equivalent of modern blueprints, could be seen
assigning to special groups of workers the responsibility of
either quarrying or preparing stones of a particular size and
shape, or cutting wood for boards, beams or panels.  When
all was prepared, the materials were transported to
Jerusalem.

The site of the Temple had already been determined
(I Chronicles 22:1), and though the Temple itself would not
be large by the standards of today, it would be twice the
size of the Tabernacle that had been erected by Moses.

## Preparations for the Temple (2:1-18)

Initially Solomon raised a levy[1] of men to do the
work. Seventy thousand men were to carry the material,
80,000 were to quarry stone from the mountains, and 3,600
were to supervise the work. But Solomon also needed
highly trained artisans and so he sought help from Huram
(spelled Hiram in the Book of Kings), King of Tyre. He
sent the following letter to him by the hand of one of his
ambassadors:

> As you dealt with David my father, and
> sent him cedars to build him a house to live in, [so
> deal with me]. Behold, I am building a house to
> the name of Yahweh my God, to dedicate to Him,
> to burn before Him fragrant incense (lit. the
> smoke of perfume] and to set out continually the
> showbread, and [to offer] burnt offerings morning
> and evening, on sabbaths and on new moons and
> on the appointed feasts of Yahweh our God, [this
> being required] forever in Israel. And the house
> which I am building [will be] great, for greater
> [is] our God than all the gods. But who is able to
> build a house for Him, since the heavens and the
> highest heavens (lit. 'heavens of heavens') cannot
> contain Him? So who [am] I, that I should build a
> house for Him, except to burn incense before
> Him? And now, send me a man skilled to work in
> gold, silver, bronze and iron, and in purple, and

---

[1] See A. Kapelrud, *Orientalia* 32 (1963), 56-62; N. Avigad,
*Israel Exploration Journal* 30 (1980), 170-73; I. Mendelsohn, *Bulletin
of the American Schools of Oriental Research* 167 (1962), 31-35; idem,
*ibid* 85 (1942), 14-17; A. Rainey, *Israel Exploration Journal* 20 (1970),
191-202. Cf. Herodotus, II:124.

*crimson, and violet [fabrics], and knowing how to*
*engrave engravings, [to work] with the skilled*
*men who [are] with me in Judah and Jerusalem,*
*whom David my father provided. And send me*
*also cedar, cypress and algum[2] timber from*
*Lebanon, for I know that your servants know how*
*to cut the trees of Lebanon; and indeed my*
*servants will work with your servants, to prepare*
*timber in abundance for me, for the house that I*
*am about to build [will be] great and wonderful.*
*And behold, I will give to your servants, the*
*woodsmen who cut the timber, 20,000 kors of*
*crushed wheat and 20,000 kors of barley, and*
*20,000 baths of wine and 20,000 baths of oil (2:3-*
*10).*

Solomon's opening remarks appear tentative.[3]  A
quick survey of his letter reveals that it contains two
requests. These are marked by the repeated use of *"send
me"* (2:7, and 8-10). The majority of Bible scholars are of
the opinion that a treaty existed between Israel and Tyre,
and that Israel was in effect the "senior partner."[4] It is
more likely that the treaty between David and Huram was a
"parity treaty," with each partner being equal. Solomon's

---

[2] The identity of "algum" is uncertain. See M. Zohary, *Plants
of the Bible* (New York:  Cambridge University Press, 1982), 125; and
J. C. Greenfield and M. Mayrhofer, *Supplement to Vetus Testamentum*
16 (1967), 83-89. Algum was evidently a precious wood used in
making furniture.

[3] For a discussion of ancient letter writing, see D. Pardee,
*Journal of Biblical Literature* 97 (1978), 321-46.

[4] E.g., McConville, *I & II Chronicles*, 115.

words, *"As you have dealt with David my father ..."*[5]
would seem to tacitly ratify this treaty while also requesting
the things he needed in order to build the Temple.

Solomon states that the Temple to be built will be
*"for the **name** of Yahweh,"* and he assumes that Huram
will be familiar with all that this expression implies.
Basically, whenever we come across the phrase *"the **name**
of Yahweh,"* it implies all that He is (i.e., the totality of His
being. Cf. Exodus 3:13-14). This is a sobering thought
when we realize that we often conclude our prayers *"in
Jesus name"* (for we are praying in recognition of all that
He is, was and will be).

With great humility Solomon emphasizes the
omnipresence of God who inhabits eternity, and is
worshipped by his people. He cannot be confined within a
building. But if this is impossible, why is Solomon going
to all the trouble and expense of building Him a Temple?
Solomon answers this natural question by pointing out that
this Temple is to serve as a place in which God's people
can worship Him.

To erect this building, however, Solomon needs
help. His first request is for a skilled craftsman who will
work with Israelites to prepare the materials and build the
Temple. The Chronicler specifies the skills required. Then
he details the payment: *"Now behold, I will give to your
servants, the woodsmen who cut the timber, 20,000 kors of
crushed wheat and 20,000 kors of barley, and 20,000 baths
of wine and 20,000 baths of oil."* This catalog of

---

[5] F. C. Fensham, *Vetus Testamentum Supplement* 17 (1968),
71-87.

Solomon's payment for "services rendered" is important as we shall see shortly.

Huram's reply to Solomon's letter is most interesting. A careful reading of it will reveal that the Chronicler has excerpted only those details that further the point he wishes to make:

> *Then Huram, King of Tyre, replied in writing to Solomon: "Because Yahweh loves His people, He has made you king over them"[6]. And Huram continued (lit. 'said'), "Blessed be Yahweh, the God of Israel, who has made heaven and earth, who has given to King David a wise son, endowed with discretion and understanding, who will build a house for Yahweh and a royal palace for himself (lit. 'his kingdom'). And now I have sent Huram-abi [7], a skilled man, endowed with understanding. [He is] the son of a woman of the daughters of Dan, and a man of Tyre, who knows how to work in gold, silver, bronze, iron, stone and wood, in purple, violet, linen and fine*

---

[6] First, such expressions of "love" were not unusual in ancient Near Eastern treaties, cf. W. Moran, *Catholic Biblical Quarterly* 25(1963), 77-87; and second, Huram may well have been aware of the problems Solomon faced as he succeeded his father and wrote to encourage him.

[7] In the Book of Kings this craftsman is simply referred to as Hiram (1 Kings 7:13, 40, 45), the same name as the king. Here the word *abi* is added. Was this a part of Huram's name or a title? *Abi* means "my father." Huram could have held the same relation to the king as Joseph held to Pharaoh, king of Egypt (Genesis 45:8), or *abi* could have been a title corresponding to "master craftsman." This latter suggestion seems most likely, for toward the end of the list of things he made he is spoken of simply as "Huram."

*linen, and in crimson, and who knows how to
make all kinds of engravings and to execute (lit.
'invent') any design that may be assigned to him,
to work with your skilled men and [with] the
skilled men of my lord David your father. And
now, let my lord send to his servants wheat and
barley, oil and wine, of which he has spoken. And
we will cut timber from Lebanon, according to
your need, and bring it to you [on] rafts by sea to
Joppa; and you shall carry it up to Jerusalem"
(2:11-16).*

Although this is sufficiently straightforward, Bible
critics have imagined certain discrepancies in the text. The
first has to do with the identity of Huram-abi's mother, and
the second concerns the matter of payment.[8]

In King Huram's letter, his master craftsman is
described as "the son of a woman of Dan," whereas in I
Kings 7:14 he is referred to as the *"son of a widow woman
of Naphtali."* The apparent contradiction is easily
explained. Huram-abi was a native of Tyre. His mother was
a Danite who had married a man of the tribe of Naphtali.
When her husband died she became *"a widow of the tribe
of Naphtali."* Later she married a man of Tyre, and
became the mother of Huram-abi, the famous artisan.

---

[8] A third supposed discrepancy has to do with the number of
workers. Kirk, *Studies in the Books of Kings*, I:87-90, has ably
correlated the accounts of Kings and Chronicles and has shown that
when the nationality of the workers is kept distinct from matters of
authority, the numbers of people comprising the levy are
complimentary and not contradictory.

The second matter has to do with remuneration. In II Chronicles 2:10, the Chronicler states that Solomon will give to Huram's *workers* a specified quantity of food. In I Kings 5:11, Solomon agrees to pay the King of Tyre a certain quantity of the food *"year by year."* The two statements are very different. It is not necessary to suppose a corrupt text, for both statements are accurate. One way to account for the difference is to note the difference between the compensation given the hewers of wood, and that which was specifically designated for the household of King Huram.[9]

This is a plausible explanation and shows that the problems imagined by the Bible's critics can easily be explained.

### The Building of the Temple (3:1-5:1)

When all of preparations have been made, Solomon is ready to begin to build the Temple. This segment of text is marked off by the words *"Solomon began to build..."* (3: 1) and *"thus the House of Yahweh was finished"* to (5: 1).

The day when the foundation stones were laid must have been a most memorable one. We are told it was in the month of April/May, 966 B.C. And the location, *"on Mount Moriah,"* was the very spot where the Lord had sent down fire from heaven to consume David's sacrifice (I:21:18, 26). It was also on the very site where, at an earlier time, Abraham had offered up Isaac (cf. Genesis 22:2).

---

[9] On the other hand, it is possible that the one sum mentioned by the Chronicler held good for the first year whereas the amounts mentioned in Kings specify what was paid afterwards "year by year."

The building of the Temple followed an orderly plan. The ground was leveled and the huge foundation stones were hauled into place. As we have noted, the size of the Temple was not large according to the standards of the day, but what it lacked in its overall dimensions it made up for in grandeur. It was 60 cubits long by 20 cubits wide (or approximately 90 feet long by 30 feet wide [2:3]).

The Temple that Solomon built was divided into three parts: the porch[10] was in the front and measured 20 cubits by 20 cubits, and it was probably 20 cubits high.[11] It was overlaid with pure gold (3: 4) and opened into the Holy Place (3: 5-7) that was paneled with cypress wood and then overlaid with the finest gold.[12] After this it was hand-decorated with various carvings before being embellished

---

[10] There has been considerable debate over the length of a cubit. It seems evident that the Chronicler was citing the "old standard" used by Ezekiel (Ezekiel 40:5; 43:13). Modern research has shown that this cubit was 17.5 inches long. For our purposes, it will be convenient to use 18 inches. See P. L. Garber, *Biblical Archaeologist* 14 (1951), 2-24; D. Gooding, *Vetus Testamentum* 17 (1967), 143-72; G. E. Wright, *Biblical Archaeologist* 4 (1941), 17-31; idem, *Biblical Archaeologist* 18 (1955), 41-44. By the time of the exile the cubit had been lengthened by a handbreadth (approximately 3 inches).

[11] The Hebrew text reads 120 cubits high, but this would make the front approximately 180 feet high—completely dwarfing the Holy of Holies and the Shekinah glory. It is preferable to conclude that this is a copyist's error. Then, as copies were made of the copy, an error could easily be perpetuated. Such instances do not invalidate the doctrine of inerrancy, for inerrancy applies only to the original "autographs."

[12] The gold is specifically stated as having come from *Parvaim*. This place is unknown. It may have been *el-Farwain* in north-eastern Arabia.

with precious stones.[13]  The most sacred part of Temple was the Holy of Holies (3: 8-9).  It was hidden from human sight, and only the high priest could enter this part of the sanctuary, and this only once a year on the Day of Atonement.  The Ark of the Covenant with its mercy seat was kept in this room, and the high priest's duty was to carry in the blood of a sacrificial animal and pour it onto the mercy seat.

The Holy of Holies was a perfect cube, signifying the perfection of God's person.  An enormous amount of gold was used to cover the room.  The biblical text states that six hundred talents of pure gold were lavished on its embellishment.  This would equal about 720,000 ounces or 22.5 tons, and would be valued at approximately 3.5 billion dollars.

The repeated use of *"and he made"* might lend one to conclude that Solomon actually made all of the vessels and utensils mentioned in chapters 3 and 4.  In actual fact, Solomon had all these things made by Huram-abi and those who worked with him.

Mention of the golden "nails" recalls the hooks which held up the veil of the Tabernacle (Exodus 26:32, 37). The word for *"veil"* is *paroket* and means "divider, barrier." Only here in the Old Testament do we read of the veil of Solomon's Temple. *"He [Solomon] had made the veil of violet, purple, crimson and fine linen, and he worked cherubim on it"* (3:14). The New Testament informs us that the *"veil"* of (Herod's) Temple was torn in two from top to bottom (see Matthew 27:51; Mark 15:38; Luke

---

[13] If I Peter 2:5 has reference to this embellishment, then it indicates the great privilege of all who own Christ as their Savior.

20:45) when the Lord Jesus died. Only God could have done that. What happened on the day of the crucifixion was intended to show that direct access into the Holy of Holies (and the presence of God the Father) was now possible without the need of a priest or other intermediary (Hebrews 9:8; 10:19-20. See also Hebrews 4:16).

> *Outside the Temple stood two large, decorated bronze pillars.[14] These were cast by Huram-abi. We read: "He also made two pillars for the front of the house, thirty-five cubits high, and the capital on the top of each was five cubits. He made chains in the inner sanctuary and placed them on the tops of the pillars; and he made one hundred pomegranates and placed them on the chains. He erected the pillars in front of the temple, one on the right and the other on the left, and named the one on the right Jachin and the one on the left Boaz" (3:15-17).*

We do not know the purpose or function of these pillars. Their names possibly mean "He establishes" and "In Him is strength." If so, then they may have been intended to remind each generation of Israelites of the greatness and power of the One whom they had the privilege of worshiping.

Chapter 4 details for us the equipment used in the worship of the Lord. The most prominent of these was the altar. *"Then he [Huram-abi] made a bronze altar, twenty cubits in length and twenty cubits in width and ten cubits in*

---

[14] Cf. R. B. Y. Scott, *Journal of Biblical Literature* 58 (1939), 143ff.; J. Ouelette, *Journal of Near Eastern Studies* 31 (1972), 187-91.

*height"* (4:1). It was almost 30 feet square, and stood almost 15 feet high. A broad staircase led up to it.

The next item to catch a person's attention would be the huge laver that, when full, contained about 18,000 gallons[15] of water. *"Also he made the cast metal sea, ten cubits from brim to brim, circular in form, and its height was five cubits and its circumference thirty cubits. Now figures like oxen were under it and all around it, entirely encircling it. The oxen were in two rows, each cast in one piece. The laver stood on twelve oxen, three facing the north, three facing west, three facing south and three facing east; and the 'sea' (i.e., the laver) was set on top of them and all their hindquarters turned inwards. It (the laver) was a handbreadth thick, and its brim was made like the brim of a cup, like a lily blossom; it could hold 3,000 baths"* (4:2-5). The laver was used by the priests for washing.

Next Huram-abi made ten basins. These were used for washing those parts of animals given as a burnt offering (4:6. Cf. Exodus 29:17; Leviticus 1:9, 13; Ezekiel 40:38).

Whereas the Tabernacle had only one seven-branched lampstand and one table for the *"Bread of the Presence"* (Exodus 25:23-40), Solomon's Temple, being longer, had ten lampstands and ten tables for the *"showbread"* (4:7-8). The light and the bread testified to

---

[15] The question naturally arises, How were the priests able to fill such a large laver? The answer lies in Solomon's elaborate scheme to bring water into Jerusalem via an aqueduct from as far away as Bethlehem. Cf. *New International Dictionary of Biblical Archaeology*, eds. E. M. Blaiklock and R. K. Harrison (Grand Rapids: Zondervan, 1982), 34.

God's continual instruction of, and continuous provision
for the needs of His people.

Mention of the courtyards interrupts the recitation
of the things Huram-abi made (4:9). Their inclusion is
justified because they were a part of the Temple, and had
we not been told about them, we would have had an
imperfect understanding of the events that would soon take
place in Jerusalem at the dedication of the Temple.

The Chronicler then details for us the utensils made
of bronze that were used by the priests:

> Huram[-abi] also made the pails, the
> shovels and the bowls. So Huram[-abi] finished
> doing the work which he performed for King
> Solomon in the house of God: the two pillars, the
> bowls and the two capitals on top of the pillars,
> and the two networks to cover the two bowls of the
> capitals which were on top of the pillars, and the
> four hundred pomegranates for the two networks,
> two rows of pomegranates for each network to
> cover the two bowls of the capitals which were on
> the pillars. He also made the stands and he made
> the basins on the stands, and the one sea with the
> twelve oxen under it. The pails, the shovels, the
> forks and all its utensils, Huram-abi made of
> polished bronze for King Solomon for the house of
> Yahweh. On the plain of the Jordan the king cast
> them in the clay ground between Succoth and
> Zeredah[16]. Thus Solomon made all these utensils

---

[16] Cf. F.-M. Abel, *Geographie de la Palestine*, 2 Vols. (Paris:
Gabalda, 1933-38), II:457.

*in great quantities, for the weight of the bronze*
*could not be found out (4:11-18).*

Though the location of King Solomon's copper
mines is uncertain,[17] it seems likely that they were in
reasonable proximity to Succoth and Zeredah where
Huram-abi prepared the molds for the things he made.

Finally, by way of review, the Chronicler mentions
that Solomon also made *"all the things that were in the*
*house of God: even the golden altar, the tables with the*
*bread of the Presence on them, the lampstands with their*
*lamps of pure gold, to burn in front of the inner sanctuary*
*in the way prescribed; the flowers, the lamps, and the tongs*
*of gold, of purest gold; and the snuffers, the bowls, the*
*spoons and the firepans of pure gold; and the entrance of*
*the house, its inner doors for the holy of holies and the*
*doors of the house, that is, of the nave, of gold"* (4:19-22).

The recounting of all this activity brings to a
conclusion the building of the Temple (5:1). The
Chronicler then reminds his readers that it was in a very
real sense a joint effort on the part of David (now dead) and
Solomon. That Solomon had contributed largely to the
embellishment of the Temple is evident from the wealth of
material contributed by David that is left over and is now
stored in special rooms in the Temple. It becomes part of
the *"treasures of the House of the Lord"* (5:1).

## IN RETROSPECT

It is so easy to become bogged down in the details
of the Temple—the exact length of a cubit, the weight of

---

[17] Cf. J. J. Brimson, *Tyndale Bulletin* 32 (1981), 1123-49; F.
Singer, *Biblical Archaeology Review* 4 (1978), 11-25.

the gold, where the water came from to fill the laver and issues that arise when the Chronicler's account differs from the record in the Book of Kings—that we forget that God's Word has relevance for every age. The Chronicler wrote to encourage people who had become discouraged on account of the opposition they faced. We can only guess at the lessons they drew from these chapters. Our task is to look for principles of application that can be of encouragement to us today.

### The Importance of Our Priorities

First, Solomon began to make preparations for building the Temple as soon as he was elevated to his father's throne. His actions illustrate the principle found earlier in God's Word, *"Those who honor Me I will honor, and those who despise Me will be lightly esteemed"* (I Samuel 2:30). There was plenty to distract Solomon from the building of the Temple. Those who had sworn allegiance to him plotted to overthrow him and seize the throne. And there was the need for Solomon to develop confidence in the hearts of those who, on account of his youth, may have doubted his ability to rule the empire. It took time, therefore, before he felt secure in his new role as king.

David had given him the outline of the plan of the Temple. Solomon, however, had to assess how the land could be leveled, the size and number of the foundation stones, the quantity of wood he would need and how it would be embellished, and the number and size of the vessels that would be used by the priests. And so, while wood was being cut in Lebanon and shipped to Joppa, Solomon was busy planning (i.e., accurately estimating the number of workmen he would need in each location, the kind of work they would do; the strength of the materials he would be using; how the heavy brass vessels could be and still be brought up from the Jordan Valley; and much more). This was followed by the delegation of responsibility to the overseers of the different levees; the supervision of the work to insure that everything was done in accordance with the plans he had made available to them; and the coordination of the different activities. All of this took time. Only when everything was ready, was Solomon able to proceed with the actual building of the Temple.

The fact that Solomon accomplished all of these tasks without becoming distracted or faltering in his commitment shows how important the building of the Temple was to him. It received top priority on his list of things to be done.

And let us not overlook the fact that in bringing the project to completion every worker was important. It is easy for us to look at the key players (e.g., Huram-abi) and conclude that, because we are not gifted in the same way, we are unimportant. Everyone who worked on the Temple had an important part to play. This principle is highlighted throughout Scripture (e.g., in Paul's teaching on spiritual gifts [I Corinthians 12:8-11; and his emphasis on the importance of each part of the body of Christ, I Corinthians 12:12-27]).

It is also necessary for us to constantly take inventory of our priorities and insure that the Lord remains in first place in our lives (Psalm 16:8). Our next most important priority should be our spouse (Ecclesiastes 9:9), followed by our children (Deuteronomy 6:5-7; Colossians

3:16), and only then the work that we do to earn a living
(Colossians 3:17).

## The Importance of Our Gifts

The second principle to emerge from a consideration of these chapters has to do with the embellishment of
the Temple. Solomon gave the Lord the best and purest
gold and silver he could obtain even though the purest gold
had to be imported. Solomon spared no expense. His letter
to King Huram reveals his view of the surpassing greatness
and glory of the One whom he worshipped. The value of
the Temple's adornment boggles our minds.

The late Dr. Karl Menninger once said, "Money-
giving is a good criterion of a person's mental health.
Generous people are rarely mentally ill people." God is
gracious. He not only gives us the ability to earn money so
that we can support ourselves and our families, but when
we set aside a portion to give back to Him in gratitude for
what He has given us, He blesses us even more (Luke
6:38). Alas, all too often we tend to be tight-fisted when it
comes to giving to the Lord's work. I cannot vouch for the
accuracy of the following statement, but one church
bulletin is reputed to have included the following line on
stewardship: "The Lord loveth a cheerful giver, but He
also accepteth from a grouch."

Solomon set an example of liberality that could
have inspired the exiles, and is of no less importance to us.

## The Importance of Perseverance

Those of us who have worked with people in a
variety of situations know how easy it is for them, when a

task seems to be interminable, to give up. It took four years of preparation before the building of the Temple commenced, and there may have been some who, during this time, voiced their skepticism to one another by stating, "We hear a lot of talk about preparations being made for the Temple, but do you think it will ever be built?" And after the actual work began, there may have been others who begrudged the time spent on the construction site because what was required of them was more than they were prepared to give. And still others might have complained about the "waste" of gold and man-hours given to the embellishment of the Temple, and especially the Holy of Holies. We've all heard such comments. Solomon persevered in spite of his critics. He was not dependent upon the approval of people for his sense of wellbeing.

When we consider the importance of perseverance, all we have to do is take a good look at a little child as he or she tries to walk. We see in the infant tremendous perseverance. If a child only tried to walk once or twice and then gave up, he or she would never succeed. But they stick to it, and eventually master the art. And later in life, it is the perseverance that is often the difference between failure and success.

Sometimes it is very hard to keep on when we do not seem to be getting anywhere. When Thomas Carlyle had finished the first hand-written copy of his book, *The French Revolution*, he gave the manuscript to his friend John Stuart Mill and asked him to read it. It took Mr. Mill several days to finish it. As he read what Carlyle had written he realized that this was truly a great literary achievement. Late one night as he finished the last page, he laid the manuscript beside his chair that occupied a place in front of the fireplace. The next morning the maid came in, and seeing these papers lying on the floor, thought that they had been discarded.  She picked them up and threw them into the fire, where they were burned.

Imagine Mr. Mill's consternation when he found out what had happened.  In deep agony of heart he walked to Thomas Carlyle's home and told him what had happened.  "It's all right," Carlyle replied,  "I'm sure I can start over in the morning and do it again."

After finally apologies had been made, John Stuart Mill left and started back to his home.  As the great author and historian watched his friend walking away, he said to his wife, "Poor Mill.  I feel so sorry for him.  I did not want him to see how crushed I really am."  Then heaving a sigh, he said, "Well, the manuscript is gone, so I had better start writing again."

It was a long, hard process.  The initial enthusiasm that accompanies the beginning of a new work was gone.  The creative "juices" do not "flow" as readily as before, and it is hard to recapture the verve of a project when it has to be done over again.  Thomas Carlyle, however, set out to do it again and he finally completed the work.[18]  Today *The French Revolution* is regarded as a classic.

Carlyle refused to be overcome by disappointment, and persevered until his two-volume work was finished.  In like manner, Solomon persevered through many difficulties, and after many years of intense effort, brought the building of the Temple to a satisfactory conclusion.

---

[18] Adapted from W. Barclay's *The King and the Kingdom* (Philadelphia:  Westminster, 1968), 161.

# CHAPTER THREE

# A CONCLUSION, AND A NEW BEGINNING

## II CHRONICLES 5:1-7:22

The worship of God lies at the very heart of Christianity. Contemporary historians, however, are prone to look upon our present era as the age in which the church has lost its way, forgotten its mission and become irrelevant. Then, fearing that they may have been unduly harsh, they concede that the church has belatedly begun to search for a semblance of significance. Such a search, however, they predict will end in failure for the church as they see it, is self-serving and hopelessly out of step with the times.

Of course, this isn't the first time the church has been considered irrelevant. In earlier centuries it succumbed to a stifling orthodoxy that manifested itself in a crippling formalism. Reacting against the contours of a lifeless dogma some leaders began to embrace contemporary fads mingled with Eastern mysticism. Others began to look for guidance to the beliefs and practices of early Christians. Instead of these quests producing spiritual satisfaction, they have had a polarizing effect. And all because the teaching of the Bible has been ignored! (cf. Isaiah 5:11; Hosea 4:6. See also Amos 8:11). Our present predicament highlights the importance of these chapters in II Chronicles. Here we have the opportunity to witness the

inauguration of a worship service in which Yahweh, the
Lord of glory, occupied the central position. His people
approached him through confession (i.e., the offering of
sacrifices), were quickened in their hearts by the singing of
spiritual songs, and then worshipped Him as Solomon led
them in prayer. The result was that God was honored and
lifted up in the hearts of His people.

A careful look at these chapters reveals that there
was order to all that took place in Jerusalem. No part of the
preliminaries was allowed to overshadow the central theme
of the people's reverence for God. In other words, *these
chapters are not so much about the Temple of God as the
worship of the One to whom the Temple belonged.*

## OUTLINE

Our discussion of the contents continues where our
last chapter left off. All six chapters (2:1-7:22) deal with
(1) the construction of the Temple, and (2) its dedication.

We now continue our discussion of the events.

## THE DEDICATION OF THE TEMPLE (5:1-7:22)

### *The Entrance of the Lord into His Temple (5:1-14)*

**The Completion of the Work (5:1).** Verse 1 is
transitional: *"Thus (lit. 'and [it] was finished, namely) all
the work that Solomon made for the house of Yahweh"*
(5:1*a*). Four years were spent in preparing materials for the
building of the Temple. Another seven years were spent in
building the Temple (I Kings 6:37-38). Only then did
Solomon set in motion his plans for the Temple's
dedication. *"And Solomon brought in the things that David*

*his father had dedicated, even the silver and the gold and all the utensils, [and] he put them in the treasuries of the house of God"* (5:1b).

**The Gathering of the People (5:2-3).** Solomon probably knew intuitively that leaders lead by example, and so as the nation's "chief executive" he invited all of the other leaders of the people to meet with him in Jerusalem for the dedication ceremony. An open invitation probably also went out to the people, for they, too, came to join in the proceedings.

> *Then Solomon assembled [to Jerusalem] the elders of Israel and all the chiefs (or heads) of the tribes, the rulers (i.e., leaders) of the fathers' [households] of the sons of Israel, to bring up the Ark of the Covenant of Yahweh out of the city of David, which is Zion. And all the men of Israel assembled themselves to the king at the feast ... (5:2-3).*

This event took place in the seventh month and was arranged to coincide with the Feast of Tabernacles.

**The Final Journey of the Ark (5:4-6).** The Feast of Tabernacles reminded the people of their ancestor's exodus from Egypt and subsequent wandering in the desert. On this occasion, it focused on the Ark for it had shared in the nation's travels. Now it took its final journey up from the city of David to the Temple on Mount Moriah.

> *Then all the elders of Israel came, and the Levites lifted the Ark, and they brought up the Ark and the Tent of Meeting [i.e., the Tabernacle] and all the holy utensils that [were] in the tent; the Levitical priests brought them up. And King Solomon and all the congregation of Israel who*

*were assembled with him before the Ark, were*
*sacrificing sheep and oxen, [so many] that they*
*could not be counted for multitude.*

Solomon may have heard of his father's mistake in
not involving the Levites when he attempted to bring up the
Ark from Kiriath-jearim (I Samuel 6:1-11. Cf. Numbers
4:15). Not wishing to make the same mistake, he has the
Levites carry the Ark on long poles. The procession up the
slope from Zion to the Temple must have been one the
people would never forget. The priests and Levites, of
course, were dressed in their official attire. The Ark was
covered, and this added to its mystery. The people,
however, could probably see the outline of the wings of the
cherubim as the covering hung on them.

The transportation of the Ark was accompanied by
the offering of sacrifices, and the biblical writer says that
they were so many they could not be counted. Given the
nature of the Kidron Valley and the constant movement of
the animals, anyone wishing to count them would be at a
loss to know where to start or how to proceed.

In addition to the entrance of the Ark into the
Temple, the Tabernacle of Moses was placed in one of the
storage rooms. It had probably been brought from Gibeon
that morning.

**The Final Resting-Place of the Ark (5:7-10).**
Outside the beautiful Temple that Solomon had built, the
Levites stop and lower the Ark. Only priests could carry it
into the Temple.

*Then the priests brought the Ark of the*
*Covenant of Yahweh to its place, into the inner*
*sanctuary of the house (lit. 'to the house of the*
*oracle'), to the Most Holy place, under the wings*

*of the cherubim.[1]  And the cherubim spread out
their wings over the place of the Ark, so that the
cherubim made a covering over the Ark and its
poles.  The poles were so long that the ends of the
poles of the ark could be seen in front of the inner
sanctuary, but they could not be seen outside; and
they are there to this day.  There was nothing in
the ark except the two tablets, which Moses put
there at Horeb, where Yahweh made (lit. 'cut') a
covenant with the sons of Israel, when they came
out of Egypt.*

There are four notable features to observe in these
verses. (1) The Ark of the Covenant was placed in the Holy
of Holies, (2) it was symbolically protected by the
cherubim that stood guard over it, (3) the poles were so
long they jutted out beyond the veil, and (4) the Ark
contained only the two tablets of the Law given by God to
Moses on Mount Sinai.  At an earlier time, the Ark had
contained the golden pot of manna and Aaron's rod (Hebrews 9:4).  What happened to these items we do not know.

From this brief review, the Chronicler moves to
discuss the actual dedication of the Temple.

**The Manifestation of God's Glory (5:11-14)**. Two
things happen as the priests come out of the Temple:  (1) A
large choir made up of the three branches of Levitical
singers began their hymn of praise, and (2) a cloud
(signifying God's presence) settled over the Temple.

*And it was (i.e., it came to pass) when the
priests came forth from the sanctuary (for all the
priests who were present had sanctified*

---

[1] *Cherubim* is the plural form of "cherub" in Hebrew.

*themselves, without regard to divisions), and all
the Levitical singers, of Asaph, of Heman, of
Jeduthun, and their sons and brethren, clothed in
fine linen, with cymbals, and with harps and lyres,
stood to the east of the altar, and with them one
hundred and twenty priests blowing trumpets-
when the trumpeters and the singers made
themselves heard with one voice to praise and to
glorify Yahweh, and when they lifted up their
voice accompanied by trumpets and cymbals and
instruments of music, and when they praised
Yahweh [saying], "Good (i.e., He is good) for His
lovingkindness [endures] forever"-then the house,
the house of Yahweh, was filled with a cloud, and
the priests were not able stand to minister because
of the cloud, for the glory of Yahweh filled the
house of God.*

The Levitical singers from Gibeon were under the
direction of Heman and Jeduthun, and those from
Jerusalem were under the oversight of Asaph. Their song
of praise appears to have been taken from Psalm 107:1;
118:1; and 136:1. What is unique is the absence of
competition. Each division was committed to singing the
praises of the Lord and worshipping Him in an appropriate
manner. And they praise Him for His *hesed ("lovingkindness, covenant faithfulness")* had brought the entire
building project to completion.

When God's people set themselves apart to worship
Him in an appropriate manner, He will most assuredly
respond with some indication of His approval. On this
occasion, it was His descent in a cloud. The rabbis called
this the *Shekinah,* for it veiled His glory while indicating in
a definite manner His presence in the midst of His people.

The Lord does not always manifest Himself in the same way, and so we should not look for outward phenomena as a sign of His blessing nor for some emotional reaction. Our responsibility is to worship Him, not to seek for some special feeling.

The descent of the cloud calls to mind a similar event at the dedication of the Tabernacle nearly five hundred years earlier (I Kings 6:1). On that occasion, the cloud settled over the Tabernacle and Moses could not minister in it because the glory of the Lord filled the place (Exodus 40:34-35). Now, in Jerusalem, the glory of the Lord so filled the Temple that the priests, though they had sanctified themselves, were unable to carry out any of their regular duties.

### *The Worship of the Lord in His Temple (6:1-42).*

Solomon's prayer forms the heart of the dedication service. Some well-meaning individuals will most certainly challenge this statement. "Surely," they will say, "the singing of choruses is the heart of the 'worship service' today."[2] The singing of God's praise was a definite part of the service Solomon had planned, but it did not dominate what took place; and in defense of Solomon's actions, the Lord Jesus Himself said that His house was to

---

[2] A further argument that is often advanced is to make reference to Ephesians 5:19. This verse, interpreted in its context, has to do with the believer's relation to the Holy Spirit, and "singing and making melody with your heart to the Lord" is an individual expression of gratitude and does not apply to the worship service of the local assembly.

be a *"house of prayer"* (Matthew 21:13; Mark 11:17; Luke 19:46).

As Solomon began to pray, his opening words bore the impact of what they had all seen.  The Lord had accorded them the same privilege Moses had received at the outset of the nation's journey from Mount Sinai to the Promised Land (Exodus 40:1-38).  To assure the people of His presence a cloud hovered over the Tabernacle during the day and changed to a pillar of fire at night.  Now, to assure the people of His acceptance of the Temple that Solomon had built, the Lord of Glory was seen to have taken up residence in the Temple (a remarkable act of condescension on His part!).

As Solomon explains to the people what they have just seen  (6:1-2), he testifies to God's faithfulness to His word (6:3-11), and then formally dedicates the Temple (6:12-42).

## Response to the Manifestation of God's Glory (6:1-2).

*"Then Solomon said, 'Yahweh has said that He would dwell in darkness.  And I have built You a lofty house, a place for You to dwell [in] forever.'"*  His opening remarks are very brief, and it is possible that he was still reacting to what has just happened, for it is likely that the descent of the cloud on the Temple had taken him and everyone else completely by surprise.

On those occasions when we are surprised by some special intervention of God on our behalf, words seem totally inadequate.  In Solomon's case, his knowledge of history helped him.  He could immediately identify what had just happened with what had taken place at the time of the dedication of the Tabernacle (Exodus 40:34-35). But how could he possibly respond appropriately to this manifestation of God's grace?

While overwhelmed at God's condescension, Solomon nonetheless realizes that this is in fulfillment of His express desire to live in the midst of His people. And the Lord of glory still desires to be the center of His people's lives. But how? Is the church the New Testament counterpart to the Old Testament Temple? And if so, then why isn't there a cloud over the church we attend signifying that God is there?

These are important questions. And the answer is just as simple. *The local church is **not** the counterpart of the Old Testament Temple.* We are. The New Testament makes this clear in I Corinthians 3:16; 6:19 and in Ephesians 2:21. As the second century church Father, Irenaeus, said: "The glory of God is a living man; and the life of man consists in beholding God." How this happens is a testament to God's grace. As the Shekinah came down on the Temple and took possession of it, so it is that at the time we accept Jesus Christ as our Savior, God the Holy Spirit comes and indwells us (John 14:17; Romans 8:9, 11; I Corinthians 3:16; 6:19). In a very real (though less visible) way, He causes the glory of God to be seen in us (cf. II Corinthians 3:8, 18).[3] This takes time. However, as the Apostle Paul pointed out, we have this treasure (God the Holy Spirit living in us) in earthen vessels (II Corinthians 4:7).

---

[3] See the excellent discussion by C. C. Ryrie in *Transformed by His Glory: Regaining a Sense of the Wonder of God* (Wheaton, IL: Victor, 1990), 144pp.

The events of this chapter, therefore, merely illustrate and underscore the magnitude of God's gift to us.

## Solomon's Thanksgiving for God's Presence (6:3-11).

In Solomon's "second" prayer, he turned from facing the Lord in the Temple to face the people. His words again look back on the past.

> *Then the king faced about and blessed all the assembly of Israel, while all the assembly of Israel was standing. He said, "Blessed be Yahweh, the God of Israel, who spoke with His mouth to my father David and has fulfilled it with His hands, saying, 'Since the day that I brought My people from the land of Egypt, I did not choose a city out of all the tribes of Israel in which to build a house that My name might be there, nor did I choose any man for a leader over My people Israel; but I have chosen Jerusalem that My name might be there, and I have chosen David to be over My people Israel.' Now it was in the heart of my father David to build a house for the name of Yahweh, the God of Israel. But Yahweh said to my father David, 'Because it was in your heart to build a house for My name, you did well that it was in your heart. Nevertheless you shall not build the house, but your son who will be born to you, he shall build the house for My name.' Now Yahweh has fulfilled His word that He spoke; for I have risen in the place of my father David and sit on the throne of Israel, as Yahweh promised, and have built the house for the name of Yahweh, the God of Israel. There I have set the Ark in which is*

*the covenant of Yahweh which He made with the*
*sons of Israel."*

Those who had returned from exile and read this
recounting of their past could hardly miss the Chronicler's
emphasis on the faithfulness of God. He had been faithful
in fulfilling His promise to David; He had been faithful in
helping Solomon with all of the details of the Temple's
construction; and He had fulfilled His word by selecting
Jerusalem as the place for His Name.

There is an unmistakable emphasis in Solomon's
prayer to the *"whole assembly"* (6:3, 12-13). The Temple
and its services were for all the people. The returned exiles
had built a second Temple that lacked the beauty and
adornment of the one Solomon built, and they had spoken
disparagingly of its smallness and seeming insignificance
(cf. their remark about a *"day of small things"* in Zechariah
4:10). God, however, is not impressed with the size or the
munificence of the place where He is worshipped. He does
want to be the center of His people's lives.

When we consider the central duty of believers
today, we need to remember the words of the late Dr. A. W.
Tozer: "God wants worshippers before workers; indeed the
only acceptable workers are those who have learned the art
of worship."

In reflecting on the past, Solomon thanks God that
He has indeed enabled him to ascend his father's throne
(6:10); that he has been able to bring the building of the
Temple to a successful conclusion (6:10); and that the Ark
of the Covenant now has a permanent home. He sees all
this as evidence of the faithfulness of God.

A careful reading of Solomon's prayer reveals
several anthropomorphisms. This is a term theologians like

to toss about to impress people with their sophistication. Actually, there is no reason why we should be impressed with such sophistry. The word comes from two Greek words, *anthropos*, "man," from which we derive the discipline of anthropology (i.e., the study of human life), and *morphe*, "form," as in "morphology" (the study of forms). When applied to God it means that we, because we cannot fully understand God, attribute to Him certain physical characteristics (e.g., hands, feet, eyes and ears). A second use of anthropomorphism is to ascribe to God human non-physical traits (e.g., emotions like love or anger). In Solomon's prayer, he speaks of God having fulfilled with His *hands* what He promised with His *mouth*, et cetera (cf. 6:4, 10. See also vv. 16, 20, 40).

It should also be observed that in this recounting of the reason why God disallowed David to build the Temple and chose instead his unborn son, it was not David's sins or frequent wars that disqualified him, *but because God's idea of rest could best be illustrated by the life of Solomon* who was spared the emotional turmoil of war.

### Solomon's Prayer of Dedication (6:12-42).

Solomon now turns and faces the altar. And kneeling down, he raises his arms toward heaven. In preparation for this event, he had had made a bronze platform, five cubits long, five cubits wide (i.e., approx. 7.5 feet square) and three cubits (i.e., approx. 4.5 feet) high. This he set in the middle of the court. Solomon now stood on this platform and, in the sight of all the people, knelt down and began to pray (6:13).

But why face the altar? Why not continue to face the Temple where God had so recently taken up residence?

The altar was the place of sacrifice, and Solomon's actions remind all of us that the only basis of true worship is the death of Christ. But the altar also reminds us that we are to present ourselves to God as a living sacrifice (Romans 12:1-2). Then, with the assurance of our acceptance, we can offer our prayers with the assurance that He hears us.

We next read of Solomon's request for God's continuing fulfillment of His promises (6:14-17). He said:

> *"O Yahweh, the God of Israel, there is no god like You in heaven or on earth, keeping covenant and showing lovingkindness to Your servants who walk before You with all their heart; who has kept with Your servant David, my father, that which You have promised him; indeed You have spoken with Your mouth and have fulfilled it with Your hand, as it is this day. Now therefore, O Yahweh, the God of Israel, keep with Your servant David, my father, that which You have promised him, saying, 'You shall not lack a man to sit on the throne of Israel, if only your sons take heed to their way, to walk in My law as you have walked before Me.' Now, therefore, O Yahweh, the God of Israel, let Your word be confirmed which You have spoken to Your servant David."*

Let us note that for our worship of the Lord to be truly biblical, we must allow the uniqueness of God's person and work to permeate out minds. Solomon reminds us that our God is unique. There is no one and nothing that can compare with Him. And this includes things on earth as well as in heaven. Such a realization of His greatness and wisdom and majesty should fill us with awe. He is also faithful and will perform all that He has promised (6:14*b*-

15). Solomon then reminds the people of the fact that God had kept His covenant with David. If God had not done so, Solomon would not now sit on David's throne.

Solomon's use of *"Now"* (6:16) brings him to his first request. He prays that God will keep His promise that someone of David's line (i.e., dynasty) will continue before Him. His prayer also illustrates for us the basic principles of intercession (6:18-21). He begins with a rhetorical question. *"But will God indeed dwell with mankind on the earth? Behold, heaven and the highest heaven cannot contain You; how much less this house that I have built."* If we would understand what prayer really is, then we must also understand who God is and what He is like. The highest heaven cannot contain Him. But does this mean that He is far away and either cannot hear us or is disinterested in our prayers? Because He is omnipresent (i.e., He is everywhere present) He can and will hear the prayers of every person the world over. In Solomon's time, He also dwelt on earth and His Temple served as a physical dwelling-place even though He was also in heaven.

In verses 19-21 we have the basic essentials of prayer: (1) Sincerity coupled with a sense of urgency; (2) a call for God not only to see us, but also to hear us; (3) that no one be excluded (cf. Luke 18:9-14); and (4) that the Lord forgive the sins of the penitent and those who come earnestly seeking Him. Let us take note of the Chronicler's emphasis. Solomon was not a prima donna. He asked the Lord to have regard to his prayer and to his supplication, and *"to listen to the ...supplications ... of [His] people Israel when they pray toward this place."* Then he concluded with a reminder of God's greatness: *"Lord, hear from Your dwelling place, from heaven; hear and forgive."*

From this, Solomon immediately launched into describing the kinds of situations in which prayer might be offered (6:22-40).

> *"If a man sins against his neighbor and is made to take an oath, and he comes and takes an oath before Your altar in this house, then hear from heaven and act and judge Your servants, punishing the wicked by bringing his way on his own head and justifying the righteous by giving him according to his righteousness. If Your people Israel are defeated before an enemy because they have sinned against You, and they return to You and confess Your name, and pray and make supplication before You in this house, then hear from heaven and forgive the sin of Your people Israel, and bring them back to the land which You have given to them and to their fathers. When the heavens are shut up and there is no rain because they have sinned against You, and they pray toward this place and confess Your name, and turn from their sin when You afflict them; then hear in heaven and forgive the sin of Your servants and Your people Israel, indeed, teach them the good way in which they should walk. And send rain on Your land, which You have given to Your people for an inheritance. If there is famine in the land, if there is pestilence, if there is blight or mildew, if there is locust or grasshopper, if their enemies besiege them in the land of their cities, whatever plague or whatever sickness there is, whatever prayer or supplication is made by any man or by all Your people Israel, each knowing his own affliction and his own pain, and spreading his hands toward this house, then hear from*

*heaven Your dwelling place, and forgive, and*
*render to each according to all his ways, whose*
*heart You know for You alone know the hearts of*
*the sons of men, that they may fear You, to walk in*
*Your ways as long as they live in the land which*
*You have given to our fathers. Also concerning*
*the foreigner who is not from Your people Israel,*
*when he comes from a far country for Your great*
*name's sake and Your mighty hand and Your*
*outstretched arm, when they come and pray*
*toward this house, then hear from heaven, from*
*Your dwelling place, and do according to all for*
*which the foreigner calls to You, in order that all*
*the peoples of the earth may know Your name, and*
*fear You as do Your people Israel, and that they*
*may know that this house which I have built is*
*called by Your name. When Your people go out to*
*battle against their enemies, by whatever way You*
*shall send them, and they pray to You toward this*
*city which You have chosen and the house which I*
*have built for Your name, then hear from heaven*
*their prayer and their supplication, and maintain*
*their cause. When they sin against You (for there*
*is no man who does not sin) and You are angry*
*with them and deliver them to an enemy, so that*
*they take them away captive to a land far off or*
*near, if they take thought in the land where they*
*are taken captive, and repent and make*
*supplication to You in the land of their captivity,*
*saying, 'We have sinned, we have committed*
*iniquity and have acted wickedly;' if they return to*
*You with all their heart and with all their soul in*
*the land of their captivity, where they have been*
*taken captive, and pray toward their land which*

*You have given to their fathers and the city which
You have chosen, and toward the house which I
have built for Your name, then hear from heaven,
from Your dwelling place, their prayer and
supplications, and maintain their cause and
forgive Your people who have sinned against You.
Now, O my God, I pray, let Your eyes be open and
Your ears attentive to the prayer offered in this
place."*

No matter what the situation, Solomon asked the
Lord to incline His ear and hear the prayers of His people,
forgive their sin, and help them. And so he listed seven
different scenarios, each describing a situation in which
prayer could be made. These included a breakdown in
interpersonal relationships, national defeat, drought,
disasters and/or disease, the need(s) of foreigners, or the
needs of God's people in wartime or exile. In each case, he
asked that confession of sin and repentance be the prelude
to God's forgiveness and intervention.

Solomon's long prayer concludes with his request
for God's continuing presence and power (6:41-42). *"Now
therefore arise, O Yahweh God, to Your resting place, You
and the Ark of Your might. Let Your priests, O Yahweh
God, be clothed with salvation and let Your godly ones
rejoice in what is good. O Yahweh God, do not turn away
the face of Your anointed; remember the good deeds of
Your servant David."*

It is interesting to notice Solomon's emphasis on
God's *"resting place."* The imagery conjures up before
our minds the wandering of the children of Israel in the
desert. Though God's presence was always there in the
cloud by day and the pillar of fire by night, yet the tribes
lacked permanence. Now that the Temple has been built,

and the Ark is safely ensconced in the Holy of Holies, God can figuratively enjoy His *"rest."*

Also of interest is Solomon's prayer for the priests. He prayed that they might be *"clothed with salvation"*— i.e., fully committed to their ministry of bringing salvation to Israel; that God's people could rejoice in His goodness to them; that His people experience the joy of fellowship with Him, and that He would remember His covenant with David.

Before we consider the contents of chapter 7, we need to pause and consider how this chapter applies to our hearts and lives. What is it to truly worship God?

To truly worship God, we need to consciously realize that, when we pray, we enter the presence of the Creator and Sustainer of heaven and earth. When this happens, we undergo a change. We cannot remain the same. For us, worship begins with awe and ends with obedience. As the late Dr. William Temple used to say, "To worship is to quicken the conscience by the holiness of God, to feed the mind with the truth of God, to purge the imagination by the beauty of God, to open the heart to the love of God, and to devote the will to the purpose of God."

### The Response of the Lord to His Worshippers (7:1-22)

Chapter 7 is central to the Book of Chronicles. It is also one of the most important in the entire Old Testament. It is based on 6:32-33 and has application to God's people of every age. In place of a physical Temple, they have direct access to the throne of grace in heaven (Hebrews 4:13-16).

The altar reminded the Israelites of God's willingness to forgive their sins and His desire to restore them to His favor. And that is why there is such an important link between confession of sin and forgiveness. These truths would have been readily understood by the returned exiles. They knew that the captivity had been occasioned by the sins of their forebears. Now, as they read Solomon's prayer, their hearts would be encouraged to turn to the Lord in humility and contrition, asking for His mercy, forgiveness and blessing.

## God's Acceptance of His People's Worship (7:1-3).

> *"Now when Solomon had finished praying, fire came down from heaven and consumed the burnt offering and the sacrifices, and the glory of Yahweh filled the house. The priests could not enter into the house of Yahweh because the glory of Yahweh filled Yahweh's house. All the sons of Israel, seeing the fire come down and the glory of Yahweh upon the house, bowed down on the pavement with their faces to the ground, and they worshipped and gave praise to Yahweh, saying, 'Truly He is good, truly His lovingkindness is everlasting.'"*

In the same way that the Lord had sent down fire from heaven to consume the sacrifice at the time of the dedication of the Tabernacle (Leviticus 9:24), so now He signified His acceptance of the Temple as His abode, and His acceptance of His people's commitment to Him.

It is important to notice that the people worshipped the Lord as a result of His gracious acceptance of the sacrifice. They could not do otherwise, for they were filled

with awe. And God's glory that had already filled the
Temple now overflowed, so that it was not only seen above
the Temple and inside it, but outside as well.

## The People's Sacrifices and Praise (7:4-10).

*Then the king and all the people offered
sacrifice before Yahweh. King Solomon offered a
sacrifice of 22,000 oxen and 120,000 sheep. Thus
the king and all the people dedicated the house of
God. The priests stood at their posts, and the
Levites also, with the instruments of music to
Yahweh, which King David had made for giving
praise to Yahweh—"for His lovingkindness is
everlasting"—whenever he gave praise by their
means, while the priests on the other side blew
trumpets; and all Israel was standing.*

*Then Solomon consecrated the middle of
the court that was before the house of Yahweh, for
there he offered the burnt offerings and the fat of
the peace offerings because the bronze altar which
Solomon had made was not able to contain the
burnt offering, the grain offering and the fat. So
Solomon observed the feast at that time for seven
days, and all Israel with him, a very great
assembly who came from the entrance of Hamath
to the brook of Egypt. On the eighth day they held
a solemn assembly, for the dedication of the altar
they observed seven days and the feast seven days.
Then on the twenty-third day of the seventh month
he sent the people to their tents, rejoicing and
happy of heart because of the goodness that*

*Yahweh had shown to David and to Solomon and
to His people Israel.*

To the amazement of the people (as they saw fire
come down from heaven) was added the joy of worshipping their great and awesome God. Their praise was given
additional impetus as the priests and Levites provided
appropriate music for the occasion. Dr. A. W. Tozer
captured the essence of this when he applied what we read
in this chapter to the experience of the Christian. He wrote:
"There are delights that the heart may enjoy in the
awesome presence of God that cannot find expression in
language; they belong to the unutterable element of
Christian experience. Not many enjoy them because not
many know that they can. The whole concept of ineffable
worship has been lost." And because we have largely lost
the art of worship, we try to replace it with liturgical prayer
and feel-good routines. As beautiful as these elements of a
service may be, they miss the whole point of worship.

The intent of the Chronicler in recounting these
events may have been to encourage the returned exiles to
greater devotion and to show them that they had freedom in
their worship. But everything should be done decently and
in order. To quote Dr. Tozer again, "By making a lot of
religious din we assure our faltering hearts that everything
is well, and conversely, we suspect silence and regard it as
proof that that [a particular] meeting is 'dead.'" Much of
modern religious music is anything but worshipful, and
when compared with the psalms of David or Asaph or any
of the others that were used in Israel's worship, modern
choruses (even when they are based on a verse of Scripture)
are a very poor substitute.

At the dedication of the Temple, Solomon
specifically dedicated the altar (7:9). This involved more

than a ceremony. The offering of sacrifices on it in effect
sanctified it for a special purpose. Then other sacrifices
were offered. So many animals were killed that Solomon
had to sanctify the middle court of the Temple, and erect
other (temporary) altars on which the people could offer
their peace offerings. The worshipper could take part of
this sacrifice to his family, so there was plenty of food for
everyone.[4]

There is a small matter of chronology in verses 8-
10. The entire celebration lasted fifteen days. Seven days
were devoted to offering sacrifices to the Lord before the
week-long Feast of Tabernacles (that lasted from the 15th to
22nd of the seventh month. See Leviticus 23:34-36, 39-
43). This was followed by a day devoted to a solemn
assembly (Numbers 29:35), and then Solomon sent the
people away.

Of significance is the fact that the people
participated wholeheartedly in the events. They had come
from all parts of the nation—from the Wadi of Egypt in the
south to the entering in of Hamath in the north. Their
hearts were full of joy and gladness as they participated in
the activities, for the Lord had been good to them.

---

[4] Those who are inclined to minimize the large number of
sacrifices have pointed out that to offer up all of these animals would
require that the priests offer a new sacrifice every three seconds, ten
hours a day, for twelve days. Cf. J. Wenham, *Tyndale Bulletin* 18
(1967), 19-53, noting esp. p. 49. We have no means of knowing how
many hundred additional (temporary) altars were set up in the court or
how many priests and Levites were involved in this work.

## Rehearsal of God's Promises (7:11-22).

This concluding paragraph begins with a summary of all that Solomon had been able to accomplish. His palace took thirteen more years to finish, and so what is recorded here probably did not happen immediately.

> *Thus Solomon finished the house of Yahweh and the king's palace, and successfully completed all that he had planned to do in the house of Yahweh and in his palace. Then Yahweh appeared to Solomon at night and said to him, "I have heard your prayer and have chosen this place for Myself as a house of sacrifice. If I shut up the heavens so that there is no rain, or if I command the locust to devour the land, or if I send pestilence among My people, and My people who are called by My name humble themselves and pray and seek My face and turn from their wicked ways, then I will hear from heaven, will forgive their sin and will heal their land. Now My eyes will be open and My ears attentive to the prayer offered in this place. For now I have chosen and consecrated this house that My name may be there forever, and My eyes and My heart will be there perpetually. As for you, if you walk before Me as your father David walked, even to do according to all that I have commanded you, and will keep My statutes and My ordinances, then I will establish your royal throne as I covenanted with your father David, saying, 'You shall not lack a man to be ruler in Israel.' But if you turn away and forsake My statutes and My commandments which I have set before you, and go and serve other gods and worship them, then I will uproot*

*you from My land which I have given you, and this*
*house which I have consecrated for My name I*
*will cast out of My sight and I will make it a*
*proverb and a byword among all peoples. As for*
*this house, which was exalted, everyone who*
*passes by it will be astonished and say, 'Why has*
*Yahweh done thus to this land and to this house?'*
*And they will say, 'Because they forsook Yahweh,*
*the God of their fathers who brought them from*
*the land of Egypt, and they adopted other gods*
*and worshipped them and served them; therefore*
*He has brought all this adversity on them.'"*

The lapse in time between the dedication of the
Temple and this appearance of the Lord to Solomon is not
important. What is important is the fact the Lord indicated
that He had heard and accepted Solomon's prayer (6:14-
42). His message was clear. His house was to be a house
of prayer. Furthermore, He invited His people to take
advantage of the unprecedented benefits that could be theirs
if they would approach Him in the right way (i.e., humbly,
prayerfully, devotedly and in a spirit of repentance). When
these elements are present, He promises to hear and forgive
them and heal their land. And what is more, His words to
Solomon indicate that He is attentive and near those who
come to Him in contrition, and intercede before Him
believing that He will do as they have asked.

God also confirmed the covenant He had made with
David and assured Solomon of the continuation of his
dynasty (7:17-18; cf. 6:16-18). He may reject the Temple
(*"if you [plural] turn away and forsake My statutes..."* for
the Temple was only of secondary importance, 7:19) and
send His people into exile but, if they repented, He would

hear from His throne in heaven and restore them to their land. And this He had done with the returned exiles!

## IN CLOSING

Whatever is outward in worship must come as a direct result of what is within us, otherwise it will deteriorate in legalism and/or a meaningless routine. The Lord Jesus told the woman at Jacob's well that true worship is in spirit and truth (John 4:24). Real worship has its foundation in adoration, and this is an attitude of the heart. If the dedication of the Temple teaches us anything, it should be that God is honored when we hold Him in awe and bring before Him our prayers as well as our thanksgiving (Psalm 50:23; Philippians 4:6; Colossians 4:2). And when we consider God's admonition to Solomon to be faithful and not go after other gods, it is given because within the human heart is the tendency to become like the things we worship. But surely it could never be said of us that we are guilty of *"going after other gods"*? Yes, it can. These *"other gods"* often take the form of material possessions, wealth, fame, power or anything that we covet.

*True praise is to be taken up with who God is, the excellency of His person, the evidences of His grace, the greatness of His works, and His abiding love.* The Book of Psalms contains both praise and lament. The opportunity we have to praise the Lord and bring before Him our troubles is a priceless privilege!

# CHAPTER FOUR

# MID-CAREER AND BEYOND

II CHRONICLES 8:1-9:31

Scott is a member of the church where I am one of the pastors. He is in his early 40's, has a wife and two daughters and is successful without being ostentatious. As he and I were chatting on the patio after church one Sunday, he shared with me the fact that he had achieved all the goals he set for himself since he obtained his CPA. He also told me that was praying that the Lord would show him what do with the rest of his life.

Marion is in a different position. Her husband has recently left her and their children for a younger "single, no children" woman he met while attending a business seminar. He has been seeing this "other woman" on the sly, and has now filed for divorce. At 38, Marion feels as if she has been cast adrift on the sea of her emotions. Loneliness, rejection, anger, frustration, doubts about the future and financial worries weigh heavily upon her and she wonders how long she can continue to persevere.

Marshall is in his early 50's. His investments have paid off, and he is thinking of taking early retirement at 55 so that he can devote his remaining years to some form of ministry.

As a child, Elwood had ambitions of becoming the President of the United States. After college, he modified his goals and determined that he would settle for being president of his company. Now at 42 and in mid-career, his early aspirations have vanished. He brings home enough money to support his wife and sons, but seriously questions if he will be able to send his boys to college. To avoid giving way to discouragement he has, of necessity, established new, realistic goals for himself. But what of the future? Much depends on the economy.

In II Chronicles, the Chronicler wraps up his discussion of the life of Solomon by assessing his accomplishments. He is about 40 years old. He will die around age 60. What will he do with the remainder of his life?

## OUTLINE

Chapters 8 and 9 resemble a potpourri of events. At first glance, there seems to be little thematic unity in their content. We will treat the data in the following way:

### Summary of Solomon's Accomplishments (8:1-9:31)

Defense of the Kingdom (8:2-6)

Organization of the Kingdom (8:7-11)

. Division of Labor (8:7-8)
. Delegation of Authority (8:9-10)
. Domicile of Pharaoh's Daughter (8:11)

Worship within the Kingdom (8:12-16)

Prominence of the Kingdom (8:17-9:28)

Obituary (9:29-31)

As we shall see, the emphasis of the Chronicler is on all that God did. He helped Solomon with his building projects; He assisted Solomon in extending the borders of the nation; He gave wisdom to Solomon so that his economic plans brought great wealth to his people; and in the end, He is seen to have fulfilled all His promises to Solomon. In all of this, we have brought before us the faithfulness of God. This truth would be of considerable encouragement to the returned exiles. The Lord honors His word and will meet the needs of those who trust in Him and obey Him.

We are so prone to look at the effort we expend to accomplish a particular task that we seldom stop to thank the Lord for His enabling grace. A sub-theme, therefore, that runs through chapters 8 and 9 emphasizes the need for praise.

The Chronicler presumes that his readers are familiar with the Book(s) of Kings and so does not enlarge upon events or circumstances mentioned there. His focus is on the relevance of Israel's history to the people of his time. And because the books of the Bible were written under the direction of the Holy Spirit, principles drawn from the events described in them can be applied to the people of God in every age.

## RECAP OF SOLOMON'S ACCOMPLISHMENTS (8:1)

In summarizing Solomon's activity for the first half of his reign, the Chronicler concentrates on his building projects. He had successfully brought to completion the construction of the Temple and *"his own house"* as well. That this emphasis on building (or rebuilding) was in the mind of the biblical writer is evident from 8:1, 2, 4 (twice), 5 and 6. And when we consider the magnificence of the Temple and Solomon's palace—the splendor of which aroused the envy of the ancient world—we realize that their completion was no mean accomplishment.

But were they designed to bring glory to Solomon? No. They were intended to bring glory and honor to the Lord, and as opportunity presented itself, Solomon emphasized the fact that he was merely God's regent (cf. 9:8).

## DEFENSE OF THE KINGDOM (8:2-6)

God had promised to bless His people if they would faithfully walk in His ways, and He had done so. Solomon, however, did not take the present peace for granted. The surrounding nations were gradually gaining in power. Though Egypt at that time was an ally, Solomon knew that when his father-in-law died, a future king might not view Israel with the same kindness. And Assyria was also gaining in strength. It would be many years before she became a formidable power in the Middle East, but Solomon wanted to be prepared. He knew that after his passing the status quo might change. As he looked ahead to a time when his son would sit on his throne, he knew that Israel's defenses would be of the utmost importance. And so ...

> *he built the cities which Huram had given to him, and settled the sons of Israel there. Then Solomon went to Hamath-zobah and captured it. He built Tadmor in the wilderness and all the storage cities that he had built in Hamath. He also built upper Beth-horon and lower Beth-horon, fortified cities with walls, gates and bars; and Baalath and all the storage cities that Solomon had, and all the cities for his chariots and cities for his horsemen, and all that it pleased*

*Solomon to build in Jerusalem, in Lebanon, and in
all the land under his rule.*

For some reason the Chronicler makes reference to
the cities that Huram had given to Solomon.  At first this
seems to flatly contradict I Kings 9:11-14.  There we read
that Solomon gave to Huram certain cities in payment of a
debt, whereas here it is Huram giving certain cities to
Solomon.  Is there a discrepancy in the text, or is the
Chronicler purposefully rewriting history to make Solomon
look good in the eyes of his readers?  There are several
possible explanations, and it is not necessary to imagine (as
some writers have done) that the Chronicler put a "spin" on
this event because the truth would be damaging to
Solomon's reputation.

The central question that must be answered is,
"Were these cities the same as the ones Solomon had given
the Tyrian king?"  The thought of Solomon giving away
part of the Promised Land is unthinkable.  It would have
been easier for the biblical writer to ignore what happened
and omit all mention to these cities.  If the cities are the
same as those mentioned in I Kings 9:12-13, then it seems
likely that they were returned to Solomon because they had
first been ceded to Tyre as collateral for a loan (I Kings
9:14).  When the loan had been paid, the cities were
returned.  On the other hand, these may be cities given to
Israel as payment for the right to travel untaxed along
highways held by Israel.

The next matter to occupy the writer's attention is
the capture of Hamath-zobah.[1]  Apparently the king of
Zobah was intent on establishing his claim to the lucrative

---

[1] *Macmillan Bible Atlas, 105, 115.*

trade of the Tigris-Euphrates River valley. Revenue from caravans that used this route had poured into Israel from the time of David. Solomon immediately seized the principal city of Hamath-zobah so as to guarantee Israel's revenues.

Next, Solomon built (or rebuilt) Tadmor,[2] about 125 miles north east of Damascus. He also built storage cities in Hamath. When Assyria began to flex its muscles, this was one of the first sections of the country to fall before the might of their human war machine. For the present, however, Solomon placed the entire area under tribute.[3] Then he built (or rebuilt) Upper Beth Horon and Lower Beth Horon,[4] and Baalath (Joshua 19:44-not to be confused with the city of the same name mentioned in Joshua 19:8).[5] These cities were also situated on trade routes linking Jerusalem with the coast.

Once these cities were fortified and well provisioned, they could withstand a siege. And depending on the terrain, some of them had in them chariots and charioteers (e.g. Hazor, Megiddo, Gezer) and cavalry.

---

[2] *Ibid.*, 9, 43. For a brief history of the trade between Egypt and Israel with "the land between the rivers" (i.e., the Tigris and Euphrates), see A. Malamat, *Biblical Archaeologist* 21 (1958), 101, note 22. See also D. J. Wiseman, ed., *Peoples of Old Testament Times* (Oxford: Clarendon, 1973), 142-43.

[3] Z. Kallai has pointed out that to keep open such trade routes and prevent the caravans from being robbed, it would have been necessary for Solomon to maintain strong defenses (see his *Historical Geography of the Bible* [Jerusalem: Magnes, 1986] 73-74.

[4] *Macmillan Bible Atlas*, 56, 71, 73.

[5] *Ibid.*, 107.

When all of this had been done, the nation was more secure that ever before.

## ORGANIZATION OF THE KINGDOM (8:7-11)

Next, we consider Solomon's organization of the kingdom. This falls into three parts: The division of labor, the delegation of authority, and the domicile of Pharaoh's daughter.

### *Division of Labor (8:7-8)*

*All of the people who were left of the Hittites, the Amorites, the Perizzites, the Hivites and the Jebusites, who were not of Israel, from their descendants who were left after them in the land whom the sons of Israel had not destroyed, them Solomon raised as forced laborers for this day. But Solomon did not make slaves for his work from the sons of Israel; they were men of war, his chief captains and commanders of his chariots and his horsemen.*

Verses 7-10 mention two different groups of people. The first is the slave labor-force made up exclusively of the descendants of the pre-Israelites who lived in Canaan before the time of Joshua. It was a common practice to impose work of this kind on former enemies. Those who did not like the conditions could always leave Canaan and live elsewhere.

### Delegation of Authority (8:9-10)

The second group is mentioned in verses 9-10. *"But Solomon did not make slaves for his work from the sons of Israel; they were men of war, his chief captains and commanders of his chariots and his horsemen. These were the chief officers of King Solomon, two hundred and fifty who ruled over the people."* Some Bible scholars have imagined a contradiction between the Chronicler's record of Solomon's policies and the information presented in I Kings 5:13-14.[6] Different words are used: ***mas,*** *"forced labor,"* and ***mas 'obed,*** *"state slaves"* (cf. I Kings 9:21). Israelites worked on the Temple in a three-month rotation. One month was devoted to building the Temple and two months were spent at home. The Canaanites worked continuously, first on the Temple and then on the cities Solomon fortified for the defense of the nation.

The 250 Israelites who held rank in the military or as supervisors of construction (8:10) appear to contradict the number of 550 used by the writer of I Kings 9:23. Could this be a simple scribal error? If, however, the figure is linked with the 3,600 supervisors of II Chronicles 2:18 and the 3,300 in the parallel passage in I Kings (5:16), then the total in both books equals 3,850. The difference can be accounted for on the basis that when the Temple was finished certain individuals were assigned other responsibilities.

---

[6] Cf. I. Mendelsohn, *Biblical Archaeologist* 85 (1942), 13-14.

### Domicile of Pharaoh's Daughter (8:11)

Special mention is made of the palace built for Solomon's Egyptian wife. The reason for her move is a surprising one: The holiness of the Ark (8:11*b*).

> *"Then Solomon brought Pharaoh's daughter up from the city of David to the house which he had built for her, for he said, 'My wife shall not dwell in the house of David king of Israel, because the places are holy where the Ark of Yahweh has entered.'"*

Many commentators have speculated that Solomon's decision was based on sex, but in the light of modern advancements in our knowledge of ancient customs, this seems unlikely. Another possible reason may have been her pagan beliefs. Certainly it would be unthinkable for a worshipper of idols to live in close proximity to the Shekinah glory that filled the Holy of Holies. If, however, Pharaoh's daughter had become a believer in Yahweh when she married Solomon, then it is possible that the real issue was her retinue (both male and female) who continued to serve her needs. Whatever the real explanation, the point of this verse is Solomon's desire to keep sacred the Temple and its courts.

## WORSHIP WITHIN THE KINGDOM (8:12-16)

We now move to consider Solomon's example of piety, and his provision for the rotation of the priests and Levites:

> *Then Solomon offered burnt offerings to Yahweh on the altar of Yahweh which he had built before the porch; and did so according to the*

*daily rule, offering them up according to the
commandment of Moses, for the Sabbaths, the new
moons and the three annual feasts - the Feast of
Unleavened Bread, the Feast of Weeks and the
Feast of Booths. Now according to the ordinance
of his father David, he appointed the divisions of
the priests for their service, and the Levites for
their duties of praise and ministering before the
priests according to the daily rule, and the
gatekeepers by their divisions at every gate; for
David the man of God had so commanded. And
they did not depart from the commandment of the
king to the priests and Levites in any manner or
concerning the storehouses."*

Solomon's devotion to the Lord was evident in his
observance of the daily, weekly, monthly and annual
sacrifices. No matter what affairs of state demanded his
attention, he regularly offered up burnt offerings to the
Lord, together with incense. The former were wholly
consumed (Psalm 103:1) and intimated the entire
dedication of the individual to the Lord, while the latter
were symbolic of his prayers.

The priests and Levites performed their regular
functions, with the latter also singing hymns of praise to the
Lord, assisting the priests when necessary, and serving as
gatekeepers and treasurers (cf. I Chronicles 23:2-5, 28-31;
26:1-28). And they performed these tasks faithfully.

The Chronicler then brings this part of the nation's
history to a close by pointing out that *"all the work of
Solomon was carried out from the day of the foundation of
the house of Yahweh, and until it was finished. So the
house of Yahweh was completed."*

## PROMINENCE OF THE KINGDOM (8:17-9:28)

At the beginning of Solomon's reign, the Lord had promised him wisdom, wealth, and personal and national renown. Now, in demonstration of His faithfulness, we are given illustrations of the way in which He kept His word. The result was that Israel attained a prominence in the Near East that caused other nations to court her favor (cf. Deuteronomy 28:13).

### *Maritime Partnership (8:17-18)*

God honored Solomon's loyalty to Him, and the nation prospered. Huram had initially helped Solomon by supplying him with building materials for the Temple, and now Solomon reciprocated by allowing Huram access to the Red Sea and trade with the Orient. They joined forces to send ships from Ezion-geber (on the Gulf of Aqaba)[7] to Ophir.[8] The alliance between Israel and Tyre was beneficial to both countries. On the island of Elath just off shore, there is evidence of a large maritime complex. The pattern of the small harbors bears a striking resemblance to those of Tyre and Sidon on the Mediterranean coast,

---

[7] *Macmillan Bible Atlas*, 115, 116. Just at a time when there was no great power, either in Egypt or in Mesopotamia, that could dominate the land bridge from Asia to Africa, the newly united nation of Israel gained military and political supremacy over the principal corridors of commerce between the Euphrates and the delta of Egypt (I Kings 4:21, 24; II Chronicles 9:26). See also Blaiklock and Harrison, *New International Dictionary of Biblical Archaeology* 189-91.

[8] *Ibid.*, 346-47.

leading some archaeologists to conclude that these were
built by Huram's men.[9]

> *Then Solomon went to Ezion-geber and to*
> *Elath on the seashore in the land of Edom. And*
> *Huram by his servants sent him ships and servants*
> *who knew the sea; and they went with Solomon's*
> *servants to Ophir, and took from there four*
> *hundred and fifty talents of gold and brought them*
> *to King Solomon.*

In these verses the Chronicler is underscoring the
positive aspects of Solomon's reign. The result of this
union is the influx into Israel of an enormous amount of
gold (approx. 540,000 oz). These merchant ships also
*"brought algum trees and precious stones. From the*
*algum trees the king made steps for the house of Yahweh*
*and for the king's palace, and lyres and harps for the*
*singers; and none like that was seen before in the land of*
*Judah"* (9:10-11).

### International Recognition (9:1-12)

In appears from 8:17-9:12 that the Chronicler is
placing stress on Israel's growing fame, for Solomon now
received a visit from the Queen of Sheba (modern Yemen).
She had heard of Solomon's wisdom and came to verify
what she had heard by asking him many hard questions.

---

[9] *Ibid., 175-77*; N. Glueck, *Biblical Archaeologist* 1 (1938),
13-16; idem, *Bulletin of the American Schools of Oriental Research* 72
(1938), 2-13; idem, *Biblical Archaeologist* 28 (1965), 70-87; and the
more recent works by A. Flinders, *Secrets of Bible Seas: An*
*Underwater Archaeologist in the Holy Land* (London: Severn, 1985),
42-82; idem, *Biblical Archaeology Review* 15 (1989), 30-43.

*Now when the queen of Sheba[10] heard of
the fame of Solomon, she came to Jerusalem to
test Solomon with difficult questions. She had a
very large retinue, with camels carrying spices
and a large amount of gold and precious stones;
and when she came to Solomon, she spoke with
him about all that was on her heart.*

It is probable that her visit was also a trade mission.
Sheba[11] was a wealthy country. It had become famous for
its trade in frankincense and myrrh (cf. Ezekiel 27:22-23).
If the queen knew of Solomon's fleet that regularly sailed
to Ophir, then she may have wanted to counter competition
by entering into an alliance whereby Solomon's fleet on its
outward journey would carry spices from Sheba to distant
lands. Or she may have wanted to negotiate tariffs for the
privilege of expanding Sheba's trade along Israeli
highways to ports along the Mediterranean.

Whatever may have been the Queen's "other"
agenda, her primary goal was to ask Solomon the questions
that she desired to have answered. What these "hard
questions" were we do not know. Lacking biblical
revelation, all we can do is speculate. They may have been
about the possibility of knowing God, what constitutes
truth and about the possibility of eternal happiness after
death. Her questions may also have included the wonders

---

[10] Josephus (*Antiquities of the Jews*, VIII:6:5) identifies her as
Queen Nikaule—a similar identification to Herodotus (*History*, II:100)
who calls her Nitokris. Herodotus, however, believed that Nitokris
was Queen of Egypt and Ethiopia.

[11] Blaiklock and Harrison, *New International Dictionary of
Biblical Archaeology*, 409-10.

of God's providence, the mystery of creation and the
historic fact of the exodus when God broke the might of
Pharaoh in order to set His people free.  And so we read
that ...

> *Solomon answered all her questions;
> nothing was hidden from Solomon that he did not
> explain to her.  When the queen of Sheba had seen
> the wisdom of Solomon, the house that he had
> built, the food at his table, the seating of his
> servants, the attendance of his ministers and their
> attire, his cupbearers and their attire, and his
> stairway by which he went up to the house of
> Yahweh, she was breathless.*

> *Then she said to the king, "It was a true
> report that I heard in my own land about your
> words and your wisdom.  Nevertheless I did not
> believe their reports until I came and my eyes had
> seen it. And behold, the half of the greatness of
> your wisdom was not told me. You surpass the
> report that I heard.  How blessed are your men,
> how blessed are these your servants who stand
> before you continually and hear your wisdom.
> Blessed be Yahweh your God who delighted in
> you, **setting you on His throne** as king for Yahweh
> your God; because your God loved Israel
> establishing them forever, therefore **He made you
> king over them,** to do justice and righteousness"
> (emphasis added).*

The text makes it clear that Solomon's wisdom was
God-given.  The Lord enabled him to answer all of her
questions.  And when it is borne in mind that often in the
Middle East questions are phrased in the form of riddles,
Solomon would have had to probe the riddle before being

able to provide an answer to her question. *"Nothing was hidden from him."* The wisdom that God gave him enabled him to satisfactorily resolve all of the issues that lay heavily on the heart of Sheba's queen.

We can also imagine Solomon and the queen walking from his palace through the beautiful garden he had planted toward the Temple. The beauty of the palace would have impressed her, but when she saw the splendor of the Temple with the Shekinah glory, she was speechless. She now believed what had been told her and gave praise to the Lord.

When verses 5, 6 and 8 are linked together, there seems to be enough evidence to conclude that she became a believer in the God of Israel. But how can we be sure? In pagan cultures it was taboo to take the name of another god on one's lips. It was diplomatic to use the general term *elohim* that could be "God" or "gods" depending on the context, but to utter the name *Yahweh* would incur the anger of the god(s) whom the person professed to worship. While we may stretch the point to claim that the Queen of Sheba used the name of *Yahweh* out of awe for all that she had seen, it is more than likely that her heart had opened to the truth and she responded by acknowledging *Yahweh* as the God of all truth.

The queen also spoke of the Lord's *"love for Israel."* This was something unique. Pagan deities instilled fear in the hearts of their devotees. What the queen saw in Israel of the wealth and contentment of the people drew from her an expression of appreciation for God's elective love and the fact that His rule over them was beneficial. And if this is insufficient evidence to conclude that she came to believe in *Yahweh*, then let it be noted that she also acknowledged Solomon as the Lord's regent who sat on *"God's throne"* (9:8). She also praised Solomon's administration as *"just and righteous"* because Solomon's wisdom came directly from Him.

This testimony to the uniqueness of the nation of Israel as the people of God is followed by gifts that the queen gave to Solomon. These were in addition to the ones she would have presented at the time of her arrival (9:1). *"Then she gave the king one hundred and twenty talents of gold [approx. 144,000 oz.] and a very great amount of spices and precious stones. There had never been spice like that which the queen of Sheba gave to King Solomon."*

An exchange of gifts between heads of state had become a common practice in the ancient Near East, and Solomon reciprocated. *"King Solomon gave to the queen of Sheba all her desire which she requested besides a return for what she had brought to the king. Then she turned and went to her own land with her servants."* Her mission was a complete success.

There is an old and persistent tradition that the Queen of Sheba became Solomon's wife during her visit to Jerusalem; that she conceived, and on returning to her homeland bore a son. The Ethopians are tenacious in this belief. Apart from the information that they advance, there is no biblical evidence to support such conjecture.

### Evidence of Greatness (9:13-28)

The biblical writer now summarizes the wealth that poured into Israel (9:13-22) and the esteem in which Solomon was held by the *"kings of the earth"* (9:22-28).

**The Wealth of the Kingdom (9:13-22).** Solomon received enormous quantities of gold each year, besides exotic animals, ivory and goods from both east and west.

Now the weight of gold that came to Solomon in one year was 666 talents of gold, besides that which the traders and merchants brought; and all the kings of Arabia and the governors of the country brought gold and silver to Solomon.

*King Solomon made 200 large shields[12] of beaten gold, using 600 shekels of beaten gold on each large shield. He made 300 shields of beaten gold, using three hundred shekels of gold on each shield, and the king put them in the house of the Forest of Lebanon. Moreover, the king made a great throne of ivory and overlaid it with pure gold. There were six steps to the throne and a footstool in gold attached to the throne, and arms on each side of the seat, and two lions standing beside the arms. Twelve lions were standing there on the six steps on the one side and on the other; nothing like it was made for any other kingdom. All King Solomon's drinking vessels were of gold, and all the vessels of the house of the Forest of Lebanon were of pure gold; silver was not considered valuable in the days of Solomon. For the king had ships that went to Tarshish with the servants of Huram; once every three years the ships of Tarshish came bringing gold and silver, ivory and apes and peacocks. So*

---

[12] For an illustration, see Y. Yadin, *The Art of Warfare in Biblical Lands* (New York: McGraw-Hill, 1963), 13-15, 295, 360, 368. The large shields were used on state occasions.

> *King Solomon became greater than all the kings of*
> *the earth in riches and wisdom.*

Gold was so plentiful in Israel that silver (the usual currency) was no longer reckoned as a valuable metal. It is unnecessary to speculate on the symbolism of 666. The Chronicler attaches no significance to this figure. The Book of Revelation had as yet not been written, and would not deal with the mysterious characters and symbolism of the end times for a thousand years. What is important is the fact that Israel received nearly 800,000 ounces of gold annually as tribute from vassal kingdoms, trade with other nations, and tariffs imposed on merchants traversing highways under Israel's control.

Solomon also made large and small shields of gold, and an ivory throne that was unique throughout the world of his time. Its magnificence was enhanced by the steps that led up to the platform on which the throne was situated, and the gold lions that symbolically guarded the king's person.[13]

At the beginning of his reign the Lord had promised Solomon wisdom and riches and honor, and this record confirms that God was faithful and fulfilled His word.

**National Prestige (9:22-28)**. Verse 22 is a "hinge" verse. It summarizes verses 13-21 and explains the source of Solomon's greatness.

> *So King Solomon became greater than all*
> *the kings of the earth in riches and wisdom. And*
> *all the kings of the earth were seeking the*
> *presence of Solomon, to hear his wisdom **that God***

---

[13] Cf. A. R. Millard, *Vox Evangelica* 12 (1981), 5-18.

*had put in his heart. They brought every man his gift, articles of silver and gold, garments, weapons, spices, horses and mules, so much year by year. Now Solomon had 4,000 stalls for horses and chariots and 12,000 horsemen, and he stationed them in the chariot cities and with the king in Jerusalem. He was the ruler over all the kings from the Euphrates River even to the land of the Philistines, and as far as the border of Egypt. The king made silver as common as stones in Jerusalem, and he made cedars as plentiful as sycamore trees that are in the lowland. And they were bringing horses for Solomon from Egypt and from all countries (emphasis added).*

The fame that Solomon enjoyed was not the result of a fortuitous combination of circumstances. It was as a result of God's blessing. In addition to the gold that Solomon received, further symbols of his power and wealth were the horses, chariots and the ivory that he imported. To accommodate the horses, special stalls had to be built in certain cities. While it is common for us to think of two horses drawing a chariot, it is possible that Solomon's chariots were drawn by three horses, and that each chariot was manned by three soldiers.

OBITUARY (9:29-31)

The narrative about Solomon ends with an account of his death. In this, it follows an accepted pattern giving information where further information may be obtained, the length of his reign, his burial place and the name of his successor.

> *Now the rest of the acts of Solomon, from
> first to last, are they not written in the records of
> Nathan the prophet, and in the prophecy of Ahijah
> the Shilonite, and in the visions of Iddo the seer
> concerning Jeroboam the son of Nebat? Solomon
> reigned forty years in Jerusalem over all Israel.
> And Solomon slept with his fathers and was buried
> in the city of his father David; and his son
> Rehoboam reigned in his place.*

It is significant that no mention is made of
Solomon's spiritual lapse when he began worshipping the
gods of the nations that surrounded Israel. Solomon must
have recovered from this before he died, for he wrote the
Book of Ecclesiastes in which he warned the younger
generation of the importance of remaining faithful to the
Lord. The Chronicler knew that his readers were aware of
Solomon's fall, so there was no need to remind them of it.
What he emphasized instead was God's faithfulness in
forgiving sin. And once forgiven, Solomon's sin was
forgotten and he was restored to a position of blessing.
Such an emphasis would be of particular importance to the
returned exiles. They knew that the sins of their parents
and grandparents had caused the exile, and to be assured of
God's favor as a result of His grace (illustrated in His
pardon of Solomon) would be especially meaningful to
them.

With this summation of Solomon's glory the
Chronicler brings to an end his record of Israel's history.

## SEED THOUGHTS

We have touched on some areas of application
already. They will be mentioned again so as to bring into

one place some of the "seed thoughts" that can become the basis for future meditation. The Apostle Paul's words in Romans 15:4 should constantly be borne in mind. The entire Old Testament, including the chapters we have just covered, contains truths that can guide us on our pilgrimage by shedding light on our path.

### *Activity Should Not Be Allowed to Push Our Devotion to the Lord to the Margins of Our Lives*

Solomon's days were filled with activity. Though rich, he did not spend his time idly cavorting with his concubines. Instead, he busied himself with numerous building projects (8:1-11), organizing workers, fortifying strategic cities and insuring the continued prosperity of his people. In the end, the Chronicler could write, *"He built all that he desired"* (8:6). At no time, however, did he slacken in his devotion to the Lord.

Solomon also built a palace for Pharaoh's daughter. We may be sure that, having married her at a time when *"he loved the Lord with all his heart,"* he would not have taken her as his wife if she had not converted to Judaism. Why then did he not want her near the Ark? It seems obvious that Solomon was jealous for glory and honor of the Lord. He wanted to keep the worship of Yahweh free from all contaminating influences. Because his wife's vast retinue was made up of idolaters, he did not want their presence near the Ark. Likewise, we, in our devotion to the Lord, should keep His worship pure and unsullied from our daily contact with those who do not know the Lord and who refuse to allow Him to rule over them. This does not mean that we should have no contact with the unsaved. The teaching of the Apostle Paul is very clear on that point

(I Corinthians 5:10; II Corinthians 6:14-18). Rather it
points to the sense of reverential awe that should
characterize our worship.

### *Material Possessions Should Not be the Cause of Arrogance or Pride*

Solomon's diligence in his worship of the Lord was
not diminished as a result of the vast riches he amassed.
He was free from covetousness. He did not allow his riches
to cause him to conclude that he no longer needed God. He
reined in any temptation to pride and arrogance. Instead,
he was diligent in every aspect of His worship. This truth
is borne out by his conduct. He did not allow preoccupa-
tion with material possessions or worldly ambitions to push
to the periphery of his life the daily, weekly, monthly and
yearly requirements of the law. He took care to perform his
duty as each day required (8:14). Nor did he alter any of
the procedures that David had established. He did not
allow pride in his wisdom to lead him to think that he could
improve on what was working well. The priests and
Levites had their respective duties, and their rotation gave
each person the opportunity to serve in the Temple.

In the building of ships, he did not succumb to pride
that may have caused him to conclude that he had a
monopoly on all wisdom. He gladly availed himself of the
skills of the men of Tyre. They had the practical
knowledge of the sea that he lacked (8:18). And he
reciprocated by sharing with others the know-how the Lord
had given him.

In all things Solomon manifested befitting humility.

## *Praise from Others Affords Us an Opportunity to Witness to What the Lord has Done*

The visit from the Queen of Sheba is of particular importance for the Lord Jesus commended her for taking a long and tiring journey to visit Solomon. Her primary goal was to have her most pressing questions answered. She held nothing back, and Solomon was able to answer all of her questions because the Lord helped him. As he did so, he told her of the greatness of his God; revealed to her the principles he followed in building the Temple so that the weight of the gold did not crack the foundation; entertained her in his palace where she enjoyed a sumptuous feast and witnessed the quiet dignity of his servants; and sat her on a separate throne beside him as he tried cases and administered justice.

It is trite to say that Solomon gave glory to God for all his accomplishments. We often do the same, but with us it is often only a pious attempt to cover our pride. Solomon witnessed to the grace of God in giving him wisdom, and did so in such a self-effacing way that he impressed the Queen of Sheba with the reality of the goodness and grandeur of the One whom he worshipped. And, as we have pointed out, there is every reason to believe that she became a believer in the Lord as a result of her visit to Jerusalem.

## *Those Who Honor the Lord are in Turn Honored by Him*

Under Solomon, the Lord blessed His people so that they prospered and became the envy of the surrounding nations. Convinced of the greatness of the kingdom of Israel, kings from the surrounding nations sought

Solomon's favor. They visited him, brought gifts to him and received the same kind of witness to the truth that the Queen of Sheba received.

In these events, Solomon merely prefigured the Lord Jesus who will one day sit on David's throne as King over the nations. These monarchs will likewise bring Him gifts (9:14, 24, 28; cf. Psalm 68:29*b*; 76:11*b*; etc.).

### *Finally . . .*

Lastly, as we look back over Solomon's reign, we are reminded that God promised Solomon wisdom, riches and honor. Was His word fulfilled? It was. And in fulfilling every aspect of His pledge, the Lord showed that He is faithful to all that He vowed to do. His promises are sure! This truth is of encouragement to all believers. Often we wonder if He hears our prayers (James 1:5-8; I John 5:14). He is sovereign. Sometimes He withholds the answer to our prayers because He knows that what we have asked is not the best for us. At other times, He expects us to persevere in our prayers so that we are eventually brought to a place wherein He can give us the desires of our hearts.

God is faithful, and He will fulfill His Word. Of this Solomon is a witness.

# Chapter Five

# SUCCESSION WITHOUT SUCCESS

## II Chronicles 10:1-12:16

When King Solomon died in 931 B.C. his son, Rehoboam, succeeded him.

> *And Solomon slept with his fathers and was buried in the city of his father David; and his son Rehoboam reigned in his place (9:31).*

The Bible states his succession so matter-of-factly that we tend to pass over the event without grasping the significance of what we've read. The man to whom God gave a special name was gone. The kingdom that had its borders extended farther than at any time in the past, now had a new leader. But what kind of leader would he be? What kind of a situation did Rehoboam face when he ascended the throne? Was he prepared to lead God's people? Were there any unique problems that would require his immediate attention? And would he select wise advisors to counsel him as he made important decisions?

Rehoboam's own father, Solomon, had reigned jointly with David for a period of time. Solomon was the wisest of men and he inaugurated Israel's "golden age." The big question facing everyone was, "To what extent had Solomon prepared Rehoboam to lead the nation and carry on the Davidic tradition?"

Rehoboam knew about court life, but it would appear that he was untried and untrained in matters of leadership, administration, the implementation of justice, a wise handling of the economy and politics. And he also seems to have lacked a sound, biblically based faith. Perhaps Solomon intended to have Rehoboam rule jointly with him during the last ten years of his life, but inasmuch as he died prematurely, Rehoboam was denied the benefits of a co-regency. (This seems to be supported by the fact that there is no hint of a co-regency, and at the time of his coronation, Rehoboam did not have a cabinet to support him.)

As we read through these chapters we come across the names of several people that are both familiar and unfamiliar to us, and so a brief introduction to them will help us gain a better understanding of the biblical narrative.

## PRINCIPAL PERSONALITIES

We shall start with Solomon's son, Rehoboam.

**Rehoboam** had been given a name that meant "enlarger of the people." It would require extraordinary personal qualities for him to fulfill this desire on the part of his parents. In actual fact, under him the nation split into two unequal parts. The ten northern tribes were ruled by Jeroboam, leaving only the two southern tribes to be ruled by Rehoboam.

**Jeroboam** is an important person in biblical history. He had been an overseer under King Solomon. He was from the northern tribe of Ephraim, and was a very capable (but inordinately ambitious) young man. When Solomon suspected that he might be fomenting sedition, Jeroboam fled to Egypt. There he married the daughter of Shishak, king of Egypt. When Solomon died, Jeroboam returned to Israel and led a rebellion against Rehoboam. He was later crowned king over the ten northern tribes of Israel.[1]

As far as the present study is concerned, Jeroboam's significance lies in the fact that he provides us with an important illustration of demagoguery. He had the ability to sense the movement of the crowd (today, politicians use "polls" and "focus groups") and to run ahead so as to lead the way. Demagogues find it easy to cloak personal ambition under the guise of care for the welfare of a specific group of people (e.g., the oppressed, the persecuted, the socially deprived, the elderly, etc.). Jeroboam was skilled in this art. But he was unprincipled and is now forever remembered as *"Jeroboam the son of Nebat, who made Israel to sin."*

**Wise counselors**. These men had given counsel to King Solomon. Rehoboam sought their advice, but found it unpalatable. They did not tell him what he wanted to hear.[2]

**Young counselors**. These men had grown up with Rehoboam in Solomon's court. They were not a clearly defined "council," but were a part of the indulged aristocracy. Their advice was bold, but they lacked wisdom and discretion. They had no patience with the older generation that was dying off, and counseled Rehoboam to assert his authority.

---

[1] See M. Aberbach and I. Smoler, *Journal of Biblical Literature* 88 (1969), 69-72; and D. Gooding, *Journal of Biblical Literature* 91 (1972), 529-33.

[2] D. Evans, *Journal of Near Eastern Studies* 25 (1966), 273-79.

**Shemaiah** was the prophet who dissuaded Rehoboam from attacking the northern tribes.

**Shishak**, Pharaoh of Egypt, who reigned from 945-924 B.C., invaded Judah, took all of Rehoboam's fortified cities and carried away the treasures of the palace and the Temple.

## OUTLINE

As we have seen, II Chronicles carries forward the history begun in I Chronicles. In setting forth an outline, we must of necessity place our present study in the mainstream of the Chronicler's record. Looking back, we note a phrase in I Chronicles 10:14 that also occurs in our present chapter (10:5), namely, *"turn of events"* or *"turned over."* The former marks a division in the biblical writer's history when, following the death of Saul, the kingdom was "turned over" to David. And here the same word is used for the division of the kingdom. Our study continues, therefore, with ...

III.  THE DIVIDED KINGDOM (10:1-36:23)

A.  The Reign of the Kings of Judah (10:1-36:21)

　　　1.  Rehoboam, Son of Solomon (10:1-12:16)

　　　　　　The Evidence of His Folly (10:1-19)

　　　　　　The Value of His Obedience (11:1-23)

　　　　　　The Extent of God's Mercy (12:1-12)

　　　　　　Obituary (12:13-16)

## REHOBOAM, SON OF SOLOMON (10:1-12:16)

Rehoboam reigned over Judah from 931-910 B.C.—a much shorter reign than that of either his grandfather or father, who each reigned for 40 years. Much has been written about Rehoboam's life at court. None of it is complimentary and some of it is misleading.

As we have noted, Rehoboam was born to Solomon and Naamah, an Ammonite princess (1 Kings 14:31), whose marriage had probably been arranged by David. It strains our understanding of David as a righteous king to imagine him contracting a marriage for his son with a pagan. And it is even harder to imagine that Naamah was one of those women who turned Solomon's heart away from the Lord.[3] It is more likely that David, whose influence for good extended far beyond the borders of Israel, and through whom kings and some of their subjects came to faith in the God of Israel, had significantly influenced the king of Ammon.[4] If this is so, then he chose a bride for his son who had become a worshipper of Yahweh.

---

[3] This is the contention of F. W. Farrar in *Solomon, His Life and Times*, 8-9. 146-47, and G. Rawlinson, *The Kings of Israel and Judah*, 1-3, as well as some contemporary writers.

[4] Cf. His influence on Achish, king of Gath. In addition, Ittai and 600 Gittites followed David because they were impressed with David's leadership qualities. Ittai later became a believer in the God of Israel, and perhaps other Philistines did as well. David was also on friendly terms with Nahash, king of Ammon, and his son, Shobi, supported David when he fled from Absalom (I Kings 17:27-29). If Naamah was the daughter of Shobi, then there is even more reason to hold that she was a believer in the God of Israel.

It is true that Rehoboam grew to adulthood surrounded by wealth and luxury. However, inasmuch as Solomon probably followed the same practice as David in assigning each of his wives a separate house in which to live, the criticism that his son was adversely affected by the evils of polygamy (as a result of competition among the wives) is unfounded. What is more plausible is that, as the heir apparent,[5] he was accustomed to having slaves cater to his every wish. In other words, he was unused to being denied anything that he wanted. It is also alarming to note the absence of evidence that he was given any significant responsibility (cf. Lamentations 3:27). This leaves open the possibly that he was thoroughly spoiled—fawned over and flattered by servants and surrounded by young men who encouraged his foibles (I Kings 12:8). And as the reign of Solomon had been a peaceful one, there were no wars to test Rehoboam's courage or develop his skills.

How did the ease and comfort of court life impact Solomon's assessment of his son? There is a passage in the wise king's writings that may give us some indication of how he felt about Rehoboam. He wrote *"Thus I hated all the fruit of my labor for which I had labored under the sun,*

---

[5] Scripture does not record that any other sons were born to Solomon. At first this seems unlikely, for we are told that he had 700 wives (possibly a scribal error for 70) who were princesses and 300 concubines (I Kings 11:3; cf. Song of Solomon 6:8a), but their very number would limit conception rather than increase it. In Proverbs, chs. 1-9, Solomon does speak of the counsel he gave to his "sons," but in Proverbs 1:8, 10, 15; 2:1; 3:1, 11, 21; 4:10, 20; 5:1, 20; 6:1, 3, 20; and 7:1 he uses the singular "son," lending weight to the possibility that he had only one son. His use of the plural "sons" is less frequent and may refer to the children of his officials whom he (Solomon) instructed. These "sons" were most certainly the "young men who grew up with Rehoboam."

*for I must leave it to the man who will come after me. And
who knows whether he will be a wise man or a fool? Yet he
will have control over all the fruit of my labor for which I
have labored by acting wisely under the sun"* (Ecclesiastes
2:18-19).  Possible prolonged idleness, too many female
servants to cater to his every wish, and the lack of a godly
mentor[6] had ill-prepared Rehoboam for leadership.

### The Evidence of His Folly (10:1-19)

When Rehoboam was 41, his father died
prematurely and he found himself thrust into a position of
authority and responsibility.  There must have been
rumblings of discontent among the northern tribes and so,
as a conciliatory move, it was decided to hold Rehoboam's
coronation at Shechem[7] rather than in Jerusalem.  While
plans were underway for the ceremony, friends of
Jeroboam send to him word of what had happened.  He left
Egypt and hastened to return to Israel.  There he led the
group that came to Rehoboam asking for an easing of their
taxes and of the forced labor that Solomon had imposed on
them.

> *Then Rehoboam went to Shechem, for all
> Israel had come to Shechem to make him king.
> When Jeroboam the son of Nebat heard of it (for
> he was in Egypt where he had fled from the*

---

[6] Solomon had Nathan to mentor him, but there is no mention
of Rehoboam having someone like Shemaiah. Rehoboam's later
mistakes underscore the importance of spiritual instruction.

[7] *Macmillan Bible Atlas*, 113, 118. See also *Encyclopedia of
Archaeological Excavations in the Holy Land*, IV: 1083-94 (note
bibliography), and G. E. Wright, *Shechem, The Biography of a Biblical
City* (London:  Duckworth, 1965), 270pp.

*presence of King Solomon), Jeroboam returned
from Egypt. So they sent and summoned him.
When Jeroboam and all Israel came, they spoke to
Rehoboam, saying, "Your father made our yoke
hard; now therefore lighten the hard service of
your father and his heavy yoke which he put on us,
so that we may serve you." He [Rehoboam] said
to them, "Return to me again in three days." So
the people departed (10:1-5).*

Shechem (modern Nablus) was a very ancient city.
It had flourished long before the exodus of the Israelites
from Egypt, and it was there that the tribes (after their
conquest of the land) had renewed their covenant with the
Lord (Joshua 24:1-27). Shechem seems to have been a
place of importance for, following the death of Gideon, the
men of that city took on the role of "king maker" and made
Gideon's son, Abimelech, their king (Judges 9:1-57).

Whatever plans were made by the people of
Shechem for Rehoboam's coronation, there was one
notable omission: *God was left out.*

Sometime during Rehoboam's stay in the city, a
delegation led by Jeroboam approached him with a request
to have their taxes reduced and their compulsory labor
lightened (10:4). What could be more reasonable?
However, there was an ominous innuendo in their closing
words, "Lighten our hard service ... so that we may serve
you" (with the unexpressed threat, "If you don't, we
won't").

Rehoboam had already made a major concession in
coming to Shechem for the coronation, and he needed time
to reflect on this new demand. He, therefore, asked for
three days to think about their proposition. This does not

mean three full days (i.e., 72 hours), for in Old Testament times, up to and including the life of Christ, a part of a day was considered as a whole day. So, in effect, what he said was, "Come back the day after tomorrow."

As the new king, confronted with an important decision, Rehoboam wanted to consult with others before giving his answer to Jeroboam. After all, this would be his first official act.

> *Then King Rehoboam consulted with the elders who had served his father Solomon while he was still alive, saying, "How do you counsel me to answer this people?" They spoke to him, saying, "If you will be kind to this people and please them and speak good words to them, then they will be your servants forever." But he forsook the counsel of the elders that they had given him, and consulted with the young men who grew up with him and served him. So he said to them, "What counsel do you give that we may answer this people, who have spoken to me, saying, 'Lighten the yoke that your father put on us'?" The young men who grew up with him spoke to him, saying, "Thus you shall say to the people who spoke to you, saying, 'Your father made our yoke heavy, but you make it lighter for us.' Thus you shall say to them, 'My little finger is thicker than my father's loins! Whereas my father loaded you with a heavy yoke, I will add to your yoke; my father disciplined you with whips, but I will discipline you with scorpions'" (10:6-11).*

Did Rehoboam possess even a fraction of the wisdom for which Solomon had prayed? Did he ask God for guidance as he faced the first test of his leadership? And how carefully did he weigh the request of the northern tribes? Were their grievances valid, and how should he respond to the latent threat that was present in their words. Rehoboam's father had drawn attention to the fact that a *"soft answer turns away wrath"* (Proverbs 15:1; see also Proverbs 30:33). Would Rehoboam follow his father's counsel as he faced this volatile situation?

The counsel Rehoboam receives from the elders is wise. But it does not please the new monarch who may have felt, "I've already made one concession to the northern tribes by coming to Shechem, if I make another they may think that I am weak. Will a concession made now pave the way for more demands later on? And what of their implied threat that '…if you don't agree to our demand, we won't "serve you" (i.e., remain loyal to the crown)?'"

Feeling uneasy, Rehoboam turns to his associates and asks them what counsel they have to offer. Their response is in keeping with his way of thinking. In essence, they counsel him, "Show them who's boss. Don't let them push you around. You're king and they must be taught to respect you. So lay down the law. Reject their request. They'll fall into line. Then, at a later time, should you so desire, you can lighten their burdens and everyone will praise you for being a true humanitarian."[8]

---

[8] Rawlinson, *Studies in I and II Kings*, 5, has this observation: "Prerogative was in question, and prerogative is naturally dear to kings…. Hangers-on at court [are] more loath to yield one jot or tittle

> *So when Jeroboam and all the people*
> *came to Rehoboam on the third day as the king*
> *had directed, saying, "Return to me on the third*
> *day." The king answered them harshly, and King*
> *Rehoboam forsook the counsel of the elders. He*
> *spoke to them according to the advice of the young*
> *men, saying, "My father made your yoke heavy,*
> *but I will add to it; my father disciplined you with*
> *whips, but I will discipline you with scorpions."*
> *So the king did not listen to the people, for it was a*
> *turn of events from God that the LORD might*
> *establish His word, which He spoke through*
> *Ahijah, the Shilonite to Jeroboam the son of*
> *Nebat. When all Israel saw that the king did not*
> *listen to them the people answered the king,*
> *saying, "What portion do we have in David? We*
> *have no inheritance in the son of Jesse. Every man*
> *to your tents, O Israel; Now look after your own*
> *house, David"[9]. So all Israel departed to their*
> *tents (10:12-16).*

Rehoboam's haughtiness reveals his true character. The *"fool* (to paraphrase Proverbs 26:4) *was rightly answered according to his folly"* (cf. Proverbs 14:16; 19:1). His response was rash and served only to exacerbate an already volatile situation. The outcome was predictable. *"When all Israel saw that the king did not listen to them the*

---

of it than kings themselves. Persons of this class no doubt pointed out to Rehoboam that it was no light matter that was in question, but really the very character of the monarchy." See also Herodotus, *History*, II:124, 128.

[9] H. G. M. Williamson, *Oudtestamentische Studien* 21 (1981), 172-76.

*people answered the king, saying, 'What portion do we
have in David? We have no inheritance in the son of Jesse.
Every man to your tents, O Israel; now look after your own
house, David.'"*

The statement, *"To your tents, O Israel"* was the
equivalent of saying, "We secede from the kingdom. From
now on all allegiance to David's dynasty is a thing of the
past."[10]

Too late, Rehoboam realizes how he has misjudged
the situation. Further evidence of his propensity for folly is
to be found in what happens next. *"Then King Rehoboam
sent Hadoram, **who was over the forced labor,** and the
sons of Israel stoned him to death"* (10:18. Emphasis
added). Rehoboam probably gave Hadoram the power to
try and reach a compromise with Jeroboam and the people
from the north. His belated action gives us further
evidence of his ability to turn a problem into a catastrophe.
It was like sending a sheriff to console a family that he has
just evicted, or having the representative of the IRS try to
mollify an impoverished family after he has confiscated all
their goods for failure to pay their taxes.

In the eyes of the northerners, Hadoram was
responsible for their oppression. When he came to

---

[10] C. Knapp, in *The Kings of Israel and Judah* (New York:
Loizeaux, 1956), 32, writes: "under the government of God this
division of the kingdom was the punishment of the sins of Solomon (I
Kings 11:33), occasioned by the folly of Rehoboam." However, as we
weigh carefully God's words to Jeroboam through His prophet, we see
that the Lord did *not* promise Jeroboam an enduring dynasty (I Kings
11:37-39). His right to rule was conditioned upon his obedience to
God's commandments. This point underscores what we will read about
in the next chapter.

negotiate with them, their anger erupted and they stoned
him to death.  Rehoboam came too late to see the mess he
had made of his recent diplomatic negotiations, and he
"made haste to mount his chariot to flee to Jerusalem."   At
least there he would be safe.  Then the Chronicler (who
wrote four centuries later and had the perspective of
history) concludes by adding, *So Israel has been in
rebellion against the house of David to this day.*

### *The Value of His Obedience (11:1-23)*

Unaccustomed to such insolent insubordination,
Rehoboam determined to punish the insurrectionists.  He
hastily raised an army from the tribes of Judah and
Benjamin and marched northward.  One of God's prophets,
a man named Shemaiah,[11] is sent to stop the carnage before
it starts.

> *Now when Rehoboam had come to
> Jerusalem, he assembled the house of Judah and
> Benjamin, 180,000 chosen men who were
> warriors, to fight against Israel to restore the
> kingdom to Rehoboam.  But the word of the LORD
> came to Shemaiah the man of God, saying,
> "Speak to Rehoboam the son of Solomon, king of
> Judah, and to all Israel in Judah and Benjamin,
> saying, 'Thus says the LORD, "You shall not go
> up or fight against your relatives; return every
> man to his house, for this thing is from Me."'"*

---

[11] The "man of God" of 11:2 is later identified as a prophet of
the Lord (12:5-8).  Outward appearances can be deceiving.

*So they listened to the words of the LORD*
*and returned from going against Jeroboam....*
*Moreover, the priests and the Levites who were in*
*all Israel stood with Rehoboam from all their*
*districts.*

It would appear that Rehoboam believed he could
compel the submission of the northern tribes.  He had
entered the territory of Ephraim, just beyond the border of
Benjamin, when Shemaiah who is identified as a *"man of*
*God"* confronted him and his army.  Speaking to them in
the name of the Lord, he tells them to return to their homes.
And the people listen to the voice of the prophet and return
to their homes.[12]  The text does not say that Rehoboam
listened.  Perhaps it was only when he saw his men turning
around and walking back toward their cities and farms that
he reluctantly rode back to Jerusalem.

The situation Rehoboam now faced was an
invidious one.  He could expect hostility from Jeroboam.
And he realized belatedly (as the facts of Jeroboam's exile
were made known to him) the severity of the threat posed
his people as a consequence of Jeroboam's earlier contact
with Shishak, king of Egypt.  To meet these challenges,
Rehoboam strengthens Judah's defenses by fortifying
Bethlehem, Etam, Tekoa, Beth-zur, Soco, Adullam, Gath,
Mareshah, Ziph, Adoraim, Lachish, Azekah, Zorah, Aijalon

---

[12] It would appear as if the people are spiritually more
sensitive to a message from the Lord than their sovereign.  They
recognized the words of the prophet as God's message to them; he
apparently did not.

and Hebron.[13]  He also reinforces the fortresses and puts officers in them with stores of food, oil and wine, and military equipment so that each city is adequately equipped to withstand an attack.[14]  George Rawlinson, a renowned historian of a generation past, writes:

> The situation was critical.  The Northern Kingdom, even if left to itself and not made the object of an organized attack, would necessarily be a hostile kingdom, and would require careful watching, and the perpetual maintenance of an attitude of defense.  But this was not the worst.  It would be supported by a southern kingdom of very much greater power, which might at any moment exchange a passive support for active intervention, and which it would be difficult, if not impossible, to resist.  Egypt, which had protected Jeroboam from the hostility of Solomon (I Kings 11:40), would be likely to lend effectual aid if invited to do so ....  Awake to these perils, Rehoboam, after his return to Jerusalem, lost no time in strengthening the defenses of his kingdom.[15]

---

[13] O. R. Sellers, *Biblical Archaeologist* 21 (1958), 71-76; F. M. Cross, Jr., and G. E. Wright, *Journal of Biblical Literature* 75 (1956), 216ff.

[14] *Macmillan Bible Atlas,* 119.  The reference to "Gath" may be to "Moresheth-Gath" rather than to the Philistine city.  Cf. N. Na'aman, *Bulletin of the American Schools of Oriental Research* 261 (1986), 5-21; idem, *ibid.*, 271 (1988), 69-73; and Y. Garfinkel, *Bulletin of the American Schools of Oriental Research* 271 (1988), 74-77.

[15] Rawlinson, *Studies in I and II Kings*, 8-9.

In addition to the threat of an attack from either the north or the south, the kingdom of Judah suffered economically when the northern tribes split away, for the Northern Kingdom held almost all of the agricultural wealth. Within its borders was the fertile Valley of Jezreel; and Galilee was known for its fine olives and vine-clad hills and the abundance of fish to be caught in its lake. In addition, and for a time, they also benefited from the taxation of caravans traveling along the major trade routes. In the south, however, all of this changed. The "golden age" of Solomon quickly vanished. Judah was reduced to virtual poverty. They still had the Temple and prided themselves in their worship of the one true God, but the land to the south (the Negev) was a harsh wilderness that was only suitable for grazing sheep and goats.

God, however, did not abandon His people. Evidence of His blessing may be seen in the fact that many of the Levites in the north left their pasturelands and their property and came to Judah and Jerusalem. Jeroboam made satyrs (goat idols) and golden calves the principal objects of worship, but not all the people were happy with his new innovations. There were many from among the tribes of Israel who set their hearts to seek the Lord. They journeyed to Jerusalem in order to sacrifice to the God of their fathers in the place of His appointment. In time, they too stayed in Judah with the result that they strengthened Rehoboam's kingdom.

For three years, Rehoboam and the people of Judah walked in the way of David and Solomon (11:13-17). The Northern Kingdom was gradually weakened by defections, whereas the Southern Kingdom gained in strength. Furthermore, as Rehoboam was submissive to the will of the Lord, He blessed him. And one of the ways He chose to do this was by increasing Rehoboam's family. In this way Rehoboam was assured of a continuing dynasty.

> *Then Rehoboam took as a wife Mahalath the daughter of Jerimoth the son of David and of Abihail the daughter of Eliab the son of Jesse, and she bore him sons: Jeush, Shemariah and Zaham. After her he took Maacah the daughter of Absalom, and she bore him Abijah, Attai, Ziza and Shelomith. Rehoboam loved Maacah the daughter of Absalom more than all his other wives and concubines. For he had taken eighteen wives and sixty concubines and fathered twenty-eight sons and sixty daughters. Rehoboam appointed Abijah the son of Maacah as head and leader among his brothers, for he intended to make him king. He acted wisely and distributed some of his sons through all the territories of Judah and Benjamin to all the fortified cities, and he gave them food in abundance. And he sought many wives for them (11:18-23).*

Reflecting back on his own days at court, Rehoboam determined that his children would not spend their years in idleness. He dispersed them throughout the major cities of Judah and Benjamin, providing amply for them and insuring that each of his sons had the comfort and contentment of a wife and family. In this, he acted wisely. However, he appointed Abijah, the son of his favorite wife, as chief prince. This may not have involved a co-regency, but probably necessitated that Abijah serve as general of his army.

### The Extent of God's Mercy (12:1-12)

We have all met people who will walk humbly before the Lord when the arctic winds of adversity blow fiercely upon them. When this happens they quickly repent of any sins they have committed, and God in His grace forgives them and blesses them. After a while, however, they tire of a life of godliness and begin to assert their independence. It was thus with Rehoboam. *"When the kingdom of Rehoboam was established and strong, he and all Israel with him forsook the law of Yahweh"* (12:1).

The reference to *"Israel"* probably refers to the tribe of Judah whose numbers have been augmented by defectors from the north. What is important is the effect Rehoboam's conduct has on his subjects. They throw off the yoke of the Lord and go awhoring after other gods. God, however, is not to be mocked. What happened to Rehoboam after this is instructive. When he believed himself to be secure, the Lord showed him that apart from His protection and blessing, he was weak.

> *And it came about in King Rehoboam's fifth year, because they had been unfaithful to the LORD, that Shishak king of Egypt came up against Jerusalem with 1,200 chariots and 60,000 horsemen. And the people who came with him from Egypt were without number: the Lubim, the Sukkiim and the Ethiopians. He captured the fortified cities of Judah and came as far as Jerusalem (12:2-4).*

As we look back we note certain facts: (1) It was God who had established Rehoboam; (2) after that, Rehoboam strengthened himself; and (3) when he felt that he no longer needed the Lord (i.e., was *unfaithful* to the

Lord), he was taught that it is a very serious thing for anyone to turn his or her back on the Lord. To do so is to invite some form of chastisement. And often He shows us our weakness in the very place where we thought we were strongest.

Brenda had divorced her husband because he had begun cavorting with younger women in the church they attended. When the leaders of the church found out about his "sexcapades" they moved to discipline him. He resigned before any action could be taken. Brenda, of course, was devastated. Long before the divorce, she boldly asserted to all that would listen to her that she would not have sex until she remarried. This was a bold and commendable stand (cf. Hebrews 13:4).

A number of years passed (perhaps as many as eight) and Brenda maintained a commendable abstinence. Then, after dating a young man for several months, and desperately desiring the closeness of intimacy, Brenda willingly yielded to him each time they were together. She believed that their forthcoming marriage would make everything right. Later, when they broke up, she regretted her weakness, began to doubt her spiritual commitment, and realized that she had fallen at the very point where she believed she was strongest.

To punish Rehoboam, the Lord allowed Shishak to invade Judah. Pharaoh had strengthened his army by including Libyans and Sukkites (from western Egypt), and Cushites (Sudanese or Ethiopians) from the south. They quickly overran Rehoboam's entire kingdom. The fortified cities offered little or no resistance when their inhabitants saw the might of the armies that had come against them. And everything Rehoboam had trusted in vanished.

What were Rehoboam and the leaders of the people to do? They met to discuss their most viable human options. Their combined wisdom, however, failed to produce a solution. Fortunately for them, the Lord did not leave them without knowledge of the cause of their misfortune. All of a sudden their meeting was interrupted as they were informed that Shemaiah wished to speak to them. It is quite possible that none of them wanted to speak to the prophet, but his presence did offer them a ray of hope. When he was shown into the room where they were meeting, he came straight to the point.

> Then Shemaiah the prophet came to Rehoboam and the princes of Judah who had gathered at Jerusalem because of Shishak, and he said to them,
>
> *"Thus says the LORD, 'You have forsaken Me, so I also have forsaken you to Shishak.'" So the princes of Israel and the king humbled themselves and said, "The LORD is righteous" (emphasis added).*

On hearing the prophet's rebuke, the leaders of the people acknowledged the truthfulness of his words and confessed their sins. They also humbly entreated God's favor (cf. 7:14). Rehoboam their king, who should have taken the lead, became instead their follower. However, he, too, humbled himself.

> *When the LORD saw that they humbled themselves, the word of the LORD came to Shemaiah, saying, "They have humbled themselves so I will not destroy them, but I will grant them some measure of deliverance, and My wrath shall not be poured out on Jerusalem by means of Shishak. But they will become his slaves*

*so that they may learn the difference between My*
*service and the service of the kingdoms of the*
*countries. "*

In response to their repentance, God in His great
grace sent Shemaiah back to them. He would grant them
some relief, but because they would not willingly serve
Him, they would know the yoke of a different lord. They
would be Shishak's vassals. And, for sparing the city,
Shishak took all the treasures of the Temple and the king's
palace.

*So Shishak king of Egypt ... took the*
*treasures of the house of the LORD and the*
*treasures of the king's palace. He took everything;*
*he even took the golden shields that Solomon had*
*made. Then King Rehoboam made shields of*
*bronze in their place and committed them to the*
*care of the commanders of the guard who guarded*
*the door of the king's house. As often as the king*
*entered the house of the LORD, the guards came*
*and carried them and then brought them back into*
*the guards' room. And when he humbled himself,*
*the anger of the LORD turned away from him, so*
*as not to destroy him completely; and also*
*conditions were good in Judah.*

In a matter of a few days, the wealth that David and
Solomon had accumulated over many years, was gone.[16]
The Temple and Rehoboam's palace were stripped of their
riches.

---

[16] K. A. Kitchen, *Biblical Archaeology Review* 15, No. 3
(1989), 32-33.

The Chronicler makes specific mention of the fact that Shishak took with him the golden shields that Solomon had made. And Rehoboam, fearing a loss of face before his people, has replicas of bronze made to take their place. In the bright light of the sun, and as Rehoboam walked to the Temple and then returned to his palace, the shields look the same. In reality they are a poor substitute for the real thing. They projected the impression of wealth and signaled "All is well," but in reality they merely covered up the true situation in Judah. *Ichabod, "Your glory has departed,"* could be written over Rehoboam's reign.

After the withdrawal of the Egyptians and their allies, Rehoboam knew that he and his people were in a vulnerable position. His defenses in the south were now virtually nonexistent, and to the north Jeroboam still posed a serious threat. *"So he strengthened himself in Jerusalem and reigned"* over God's people. The might of the kingdom of David and Solomon, however, was now only a memory.

### Obituary (12:13-16)

The Chronicler concludes with a brief summary of Rehoboam's reign:

> *Now Rehoboam was forty-one years old when he began to reign, and he reigned seventeen years in Jerusalem, the city that the LORD had chosen from all the tribes of Israel, to put His name there. And his mother's name was Naamah the Ammonitess.* **He did evil because he did not set his heart to seek the LORD.** *Now the acts of Rehoboam, from first to last, are they not written in the records of Shemaiah the prophet and of*

*Iddo the seer, according to genealogical*
*enrollment? And there were wars between*
*Rehoboam and Jeroboam continually. And*
*Rehoboam slept with his fathers and was buried in*
*the city of David; and his son Abijah became king*
*in his place* (emphasis added).

The words in italics refer back to 7:14.[17]  Though
chastened by Shishak's invasion, Rehoboam did not
prepare his heart to seek the Lord.  As a result, when God
passed judgment on his life, He characterized it as evil.

The Hebrew word *ma'al,* "evil," has as its root "to
break a trust."  A trust can be broken willfully or
unintentionally.  In Rehoboam's case, it was the former.
He sinned against the Lord and involved his people in the
results of his apostasy. When weighed in the balances, he
was found wanting.

## SOMETHING TO THINK ABOUT

### Resolving Personal Difficulties

One of the first lessons we learn from the
Chronicler's record is that no human leader can bring about
a perfect society.  Solomon advanced the fortunes of his
people so that they enjoyed peace and prosperity.  He may
have been indiscreet in the way he expected people to work
on his building projects or those whom he appointed to
supervise the work may have abused the power entrusted to
them.  Whatever the case, there were those within the
empire who felt they were being oppressed.  They became
malcontented and ungrateful, and did not balance the

---

[17] See the remarks of Allen, *1, 2 Chronicles,* 239-40.

benefits of Solomon's reign against the problems of working on the things that were of advantage to all.

If we concede that the people were being exploited, we must also admit that there was a better way of resolving the problem than having someone such as Jeroboam issue demands. A reasonable statement of grievances, followed by a *speedy* investigation of the situation, with prompt action taken where necessary, is preferable to (veiled) threats and hostile ultimatums.

Learning From the Wise

Second, the wisdom of experience is a priceless heritage (cf. 10:6-7). Our young people tend to be intolerant of their elders, believing them to be out of touch with the spirit of the times. And in some respects they may be right. But many of our senior citizens possess a knowledge of the Word of God that has been tested in the marketplace. They may not be numbered among the rich and famous of this world, but their sagacious insights can prevent problems from escalating into predicaments with far-reaching implications.

Divisions (e.g., *"What portion do we have in David?"* 10:16ff.) are easily caused, but they are not as easily corrected (cf. 13:4-12). The twelve tribes of Israel constituted a unit. Now, because of the division of the tribes, brother was prepared to lift up his hand against brother. In our day many a heart-broken parent can testify to the pain of division within their home and of the difficulties of reconciliation. Unfortunately, some sundered relationships are never mended.

Obeying God's Word

Third, God speaks to us primarily through special
revelation (i.e., His Word). Sensitivity is needed to detect
what He may be saying. This involves a dependence on the
leading of the Holy Spirit. Rehoboam's men discerned in
Shemaiah's words the command of the Lord, and obeyed.
The king only went along with them when he saw the ranks
of his army beginning to thin.

Rehoboam had been reared by a father who spent
time with him and sought to instill in him biblically-based
beliefs, values and goals (Proverbs 1:1-9:18). Apparently
Rehoboam did not respond to Solomon's instruction and so
began his reign by making a series of mistakes. He
recovered, however, and for a three-year period acted
wisely. Solomon would have been proud of him. But there
came a time when, in the pride of his heart, he thought he
no longer needed to depend on the Lord and began to
indulge in questionable things. When God's judgment did
not fall on him immediately, he may have thought that he
could get away with his transgressions of God's law. This
soon led to *"forsaking the law of the Lord"* (12:1)
altogether. And having tried the patience and
lovingkindness of God, God intervened and quickly
removed the things in which he had trusted.

I have dealt with Rehoboam's substituting shields
of brass for the shields of gold that Solomon had made in
my commentary on I Kings. I shall not repeat here what I
mentioned there. Sufficient to say that each time
Rehoboam went to the Temple, he saw the evidence of
God's presence in the pillar of cloud by day and the pillar
of fire by night. These phenomena could not be duplicated
in pagan worship. And he, who should have *"established
his people,"* ended up like a frightened rabbit in its burrow

(12:13). He was reduced to such pitiful straits that he could no longer fortify the cities of Judah. All this is a sad commentary on the results of self-will.

## Preparing Our Hearts to Seek the Lord

Finally, as a pastor, I occasionally perform funeral services. When a person reaches the end of the days allotted to him or her by God, the only thing that really matters is his/her relationship with the Lord. I conducted one funeral service for a man who had been a very successful businessman. Before he died, he confided in me that his many accomplishments, numerous philanthropic activities, and scores of accolades meant nothing to him. All he wanted to know was how he stood with the Lord.

Rehoboam's obituary is precise (12:13-16). His lasting epitaph is found in the words, *"He did evil in the sight of the Lord, because he did not prepare his heart to seek the Lord."* As we shall see, this criterion will become one of the Chronicler's main points of emphasis. God had given Rehoboam ample evidence of His authority, His power and His right to be worshipped. The responsibility to seek Him rested with Rehoboam—as it does with each one of us.

# CHAPTER SIX

# ONE DAY IN THE LIFE OF A KING

II CHRONICLES 13:1-22

Have you noticed how seldom preachers preach from the Old Testament? In recent years several books have been published encouraging the use of the Old Testament in preaching. The response has been meager. The past decade has shown that *if* the Old Testament is used at all it is for illustrative purposes. Furthermore, as congregations know less and less about this portion of God's Word, these illustrations carry less and less weight. And if a preacher is bold enough to attempt a series on a portion of the Old Testament, it is often a brief study of "The Life of David" or "the Life of Elijah" or some other notable person.

One reason for the neglect of the Old Testament was brought home forcefully several years ago. I was a freshman faculty member at the time and in a faculty meeting one day one of my colleagues stated emphatically, "I cannot preach from the Old Testament. In fact, I don't even read the Old Testament anymore. I find the God of the Old Testament to be harsh and uncaring. He sends down fire and brimstone on Sodom and Gomorrah, destroys the firstborn of Egypt, commands His people to exterminate the Canaanites and Amorites, and punishes sin with unsparing severity. It is only when we come to the New Testament that we encounter a God of grace." As the years have gone by, I have found that this attitude is widespread.

Such an attitude toward the Old Testament could not be more wrong. In Numbers 14:18-19, Moses tells the Israelites, *"The LORD is slow to anger and abundant in lovingkindness, forgiving iniquity and transgression; but He will by no means clear the guilty...."* Moses then prayed to the Lord to *"pardon ... the iniquity of this people according to the greatness of Your lovingkindness ..."* and God did so.

God is a God of grace, but His grace does not give people a license to sin.

The Bible is one Book although it is comprised of sixty-six smaller books. Its unifying theme (running through the Old and New Testaments) is the *kingdom*[1] of God. And the outworking of the kingdom from the time of

---

[1] Considerable confusion surrounds the biblical doctrine of the kingdom of God. Some believe it is a non-material, spiritual kingdom. Others have concluded that it is a heavenly kingdom. Still others claim that the term "kingdom of God" is synonymous with the eternal state. And then there are those who claim that it is to be understood nationalistically—of Israel. A consideration of the usage of the word in both the Old and New Testaments leads to the conclusion that the "kingdom of God" is vitally related to God's sovereignty over all creation. This includes the world and everything in it, including spirit beings, and embraces the past, the present, and the future (cf. Psalms 10:16; 103:19; I Chronicles 29:11-12; Jeremiah 10:10; Lamentations 5:19; Daniel 4:32, to list only a few Old Testament references. In the New Testament, reference must be made to Luke 1:31-33; I Corinthians 15:24). These passages of Scripture are only a few of the hundreds that can be studied with the aid of a concordance. When interpreted literally within their context, they show that the "kingdom of God" is far-reaching in its scope. For further information, see J. D. Pentecost, *Things to Come* (Grand Rapids: Zondervan, 1964), 427-94.

Adam and Eve until now is through the theocracy.[2] One day this will culminate in the rule of the Lord Jesus Christ over the nations of the world.

In our present chapter, we have occasion to witness the grace of God in action, and see how He shows Himself strong on behalf of those who seek to honor Him.

## RELIABILITY OF THE INFORMATION

The section extending from 13:1-16:14 is a unit. It focuses on Rehoboam's son, Abijah, and his grandson, Asa. In I Kings 15:1-8 Abijah (there called Abijam)[3] is said to have walked in the ways of his father, Rehoboam, and to have committed all the sins that his father had committed before him. Here in II Chronicles, he is presented in a different light. Is this an illustration of biblical inaccuracy? Many writers believe it is. Others accuse the Chronicler of a deliberate fabrication (i.e., a rewriting) of history to serve his own purposes. These are serious accusations.

In actual fact, achieving harmony between I Kings 15 and II Chronicles 13 is quite easy. While under his father's authority, Abijah followed the dictates of the crown. This did not excuse his conduct, but it shows that the account in I Kings is correct in that it focuses on his

---

[2] See my Introduction to *Judges*. This does not involve an authoritarian rule! Rather, it is God's rule over the earth through His divinely chosen representatives who speak and act on His behalf.

[3] The difference in names is very slight and may have arisen when a scribe, copying an old manuscript, mistook the Hebrew "h," for "m," or vice versa, for the two letters are very similar. For a discussion of the differences between I Kings and II Chronicles, see D. G. Deboys, *Biblica* 71 (1990), 48-62.

public life. The conclusion, as far as God was concerned, was that he did evil in the sight of the Lord. Once Abijah became king, however, and could exercise his own initiative, he revealed what was in his heart. And this is recorded for us in II Chronicles 13. The relevance of this for us lies in the fact that those who compromise with what they know to be right do not escape the judgment of heaven. But God is just. His commendation of Abijah in our present chapter illustrates the truth of the New Testament found in I Corinthians 4:5 that Christ, at His judgment seat, will find something to commend in every believer.

Abijah reigned for only "three years" (913-911 B.C.—in all probability, one full year and portions of a year on either side).[4] His age at the time of his enthronement is not given, but he was likely in his late 30's.

There had been war between Jeroboam and Rehoboam throughout Abijah's life.

When Abijah came to the throne he did not manifest any of the indecision his father had displayed at Shechem, but boldly confronted Jeroboam and his army. From whence came this confidence? When we take into account Rehoboam's policy of placing his sons in responsible positions (cf. 11:22-23; 12:15b), it seems likely that Abijah, as "chief prince," had been made general over the army (I Kings 15:6). In our present chapter, he gives every indication of being accustomed to leadership.

Abijah's "sermon on the mount" (13:4-12) raises the question, "How did he learn so much about his great

---

[4] Cf. the chronological notes in I Kings 15:1, 9.

grandfather, David, and of God's promise to him?" We do not know. We do know that he was related to David on both his paternal and maternal sides, and this may have aroused his interest in his famous ancestor. It is also probable that some unknown person in Rehoboam's court taught him the history of his people and of the great destiny God had for them.

But what are we to make of the criticism that the Chronicler fabricated the information in this chapter? Others who are kinder claim that he had a source other than the Book of Kings to draw from. Both groups, however, believe that he exaggerated the information to serve his own purposes.

Here again the explanation is an easy one. If the Chronicler was Ezra, then he most assuredly had other sources to draw on (notably Nehemiah's library), and among these manuscripts was unquestionably the history of the prophet Iddo. As such, the data he incorporated into his account of the history of Judah was accurate and reliable. It was also highly relevant to the Chronicler's contemporaries. They needed encouragement to exercise faith in God.

## OUTLINE

The information before us falls into the third division of the biblical writer's history, *viz.*, The Divided Kingdom (10:1-36:21). Chapters 13-16 form a distinct unit within this division and move forward the Chronicler's treatment of spiritual growth by emphasizing *trust* or *reliance* on the Lord. Whereas in chapters 10-12, stress is placed on *seek*ing the Lord, here it is *trust*ing Him. And these ideas will be repeated throughout this section.

Our material may be outlined as follows:

THE REIGN OF ABIJAH (13:1-14:1a)

A Unique Introduction (13:1-2a)

War Between the Tribes (13:2b-20)

    1.      Abijah's Challenge (13:4-12)

    2.      Jeroboam's Ambush (13:13)

    3.      Judah's Victory (13:14-21a)

    4.      An Honorable End (13:21b-14:1a)

### THE REIGN OF ABIJAH (13:1-14:1a)

### *A Unique Introduction (13:1-2a)*

> *"In the eighteenth year of King Jeroboam, Abijah became king over Judah. He reigned three years in Jerusalem; and his mother's name was Micaiah the daughter of Uriel of Gibeah."*

This introductory formula is common in the Book(s) of Kings, but it is unique in II Chronicles in that it occurs at the beginning of a king's reign. It is also the only introduction in II Chronicles to synchronize the reigns of the kings of Israel and Judah.

In this passage, Abijah's mother is spoken of as the daughter of Uriel, whereas in I Kings 15, she is listed as the daughter of Abishalom (i.e., Absalom). Is this a scribal error or is there some other explanation? Micaiah was the granddaughter of Absalom. His daughter Tamar had married Uriel, and Micaiah had been born to this union. At this time in Israel's history, a person could be referred to as the "son of David" even though removed from his great ancestor by several generations and, though less frequent, women could be referred to in the same way.[5] The significance of this inclusion shows that Abijah was descended from royalty on both sides of his family. And though his mother's name is spelled differently in these accounts, this is not unusual. The one is merely a shortened form of the other.

### War Between the Tribes (13:2b-20)

The only event in Abijah's reign that has been preserved for us is the war between Israel and Judah.[6] Jeroboam was probably the aggressor, for he had planned to ambush Abijah and his army. Abijah probably learned of the build up of Jeroboam's forces and realized that another war was inevitable. He, therefore, took a proactive approach and, with a much smaller force, chose the field of battle inside Jeroboam's territory. There he addressed Jeroboam and his army in an endeavor to avoid needless bloodshed and bring about the union of the tribes.

The place from which Abijah addressed Jeroboam's army is Zemaraim.[7] Its precise location is uncertain.

**Abijah's Challenge (13:2b-12).** Abijah began the battle with an army of valiant warriors, 400,000 chosen

---

[5] Cf. Myers, *2 Chronicles*, 79-80.

[6] Cf. R. Klein, *Zeitschrift fur die alttestamentliche Wissenschaft* 95 (1983), 210-17.

[7] *Macmillan Bible Atlas*, 121. See also Abel, *Geographie de la Palestine*, II:454; and Kallai, *Historical Geography of the Bible*, 401.

men, while Jeroboam drew up in battle formation against him with 800,000 chosen men who were valiant warriors.[8]

> Then Abijah stood on Mount Zemaraim, which is in the hill country of Ephraim, and said, "Listen to me, Jeroboam and all Israel: Do you not know that the LORD God of Israel gave the rule over Israel forever to David and his sons by a covenant of salt?[9] Yet Jeroboam the son of Nebat, the servant of Solomon the son of David, rose up and rebelled against his master, and worthless men gathered about him, scoundrels [lit. sons of Belial], who proved too strong for Rehoboam, the son of Solomon, when he was young and timid and could not hold his own against them. So now you intend to resist the kingdom of the LORD through the sons of David, being a great multitude and having with you the golden calves, which Jeroboam made for gods for you. Have you not driven out the priests of the LORD, the sons of Aaron and the Levites, and made for yourselves priests like the peoples of other lands? Whoever comes to consecrate himself with a young bull and seven rams, even he may become a priest of what are no gods. But as for us,

---

[8] See J. B. Payne, *Bibliotheca Sacra* 136 (1979), 109-28; J. Wenham, *Tyndale Bulletin* 18 (1967), 19-53.

[9] This signified an enduring (eternal) covenant (Numbers 18:19). See H. C. Trumbull, *The Covenant of Salt* (New York: Scribner's, 1899), 184pp.

*the LORD is our God, and we have not forsaken
Him; and the sons of Aaron are ministering to the
LORD as priests, and the Levites attend to their
work. Every morning and evening they burn to the
LORD burnt offerings and fragrant incense, and
the showbread is set on the clean table, and the
golden lampstand with its lamps is ready to light
every evening; for we keep the charge of the
LORD our God, but you have forsaken Him. Now
behold, God is with us at our head and His priests
with the signal trumpets to sound the alarm
against you. O sons of Israel, do not fight against
the LORD God of your fathers, for you will not
succeed."*

Though the story is easy to follow, there are several
important things to notice in Abijah's "sermon on the
mount." The *"worthless men"* who proved to be too strong
for Rehoboam were his father's associates who had grown
up with him. Now, in the cold light of history, they are
found to be reprobate. Rehoboam, though 41 years old at
the time of his enthronement, was inexperienced in the art
of leadership, and he must have admitted his irresolute state
to Abijah as he sought to prepare his son to assume the
throne.

It will be noted that Abijah based his appeal to the
reunification of the tribes of Israel on two facts: God's
choice of David as His theocratic representative, and His
appointment of the priests and Levites as His ministers.

Some writers object to Abijah's recounting of the
past and his attempt to show that Jeroboam reigned in Israel
by divine appointment. They even point to the words of the
prophet Shemaiah when he told Rehoboam that the schism
was of the Lord (11:4). Their criticism of Abijah's words

asks the rhetorical question, "If Jeroboam reigned over Israel by divine decree, what right did Abijah have appealing to the people to unite with Judah?"[10]

When we refer back to I Kings 11:29-40 we find that God's covenant with Jeroboam was a conditional covenant. Note His words: *"I will take you, and you shall reign over whatever you desire, and you shall be king over Israel. Then it will be, that if you listen to all that I command you and walk in My ways, and do what is right in My sight by observing My statutes and My commandments, as My servant David did, then I will be with you and build you an enduring house as I built for David, and I will give Israel to you. Thus I will afflict the descendants of David for this, but not always"* (I Kings 11:37-39, emphasis added).

Jeroboam had failed to live up to the specifics of the covenant. In fact, on closer examination, he had breached it in every particular. And Abijah, believing that the reunion of the tribes could be achieved if the people wanted it, offered them a choice. He began his address by speaking to *"Jeroboam and all Israel"* (13:4). In verse 6, however, he refers to Jeroboam obliquely. And when he concludes his remarks he omits Jeroboam altogether.

The choice the people of Israel made that day would have far reaching ramifications and affect their future in ways they could not perceive at the time.

Jeroboam's sins are presented within their historic context. He had rebelled against Solomon and, to save his life, he fled to Egypt. Later, following his return to Israel

---

[10] An unnamed writer for *Nelson's New Illustrated Bible Commentary* (1999), 547, claims that Abijah misinterpreted the truth in order to scare the Israelites.

and after he became king, he did not hold this trust from the Lord. Instead, he replaced God's appointed priests with ones from the least worthy elements of society. There was no integrity in his dealings. His idolatrous practices, learned while in Egypt, gave him a foolish confidence in the gods he had created. So great was his confidence that he even carried them into battle.

Perhaps the men of Israel had begun to jeer Abijah or in some way show that they rejected what he had to say, for verse 8 carries a stinging indictment. Their decision to follow Jeroboam was clear. We paraphrase Abijah's response as follows: *"So now you intend to resist the kingdom of the Lord through the divinely appointed Davidic line, and choose instead to trust in numbers rather than submit to God's revealed will."*

But this is not all. There is clever, yet purposeful repetition in Abijah's use of the verb *hazaq*, "resist." In verse 7, he has described his father's inability to resist his evil counselors, and now in verse 8 he indicts the northern tribes for resisting the kingdom of the Lord, and preferring instead to trust in the gods Jeroboam had made.

Verses 10-11 show the contrast between the north and the south. In the south, the people gladly followed the commandments of the Lord; His appointed priests performed their assigned duties, and this gave them confidence even though in the coming battle they would be outnumbered two-to-one. The war that was about to begin was a holy war, and the people of Judah had the confidence that, though unseen, the Lord was with them and would give them the victory.

**Jeroboam's Ambush (13:13).** The confidence of the northern tribesmen may also have lain in the strategy that Jeroboam had devised. He *"had set an ambush to come from the rear, so that Israel was in front of Judah and the ambush was behind them."* This was a common military strategy (Joshua 8:2; Judges 20:29; II Samuel 10:9).

**Judah's Victory (13:14-20).** We read that *"when Judah turned around, behold, they were being attacked from both front and rear; so they cried to the LORD, and the priests blew the trumpets. Then the men of Judah raised a war cry, and when the men of Judah raised the war cry, then it was that God routed Jeroboam and all Israel before Abijah and Judah"* (13:14-15).

The scene is not hard to imagine. In addition to being outnumbered, the men of Judah were caught in a pincers movement. To rally the tribe to action, the priests blew on their trumpets. The men then uttered their battle cry (cf. Joshua 6:16) and attacked the forces of Jeroboam. Just how God routed the army of Israel is not told us. The victory is reminiscent of other victories given the Israelites in earlier times (cf. God's promise in Leviticus 26:7-9).

> *When the sons of Israel fled before Judah, God gave them into their hand. Abijah and his people defeated them with a great slaughter, so that 500,000 chosen men of Israel fell slain. Thus the sons of Israel were subdued at that time, and* **the sons of Judah conquered because they trusted in the LORD,** *the God of their fathers. Abijah pursued Jeroboam and captured from him several cities, Bethel with its villages, Jeshanah with its villages and Ephron with its villages (13:16-19, emphasis added. Cf. Deuteronomy 20:1-4, 10-15).*

The men of Judah demonstrated trust in the Lord in spite of Israel's superior numbers, and God showed that He is trustworthy. The term used to describe Judah's victory, *"subdued,"* really means, "humbled." The army of Israel was "humbled" before the army of Judah. Israel suffered *"a great slaughter,"* and their manpower was so badly decimated that it was many years before they could again mount an offensive. This was the kind of message the Chronicler's contemporaries needed to hear. They, too, were surrounded by enemies and needed encouragement to trust the Lord and obey His word as Abijah and his army had done.

Abijah captured certain towns that formerly had belonged to Israel. The taking of Bethel is particularly ironic, for that had been one of the sites where Jeroboam had erected a golden calf. This god was powerless to protect his own sanctuary, and so are the things that men and women trust in today for their security.

The Chronicler then inserts an unmistakable contrast. Jeroboam was unable to regain power, *"and the LORD struck him and he died."* Abijah, however, became stronger and stronger (13:20-21).

### An Honorable End (13:21b-14:1a)

God's blessing of Abijah is summarized for us.

*"Abijah ... took fourteen wives to himself, and became the father of twenty-two sons and sixteen daughters. Now the rest of the acts of Abijah, and his ways and his words are written in the treatise of the prophet Iddo. So Abijah slept*

*with his fathers, and they buried him in the city of David."*

This contrast between the judgment that came upon Jeroboam and the blessings enjoyed by Abijah is purposeful. It demonstrates God's sovereignty and shows how He rewards the righteous. Abijah is blessed with a large family, and ten years of peace follow his victory over Jeroboam. In this, we have an illustration of the New Testament teaching on the *"goodness and severity"* of God (Romans 11:22).

And so passes from the scene a man whose later years were marked by devotion to the Lord.

## THE IMPORTANCE OF OUR CHOICES

This brief survey of Abijah's life illustrates for us the importance of our choices.

We make our choices based on *external* and *internal* criteria. For example, in spite of the precedent set by Rehoboam, Abijah, when he became king, chose to follow the Lord. And his obedience laid the foundation for the blessings that were experienced by his people during his lifetime and well into the reign of his son, Asa.

Abijah faced another choice when he learned of Jeroboam's planned attack. This took the form of an *external* threat. He chose the course of action we have read about because he was motivated by an *internal* trust in the Lord. This required a bold act of faith—the kind we read about in Hebrews 11.

Choices face each one of us. Every four years, we choose a new president, and we may well ask ourselves, "What is the basis of our choice?" Are we motivated solely by external considerations or do we take into account internal criteria as well? How does our choice of the person who will lead our country square with our beliefs, values and goals? Is our focus limited to what we believe will be good for the economy or the security of our nation, or do we vote for someone who also shares our moral commitments? And the person chosen by the party to run for the office of president must, of necessity, choose a vice president. What rationale lies at the base of his choice? Does he select a running mate who shares his beliefs and values, or does he select someone who will draw votes from a particular section of the country?

Choices also face our young people. While in high school, they experience peer pressure and desire popularity. They want to feel that they belong, have worth within a group and are capable of maintaining the respect of their peers. How do these pressures affect their attitudes and actions? In time, they must also select and apply to the college of their choice. Then, once they are ensconced in this academic institution, they must select a major ... and prepare for a career. And if these decisions are not enough to boggle their minds, it is often at this time that they choose the person whom they wish to marry.

After college there is marriage. Then they must choose where they will live and the church they will attend. In time, when they have children, they face another choice: Where will Brad and Susie go to school? And so the cycle begins again.

Life is full of choices. We make them every day. Some are as simple as choosing to spend an extra half-hour in bed on a Saturday morning (unless we run the risk of being late for Steve's little league game or Julie's piano lessons). Others choices are complex. Some of our larger companies use a mathematical model to make decisions. The goal is the development of a strategy (based on statistical concepts) that they hope will help them maximize gains and minimize losses. Most of us, however, make our decisions based on *internal* and *external* criteria. The more aware we are of the impact of these criteria the easier it is for us to apply the teaching of God's Word to our decisions so that we may be pleasing to Him.

Abijah chose to follow the revealed will of God and the Lord blessed him. Abijah then invited the men of Israel to reunite with Judah. They chose not to do so. This was an unfortunate choice for the northern tribes continued to engage in idolatrous practices until, in 722 B.C., they were overrun by the Assyrians and led away into captivity.

Abijah saw firsthand the evil effects of his father's apathy toward God. He also saw Judah reduced to poverty. What he witnessed (the *external* stimuli) caused him to deliberately choose to follow the Lord (an *internal* response). The promise God had made to David further stimulated his thought processes. These awakened his faith and became the basis of his hope (trust) in the Lord. And acting in faith, he and those who were with him went out to battle. As we have seen, God gave them a significant victory. Israel suffered a resounding defeat and could not again attack Judah for several decades. When our ways please the Lord, He makes even our enemies to be at peace with us (Proverbs 16:7).

Chapter Seven

# THE REFORMER

II Chronicles 14:1-16:14

Reformers come in all shapes and sizes. We do not have to monitor the news for too long before we hear or read of those seeking public office who wish to "reform Social Security," "reform education," "reform health care" or "reform campaign financing." And within the church, there are those who likewise clamor loudly for reform in matters of worship and governance. Some react against simplicity of worship and want to impose a liturgy upon the people, others launch a crusade against laxity in morals, and still others believe that the road to spiritual prosperity is to go back to the early days of the Christian church and follow the ascetic practices of those who sought to nullify the flesh.

Criticism of reformers is plentiful. The English poet, Samuel Taylor Coleridge, who gave us the *Rhyme of the Ancient Mariner*, said: "Every reform, however necessary, will by weak minds be carried to excess which will itself need reforming." Ralph Waldo Emerson remarked cynically, "Every reform is only a mask under cover of which a more terrible reform, which dares not yet name itself, advances." Edmund Burke pointed out that "It is a general error to suppose the loudest complainers for the public to be the most anxious for its welfare." And George

Byron opined, some people "...hope to merit Heaven by making earth a Hell."

From these statements, we might be tempted to conclude that reform is bad and that reformers past and present are at best fanatics and at worst motivated by ulterior motives. Alfred Tennyson, however, turned the search light on himself when he expressed his personal desire for reform:

> "Ah for a man to arise in me,
>      that the man I am may cease to be."

Asa, king of Judah (911-870 B.C.), was a reformer. Unlike John Wycliffe or Martin Luther, John Knox or Ulrich Zwingli—who lived when times were bad and sought to turn people back to the Lord—Asa lived when times were good, and so his reforms need to be studied in a different light. But opinions about the necessity and quality of the work he did differ, and many point to his closing years as providing grounds for dismissing any influence for good that he may have had.

Years ago, I had a maiden aunt who loved to read romance novels and mystery stories. One morning, I noticed her reading a lengthy book. By noon she was eagerly devouring the last chapter. I asked her how she had been able to read the entire book so quickly. With some embarrassment she admitted that she often read the last chapter before finishing a book because she wanted to find out what happened. She loved happy endings. If the book happened to be a romance, she wanted to know if the hero and heroine got married; and, if the book happened to be a mystery, she wanted to know whether the villain got his just desserts and the righteous were vindicated and rewarded. Asa's critics are like my aunt. They read Asa's

latter years back into the earlier part of his life and come up
with an erroneous conclusion.  When we read the closing
scenes of Asa's life back into his early reforms, we fail to
interpret the text in light of a logical sequence of events.
And this colors our understanding of the entire record.

Those who wish to find contradictions in the Bible
are quick to point out that in I Kings 15, Asa is judged to be
a good king, but in II Chronicles, he becomes intolerant of
those who disagree with him and is seen to be at odds with
God's messenger.[1]  Others claim that Asa "made a most
excellent beginning ... still, his character and life were not
free from faults," and while he began well, he finished
poorly.[2]  And of a similar nature are those whose partial
praise is damning.  They inform us that "the first part of
Asa's reign exemplifies faithfulness, expansion, and
security,"[3] with the implication that his closing years tell a
different story.

Before we allow ourselves to be persuaded by the
opinions of others, we should consider what God's Word
says about Asa.  Are the accounts in I Kings and II
Chronicles contradictory?  Once we have this information
before us, we can try to reconcile what may appear to be
dissenting points of view.

In I Kings 15:11, we are told that "*Asa did what was
right in the sight of the LORD, like David his father,*" and
in our present chapter where we read, "*Asa did good and*

---

[1] Allan, *1, 2 Chronicles*, 279.

[2] Jamison, Fausset and Brown, *Commentary Practical and
Explanatory on the Whole Bible* (1977), 319.

[3] Selman, *2 Chronicles*, 387.

*right in the sight of the LORD his God*" (14:2) and "*Asa's heart was blameless all his days*" (15:17*b*). These assessments of his life cover his entire reign. Any events from the latter part of Asa's life must, therefore, be interpreted in light of God's overall approval. And without looking ahead (as my aunt would have done), we shall deal with the issues as they arise.

What is important for us to notice is that the information about Asa carries forward the Chronicler's emphasis on "*seek*ing" the Lord (cf. 14:4, 7; 15:2, 4, 12-13; 16:12) and "*trust*ing" Him (14:11). These thoughts are prominent throughout these chapters.

## OUTLINE

The bulk of II Chronicles deals with the third division of the Book, namely, *The Reigns of the Kings of Judah* (10:1-36:21). The writer began with Rehoboam, then discussed Abijah, and now has brought us to Asa, the third ruler of the divided kingdom.

An outline of these chapters is difficult and some that have been proposed fail to come to grips with the Chronicler's theme. The following suggestion attempts to build on information supplied to us about the stages or epochs of Asa's reign:

| Asa's Reign | Theme |
|---|---|
| Years 1-15 | Reliance on the Lord (14:1-8) |
| Years 15-16 | Trust in the Lord (14:9-15:19) |
| Years 16-39 | Dependence on the Lord (16:1-10) |
| Years 39-41 | Physical Decline and Final Testimony (16:11-14) |

## ASA, KING OF JUDAH (14:1*b*-16:14)

Asa may have been in his early 20's when he ascended to the throne. His father had reigned for "three years," and Asa could have witnessed the remarkable victory over Israel that the Lord had given Abijah and the men of Judah and Benjamin. Such success may have prompted him to seek the Lord. His grandfather and grandmother would not have exerted a good influence on him, and this has caused some to question why he (and people like him) turned out to be good.

This question is a perennial one. It takes many forms. Why do some children, born to neglectful, abusive parents grow up to be model citizens, while others who have every material advantage pursue a lifestyle that is detrimental to themselves and everyone associated with them? Environment and education do not account for everything; nor does hereditary. In the mystery of God's dealings with every person (note John 16:8-11) some respond positively and others do not. Those who begin to seek the Lord and desire to do His will are led in the path of righteousness whereas others turn progressively away from the truth ultimately to perish in their unbelief.

Early in his life Asa must have set his heart to seek the Lord. If this is so, then he benefited from the experiences in his life, and when he became king he was prepared to lead his people righteously and justly.

### *Reliance on the Lord (14:1-8)[4]*

---

[4] The chapter and verse divisions in our English Bibles differ from those in the Hebrew Bible. Our 14:1 is 13:23 in the Hebrew text.

Initially Asa's reign is marked off by a period of time extending from his enthronement to the invasion of Zerah.

> *So Abijah slept with his fathers, and they buried him in the city of David, and his son Asa became king in his place. The land was undisturbed for ten years during his days. Asa did good and right in the sight of the LORD his God, for he removed the foreign altars and high places, tore down the sacred pillars, cut down the Asherim, and commanded Judah to seek the LORD God of their fathers and to observe the law and the commandment. He also removed the high places and the incense altars from all the cities of Judah. And the kingdom was undisturbed under him. He built fortified cities in Judah, since the land was undisturbed, and there was no one at war with him during those years, because the LORD had given him rest. For he [Asa] said to Judah, "Let us build these cities and surround them with walls and towers, gates and bars. The land is still ours because we have sought the LORD our God; we have sought Him, and He has given us rest on every side." So they built and prospered. Now Asa had an army of 300,000 from Judah, bearing large shields and spears, and 280,000 from Benjamin, bearing shields and wielding bows; all of them were valiant warriors.*

The peace referred to was an extension of Abijah's victory over Israel (cf. 13:13-20). It was also God's reward for Asa's faithfulness (cf. 14:5*b*, 6, 7*b*, and 15:15*b*). In furthering reform, Asa destroyed the heathen cult objects (14:2-3), *viz.*, the wooden pillars and standing stones used in the worship of Baal and Astarte, as well as the altars upon which pagan sacrifices were offered, and the "sacred" sites where immoral practices were performed in honor of the gods.

The Chronicler's emphasis on *"seeking the Lord"* (14:4) is important. *"Seek*ing the Lord" describes how a person may respond to God's intervention in his or her life (cf. 15:2), and become part of the community of believers. For those in Israel, it involved observing the law and the commandment whereas for believers today it necessitates trusting in Christ and obeying His revealed will. When *seek*ing the Lord is done consistently, it is the equivalent of serving Him with wholehearted devotion (note I:22:19; I:28:8-9; Jeremiah 29:12-14).

Asa's reform extended beyond the principal cities of the southern kingdom to *"all the cities of Judah."* No matter how remote these villages were, altars on which incense was burned (symbolic of prayer to Baal or Astarte) were broken down with the result that the people no longer frequented the high places. Asa also encouraged the people to take advantage of the peace and strengthen Judah's defenses. This involved rebuilding certain cities and fortifying others. And to show his preparedness for war, the Chronicler makes mention of the number of fighting men from Judah and Benjamin who could be called up at any given time.

### *Trust in the Lord (14:9-15:19)*

**The Battle of Mareshah (14:9-15).** The period of peace the people enjoyed did not last forever. At the end of a particular period, Asa's trust in the Lord was tested. Zerah, who was probably a Nubian or Cushite from the

Sudan, and a mercenary general of Pharaoh Osorkon I (Shishak's son), came against the people of Judah with a massive army. The invasion is recorded by the Chronicler to illustrate the need for complete trust in the Lord (cf. I:28:9).

Many of the Chronicler's contemporaries were trying to live godly lives. With the sudden and unprovoked invasion from the south, they faced a theological dilemma. Why had God allowed this to happen? And Asa may have experienced the same inner confusion. God, however, did not intend this invasion as a punishment. Asa had led an exemplary life. He had done nothing to warrant punishment. The invasion was allowed by God to serve a totally different purpose.

> Now Zerah the Ethiopian [5] came out against them with an army of a million men and 300 chariots, and he came to Mareshah. So Asa went out to meet him, and they drew up in battle formation in the valley of Zephathah at Mareshah. Then Asa called to the LORD his God and said, "LORD, there is no one besides You to help in the battle between the powerful and those who have no strength; so help us, O LORD our God, for we trust in You, and in Your name have come against this multitude[6] O LORD, You are our God; let not man prevail against You."

---

[5] "Ethiopia" in the Bible does not refer to present-day Ethiopia, but to the Sudan.

[6] These words form the basis of the hymn "We rest on Thee our shield and our defender."

> *So the LORD routed the Ethiopians before*
> *Asa and before Judah, and the Ethiopians fled.*
> *Asa and the people who were with him pursued*
> *them as far as Gerar; and so many Ethiopians fell*
> *that they could not recover, for they were*
> *shattered before the LORD and before His army.*
> *And they [the men of Judah and Benjamin]*
> *carried away very much plunder. They destroyed*
> *all the cities around Gerar, for the dread of the*
> *LORD had fallen on them; and they despoiled all*
> *the cities, for there was much plunder in them.*
> *They also struck down those who owned livestock,*
> *and they carried away large numbers of sheep and*
> *camels. Then they returned to Jerusalem (14:9-*
> *15).*

The armed men under Zerah are listed as "a thousand, thousand." The place where the battle takes place was near Mareshah.[7] According to 16:8, Zerah's army was made up of a coalition of tribesmen from Cush (i.e., the Sudan) and Libya, with a large, elite regiment of charioteers in the middle to break through the lines of an opposing army. Thus divided, they appeared to be invincible.

Confronted by such an intimidating army, Asa prayed to the Lord. His prayer in the presence of his men was most appropriate, for the crisis they faced impacted every one of them. From a human standpoint, they were dwarfed by the opposition. Defeat seemed inevitable. Asa's prayer followed the pattern established by Solomon at the time of the dedication of the Temple (6:34). He

---

[7] *Macmillan Bible Atlas,* 122, 154.

called upon the omnipotent God to help the powerless against the powerful.

God heard the prayer of His servant, and when the battle was joined, the vast army under Zerah fled in disarray. We are not told how the Lord "shattered" the invaders, only that the men of Judah chased them all the way to Gerar. The result was that the aggressors were *"crushed before the Lord and his forces"* (i.e., Asa's army.) Then the *"terror of the Lord"* came upon the people. This compels us to ask, Why? Had they sided with Zerah and his army? All we read is that the men of Judah destroyed all of the villages around Gerar and plundered them. They also drove off the sheep, goats and camels that Zerah's men had brought with them as well as the livestock of the villages they plundered.

**Encouragement and Further Reforms (15:1-19).** As Asa and his army returned to Jerusalem, they were met by Azariah who spoke to them in the name of the Lord.[8] Azariah is not spoken of as a prophet, though he was the son of a prophet. So who was he? His knowledge of Scripture seems to indicate that he may have been a priest (cf. 24:20) or a Levite (cf. 20:14), for he cites Deuteronomy 4:29 in his address (cf. Jeremiah 29:13-14 and Isaiah 55:6). As we read his words, we should take note of the repetitious use of *"seek, sought."* We should also observe

---

[8] It is important to note that Azariah spoke to Asa and his men "in the name of the LORD." Years later another prophet will do the same, only in his case there is every probability that he acted on his own authority. Some of what he said on that occasion was true, but much of it wasn't. Everyone who stands as "God's spokesman" has not necessarily been sent by Him. And lamentably, what was true in Asa's day is true of many who occupy the pulpits of our land today.

his use of history to illustrate his point, particularly the
history of the Judges.

> *Now the Spirit of God came on Azariah the
> son of Oded, and he went out to meet Asa and said
> to him, "Listen to me, Asa, and all Judah and
> Benjamin: the LORD is with you when you are
> with Him. And if you seek Him, He will let you
> find Him; but if you forsake Him, He will forsake
> you. For many days Israel was without the true
> God and without a teaching priest and without
> law. But in their distress they turned to the LORD
> God of Israel, and they sought Him, and He let
> them find Him. In those times there was no peace
> to him who went out or to him who came in, for
> many disturbances afflicted all the inhabitants of
> the lands. Nation was crushed by nation, and city
> by city, for God troubled them with every kind of
> distress. But you, be strong and do not lose
> courage, for there is reward for your work."*

> *Now when Asa heard these words and the
> prophecy which Azariah the son of Oded the
> prophet spoke, he took courage and removed the
> abominable idols from all the land of Judah and
> Benjamin and from the cities which he had
> captured in the hill country of Ephraim. He then
> restored the altar of the LORD that was in front of
> the porch of the LORD (15:1-8).*

While the New Testament places great stress on
God seeking us (cf. Luke 15:4-32; 19:10; see also Romans
3:11 and James 4:8) or inviting individuals to seek Him
(Acts 15:17; 17:27), here the emphasis is placed on people
seeking God with the promise that if they will do so, He
will be found by them. This provides a powerful corrective

to those who excuse their unbelief by saying, "But I'm not one of the elect" (as if God had published a list and their name wasn't on it) or, "I've tried to become a Christian but I've never felt what others have felt or had the experience that others claim to have had." Those who seek the Lord will find Him, but those who turn their backs on Him will find that He withdraws from them.

Azariah's words to Asa breathe *encouragement*. They also illustrate God's gracious actions in times past. And by referring to the period of the Judges, Azariah reminds them of an era of history that was very unstable. One city or nation was crushed by another. Anarchy prevailed, and people could not walk about freely for fear of what might happen to them. Those difficult times were a consequence of having forsaken the Lord. God permitted these acts in order to compel His people to seek Him. When they did, He helped them.

The priests had a vital role to play in the life of God's people. They were responsible to teach the people the Law of the Lord (17:7-9; cf. Leviticus 10:11; Deuteronomy 33:10; Malachi 2:7-8), but all too often they failed in this important task. A similar state of affairs prevails today. Later on, we find the Levites instructing the villagers in those portions of God's Word that were available to them. But times haven't changed. All who occupy our pulpits have been charged by the Lord to *"feed the sheep."* Instead of teaching the Word, many prefer to use a passage or text of Scripture upon which they hang their own thoughts. And so God's lament (recorded by Hosea) is still true, *"[His people] perished for lack of knowledge"* (Hosea 4:6).

Azariah inspires Asa to seek God afresh. Perhaps with such a significant victory behind them, Asa and his

men may have had lurking in their hearts the thought,
"Now we can ease up on our devotion to the Lord and
enjoy the fruits of our labors."[9]  This temptation is very
real.  Few will admit to having experienced it, but it is
especially subtle after we have received some significant
blessing.

Asa and the people of Judah and Benjamin
responded to Azariah's admonition.  With renewed
enthusiasm, they purged the land of idols, and even
destroyed pagan shrines in the hill country of Ephraim.
Then they repaired the altar in Jerusalem that for some
reason had fallen into disuse.

Asa, however, was not satisfied with these reforms.
He convened an assembly of all the people.

> *He gathered all Judah and Benjamin and
> those from Ephraim, Manasseh and Simeon who
> resided with them, for many defected to him from
> Israel when they saw that the LORD his God was
> with him.  So they assembled at Jerusalem in the
> third month of the fifteenth year of Asa's reign.
> They sacrificed to the LORD that day 700 oxen
> and 7,000 sheep from the spoil they had brought.
> They entered into the covenant to seek the LORD
> God of their fathers with all their heart and soul;
> and whoever would not seek the LORD God of
> Israel should be put to death, whether small or
> great, man or woman.  Moreover, they made an
> oath to the LORD with a loud voice, with
> shouting, with trumpets and with horns.  All Judah*

---

[9] The Hebrew text reads, "let one's hands drop."  Such an
attitude had to be resisted.

*rejoiced concerning the oath, for they had sworn
with their whole heart and had sought Him
earnestly, and He let them find Him. So the LORD
gave them rest on every side.*

*He also removed Maacah,[10] [his
mother], from the position of queen mother,
because she had made a horrid image as an
Asherah, and Asa cut down her horrid image,
crushed it and burned it at the brook Kidron. But
the high places were not removed from Israel;
nevertheless Asa's heart was blameless all his
days. He brought into the house of God the
dedicated things of his father and his own
dedicated things: silver and gold and utensils.
And there was no more war until the thirty-fifth
year of Asa's reign.*

Simeon's allotted territory had at one time been
within the border of Judah. Perhaps at some time in the
past they, like the people of Dan, had migrated northwards.

The "third month" (May-June), when the feast was
held, probably coincided with the Feast of Weeks (or
Pentecost. See Exodus 23:16; 34:22; Leviticus 23:15-21;
Numbers 28:26-31; Deuteronomy 16:9-10). A large
number of animals were sacrificed to commemorate the
victory over Zerah, and the people enter into a solemn
covenant with the Lord. It was done wholeheartedly
(15:12), and the people bound themselves to continue to

---

[10] It is not necessary to identify Maacah with Micaiah the
grandmother of Abijah. Maacah may well have been Asa's mother
who became Queen Mother when her son ascended the throne. Such
individuals invariably occupied influential positions, particularly if they
served as Regent until their son was able to assume power.

seek the Lord.  In their zeal, they even stated that anyone who did not agree to the conditions of the covenant was to be put to death.  (Is this an example of reform being carried to an extreme?)

The taking of the oath was accompanied by loud shouting and the blowing of trumpets.  Much joy was shared by all who attended the feast, and the people wholeheartedly dedicated themselves to seek the Lord and to do His will.

Such was the zeal of the king and the people that the reform continued.  And the royal family was included. Asa even deposed his mother, Maacah, because she had made an obscene image—an Asherah pole—that she worshipped.  Asa took this object of her veneration, broke it in pieces, and burned it in the Kidron Valley.  A stream ran through this valley and the ashes were probably thrown into the stream to be carried away out of sight.

This done, Asa brought into the Temple treasures of gold and silver (15:18), and for the next thirty years he continued to rule in peace (15:19).

### *Dependence on the Lord (16:1-10)*

It is a lot harder to maintain a close walk with the Lord when all is well than it is when we face times of adversity (cf. Psalm 119:67, 71, 75).  And if a period of tranquility is prolonged, we may not only become lax in our reading of the Bible and prayer, but we may become nonchalant in our church attendance as well.  When, however, someone whom we dearly love is involved in an accident or becomes deathly ill and there are daily and nightly vigils beside a hospital bed, we suddenly realize how desperately we need the Lord and His help.

The fact that Asa continued to walk with the Lord during the 20 years of peace and prosperity, without any external pressure being brought to bear upon him, is to his credit. He did not fall into the trap of thinking that he could get along without God (cf. Deuteronomy 32:15).

Then, after these acts of faithfulness, Baasha king of Israel marched on Judah's northern border.

> *In the thirty-sixth year of Asa's reign Baasha king of Israel came up against Judah and fortified Ramah in order to prevent anyone from going out or coming in to Asa king of Judah. Then Asa brought out silver and gold from the treasuries of the house of the LORD and the king's house, and sent them to Ben-hadad king of Aram [i.e., Syria], who lived in Damascus, saying, "Let there be a treaty between you and me, as between my father and your father. Behold, I have sent you silver and gold; go, break your treaty with Baasha king of Israel so that he will withdraw from me." So Ben-hadad listened to King Asa and sent the commanders of his armies against the cities of Israel, and they conquered Ijon, Dan, Abel-maim and all the store cities of Naphtali. When Baasha heard of it, he ceased fortifying Ramah and stopped his work. Then King Asa brought all Judah, and they carried away the stones of Ramah and its timber with which Baasha had been building, and with them he fortified Geba and Mizpah.*

With these verses we encounter certain problems. The first, and the one that Bible critics like the most, has to do with the dating of these events. In the "36th year" of Asa's reign, Baasha (d. 886 B.C.) had been dead for about ten years. And so, rubbing their hands with great delight, the critics point to what appears to be an obvious error in the Bible.

Is this an obvious instance of inaccuracy or was the Chronicler guilty of sloppy research?

It is always a dangerous expedient to imagine errors in the Bible. The solution to the problem may lie in the use of the word *malkut*, "kingdom"[11] rather than in the translation "reign." Let's see if it works. It should be noted that Baasha's aggression occurred exactly 36 years after the division of the *kingdom*,[12] not in the 36th year of Asa's reign. So, once again, the solution to an apparent discrepancy is easily obtained.

A second problem is posed by those who ask, "Since God had given Asa such a unique victory over Zerah, why didn't he gather his forces together and attack Baasha?" The question is a good one. In answering it, we need to point out that Asa may have had several reasons for not committing the army of Judah to the field of battle. (1) In the 20 years of peace, the army may have been reduced in size and/or become sluggish and unfit for the rigors of combat. (2) With the advance of years, Asa may have had physical limitations that in some way made it difficult for him to lead his people into battle. (We need to remember that at this time in history it was customary for a king to lead his men into battle.) And closely associated with this is a third reason: Accompanying the aging process is an awareness of how destructive war really is. Asa may have

---

[11] *Theological Wordbook of the Old Testament*, I:507 (#1199),

[12] Thiele, *Mysterious Numbers of the Hebrew Kings* (1983), 84.

wanted to protect his people and not compel the widows to sing sad songs.

Whatever his reason(s), Asa preferred a "diplomatic" solution. His error, of course, lay in the fact that he did not seek counsel from the Lord. Instead, relying on a precedent (e.g., Rehoboam's stripping the palace and Temple to buy off Shishak), he removed the treasures from his palace and the Temple, and sent a "present" to Ben-hadad I of Syria. The "gift" was accompanied by the request that he break his treaty with Israel and enter into one with Judah. Ben-hadad obliged. He attacked Israel's northern tribes. This brought an immediate end to Baasha's fortification of Ramah (about six miles north of Jerusalem). And with his attention now being directed against the Syrians, Asa had all the people of Judah mobilized to carry the wood and stones from Ramah to two other locations: Geba and Mizpah.[13]

It is quite possible that Asa congratulated himself on such a neat bit of diplomacy. He had avoided a war with its inevitable loss of life, and he had been able to fortify two important cities. As for the treasures of the Temple and his palace (he, of course, was now impoverished), Asa possibly reasoned that they could easily be replaced.

It was after his plan had succeeded beyond his wildest dreams that he received an unexpected visit from a man named Hanani. Hanani is spoken of as a seer. This was an old word for prophet used in the time of Samuel (cf. I Samuel 9:9, 19). Did its usage imply that Hanani was

---

[13] *Macmillan Bible Atlas,* 123.

descended from this old order of prophets? Was he old and
had he been in retirement for many years? Regardless of
Hanani's past, Asa did not know of him. Furthermore, as
we read the prophet's words, the usual *"thus says the
Lord"* is missing (cf. 11:4; 12:5; 18:10; 20:15). Was he
truly delivering the word of the Lord, or did he presume
that inasmuch as he still held prophetic office God would
still use him?

> *At that time Hanani the seer came to Asa
> king of Judah and said to him, "Because you have
> relied on the king of Aram [Syria] and have not
> relied on the LORD your God, therefore the army
> of the king of Aram has escaped out of your hand.
> Were not the Ethiopians and the Lubim an
> immense army with very many chariots and
> horsemen? Yet because you relied on the LORD,
> He delivered them into your hand. For the eyes of
> the LORD move to and fro throughout the earth
> that He may strongly support those whose heart is
> completely His. You have acted foolishly in this.
> Indeed, from now on you will surely have wars."*
>
> *Then Asa was angry with the seer and put
> him in prison, for he was enraged at him for this.
> And Asa oppressed some of the people at the same
> time (16:7-10).*

Because Asa had relied on human wisdom and had
not asked counsel of the Lord, that part of the rebuke was
just. But what are we to understand by Hanani's words that
if Asa had sought guidance from the Lord, he would have
been instructed to attack Baasha, the Syrians under Ben-
hadad I would have joined forces with Israel (in honor of
their treaty with Israel), and God would have given both
Israel and Syria into Judah's hands? Was this really the

word of the Lord to Asa, or was Hanani claiming that his own sentiments were God's will?

It is true that prophets spoke forcefully to apostate kings, but Asa had earnestly walked with the Lord all his life. He had led the people in a notable reform. He had maintained the worship of the Lord unsullied and uninterrupted for almost forty years. His commitment to what was right and true was known to all, and he most likely believed that did not deserve to be addressed in such a manner.

All great leaders have their critics. In all probability there were those who believed that Asa was too religious and clamored for fewer restraints. And there may well have been those who believed that he was not religious enough and should bear down on the halfhearted and lukewarm. However, before we condemn Asa as Hanani did, let us consider his situation. The pressures he faced were very real. He was getting old, and it had probably been a long, long time since anyone had spoken approvingly to him. In spite of this, he had remained true to the Lord and sought to do His will.

Hanani appears uninvited. He ignores all the good Asa has done and castigates him for what he believes Asa had not done. This probably caused Asa to feel unjustly accused. He had good reasons for not going to war, why should he now be made to feel guilty? It was bad enough feeling under-appreciated and condemned, but was this God's summary judgment of him?

We cannot excuse Asa's anger, even though we can understand it. Anger is never without a reason, but the reason for it is seldom a good one. It is caused by feelings of frustration, humiliation and rejection. Asa quite possibly felt frustrated when Hanani came before him, and denounced what he had done without ever giving him the opportunity to explain his actions. Hostile criticism was hard to bear, particularly when (as in Asa's case) it was accompanied by the threat that his remaining years would be filled with wars. This caused Asa to feel humiliated because the very thing he had hoped to avoid now seemed to be the judgment of heaven on him. And when Hanani made reference to *"the eyes of the Lord moving to and fro throughout the earth,"* Asa felt rejected (16:7-9). If God was so conscious of what was going on, couldn't He have warned him or said one word of encouragement to him?

It is easy to see how Asa became angry with Hanani. But was this sufficient cause to have him thrown in prison? It is likely that Hanani's denunciation caused Asa to experience feelings of impotence. In spite of all he had tried to do for his people, his fate and theirs had been taken out of his hands. Future wars and untimely deaths had been decreed, and Asa felt powerless to do anything about it. Now, believing that he had brought this trouble on his people, he was plagued with a growing sense of guilt. Acting out his grief and feelings of impotence and guilt, he ordered that Hanani thrown in jail.

Perhaps, once he had processed what he had been told or found out more about the seer, he sent and had him released.

But what of the predicted wars? They never came. Did the prophet speak on his own authority? It would appear as if he did, leaving us to wonder if the Lord really sent him.

We do not condone Asa's actions, but what he did shows us how easily we may give way to our all-too-human emotions.

## *Physical Decline and Final Testimony (16:11-14)*

> *Now, the acts of Asa from first to last, behold, they are written in the Book of the Kings of Judah and Israel. In the thirty-ninth year of his reign Asa became diseased in his feet. His disease was severe, yet even in his disease he did not seek the LORD, but the physicians. So Asa slept with his fathers, having died in the forty-first year of his reign. They buried him in his own tomb which he had cut out for himself in the city of David, and they laid him in the resting place which he had filled with spices of various kinds blended by the perfumers' art; and they made a very great fire for him.*

Asa lived for only a few more years. During this time he became diseased in both his feet. There has been much discussion of the nature of the disease. Some are persuaded that it was dropsy. Others believe it to have been a vascular obstruction, or gout or even gangrene.[14] Though certain cultures in antiquity possessed some medical knowledge (e.g., Egypt, China), Israel and Judah did not. The practice of medicine among God's people involved the use of magic as well as a rudimentary use of poultices and ointments. The criticism leveled against Asa is that he did not seek the Lord in his illness, but rather placed his confidence in physicians.

---

[14] Williamson, *1 and 2 Chronicles*, 276-77.

This passage should not be used to discourage our consulting with medical practitioners (cf. Colossians 4:14). There was nothing the doctors of that day could do to help the king. Asa's error lay in his failure to recognize the Lord as the true source of healing (Psalm 103:3*b*).

Why then didn't he seek the Lord?

Perhaps Hanani's words so deeply impacted Asa that he felt God had rejected him. The doctrine of forgiveness was not clearly understood in his day (cf. Psalm 145:8-9, 14, 17-19). Without doubt, Asa felt discouraged. He had spent his life trying to serve the Lord, and it was a painful thing to have a single lapse seemingly nullify all his efforts for good. His former zeal was now gone. He became chronically depressed. In time he died.

With Asa's passing, the people realized what it had lost, and they mourned for him. Before his death, Asa had set aside a great store of spices. His dead body was placed in the midst of these. If he had died of gangrene then the spices may have been used to mask the unpleasant odor that would still cling to his body. His mortal remains were placed in a tomb that he had had carved out of the rock, and a great fire was lit in his honor. This does not imply cremation, but was one of the ways the people of that day honored their dead.

As we conclude our study of Asa's life, we do not want to follow in the footsteps of those who fail to find anything significant in what he did. Their writings do not edify us nor do they challenge us with ideas that are worthy of emulation.

## OFTEN OVERLOOKED

During his lifetime, Asa was confronted by two prophets. Azariah encouraged him whereas Hanani discouraged him. Both men, however, said things that are of significance to us.

Azariah encouraged him with the words, *"Be strong and do not lose courage, for there is reward for your work"* (15:7), and Hanani's reminded him that... *"the eyes of the LORD move to and fro throughout the earth that He may strongly support those whose heart is completely His"* (16:9).

It is easy for us, in our struggle to live for the Lord, to question whether the things we attempt to do for Him are worth the effort. Does He really know of the cost to us of preserving an unblemished testimony in the place where we work? Is He aware of the difficulties facing those who try to maintain a Christian family and rear God-honoring children in the midst of a culture that has turned its back on Him? And what of our work in the church—visitation of the sick, service on the deacon board, teaching Sunday school, being involved as a Scout or Awana leader? How can we be sure it's worth the effort?

Of encouragement to us is the promise that the Lord will reward our work. And when we are tempted to conclude that we are a mere speck on the planet, it is comforting to know that the Lord's eye is in every place and He is cognizant of all that we do.

But discouragement can be devastating. Dr. William Barclay pointed out that... "one of the highest of human duties is the duty of encouragement. It is easy to laugh at men's ideals; it is easy to pour cold water on their enthusiasm; it is easy to discourage others. The world is full of discouragers. We have a Christian duty to encourage one another. Many a time a word of praise or thanks or appreciation or cheer has kept a man on his feet."

Azariah's words encouraged Asa and all Judah and Benjamin. They then entered into a covenant with the Lord that lasted throughout the reign of Asa and into the reign of his son, Jehoshaphat.

Unfortunately there are also those in our midst who discourage others. Few are as adept at this as is Lucy in Charles Schultz' cartoon, *Peanuts*. On one occasion, Snoopy was sliding across a frozen pond. He was having fun, and was evidently very satisfied with his progress. Just then Lucy stepped out on to the ice. She had her skates on. Coming up to Snoopy she said to him disdainfully, "That's not skating, that's sliding. You don't have any skates on. Skating is when you have skates on. You're not skating at all. YOU'RE JUST SLIDING!"

Crestfallen, Snoopy walked off the ice and said, "How could I have been so stupid? I thought I was having fun."

The things people say can affect us. What Hanani said to Asa discouraged him and left him feeling as if God had rejected him. To overcome the irritating putdowns of life, we need to remind ourselves over and over again that (1) the Lord has promised to reward our work, and that (2) nothing escapes His all-seeing eye.

Some years ago, I was perusing a book by Al Bryant when I came across an obviously fictitious story, but one that stuck in my mind. The devil, so the story went, advertised that he was going to sell some of his tools. On the day of the sale, they were placed on a table for public inspection. Each was priced according to its value. There, for all to see were implements designed to seduce people into committing all kinds of sins.

Hanging on a wall was a well-worn tool. It did not have a price tag, and one prospective buyer asked, "Is this tool also for sale?"

"No," was the quiet but firm reply.

"What is the name of this implement?" asked the would-be purchaser.

"Discouragement."

"Why isn't it for sale?"

"Because it is more useful to me than any of the others. With it I can pry open a person's heart. I can cause him to question himself and his abilities. I can unleash all his fears, and cause him to feel unappreciated and unloved. With it I can also get a person to turn on his loved ones and even doubt the goodness of God."

Hanani's words, while true (in part), had a negative effect on King Asa. He became discouraged. He may have prayed to the Lord and asked forgiveness, but the joy of the Lord was gone.

Our words are important. They can lift others, instructing or informing them, or leave them deflated and depressed. Let us follow the counsel of the Apostle Paul and insure that our speech is always gracious, seasoned with salt, so that we may know how we should respond to each person (Colossians 4:6).

Chapter Eight

# GOOD INTENTIONS, DANGEROUS CONSEQUENCES

II Chronicles 17:1-21:1

Are there times when you wish you could liven up the after-dinner conversation of your friends? Next time you are faced with this kind of situation, why not ask a question like, "What are the pros and cons of compromise? Can 'meeting someone halfway' be justified? Should Christians ever make concessions?"

We all know that lawyers and politicians are skilled in the art of compromise. But are the compromises they seek truly in the best interests of their clients and/or the country? And what of other kinds of compromise—with medicines, the quality of food, tires on our cars, building materials, education, et cetera—do people make?

The Bible tells us of a man who became embroiled in compromise. His name was Jehoshaphat (873-848 B.C.). As we study his life, we learn things about ourselves (cf. James 1:22-25, noting esp. v.25) that we may not have known before. Jehoshaphat was a good, gracious man. He was also well intentioned. His weakness lay in the fact that he was inclined to be too trusting. He wanted peace for his people and he presumed that others wanted it too. He could not see evil in those with whom he was dealing and so he was led to make unwise concessions.[1]

## OUTLINE

We will deal briefly with the information about Jehoshaphat's life using the following outline:

## JEHOSHAPHAT: A GRACIOUS, MISGUIDED KING

A. Wise Actions of a Godly Leader (17:1-19)

B. Unwise Alliance with an Ungodly Leader (18:1-19:1)

C. Stern Rebuke of a Godly Prophet (19:2-3)

D. Wise Reforms of a Godly Leader (19:4-11)

E. Coalition of Ungodly Nations (20:1-30)

Conclusion (20:31-21:1)

The information contained in these chapters exemplifies many of the Chronicler's themes. For example, Jehoshaphat was a man of prayer. He was also a reformer and removed the idolatrous images from the land. He broke new ground when he sent out "Bible teachers" to instruct the people in the Law of the Lord. And he developed strong defenses, engaged in building projects, accumulated great wealth, and had foreign nations enter

---

[1] An example of the kind of balance we need is to be found in the Lord Jesus. The apostle John said of Him that He was "full of grace and truth" (John 1: 17b). He was not so gracious that he compromised the truth, nor was he so zealous for the truth that he was devoid of grace. These two attributes were perfectly balanced in His personality.

into treaties with him. Like his father, he wanted to secure a lasting peace with the people of Israel.

## Wise Actions of a Godly Leader (17:1-19)

Verses 1-6 describe God's activity on Judah's behalf and Jehosophat's practical approach to his role as king. In this paragraph, we take note of another of the Chronicler's themes, *viz.*, the importance of seeking God. When King Asa died, *"Jehoshaphat his son became king in his place, and he made his position over Israel firm."* He had witnessed the hostility of the Northern Kingdom and, because Judah still held portions of Ephraim taken from Israel in battle, he may have feared that with the change in power in the south, Ahab, king of Israel, might take advantage of the situation by trying to retake the land held by Judah. So Jehoshaphat strengthened himself against Israel.

> *He placed troops in all the fortified cities of Judah, and set garrisons in the land of Judah and in the cities of Ephraim, which Asa his father had captured. The LORD was with Jehoshaphat because he followed the example of his father David[2] ... and did not seek the Baals, but sought the God of his father, followed His commandments, and did not act as Israel did. So the LORD established the kingdom in his control, and all Judah brought tribute to Jehoshaphat, and he had great riches and honor. He took great pride in the ways of the LORD and again removed the high places and the Asherim from Judah.*

---

[2] Jehoshaphat's "father" could be either David or Asa. The reference to the "former years" would seem to indicate Asa.

God's faithfulness is seen in His fulfillment of the Davidic covenant (I:17:11; 28:7), and Jehoshaphat showed his devotion by *"lifting up"* the ways of the Lord.  He also furthered the reform of his father.  The *"high places"* had once again become centers of pagan activity.  Often, after they had been destroyed, the people would rebuild them and revert back to their superstitious ways.  The immorality and idolatry that accompanied the rites performed at these *"high places"* angered the Lord to the point where He would severely chasten His people.

Verses 7-11 deal with several important issues. Mention of *"the third year"* has led some scholars to conclude that the first two years of Jehosophat's reign were spent as a co-regent with his father.[3]   This is possible.

> *"Then in the third year of his reign he sent his officials ... to teach in the cities of Judah; and with them the Levites ... and with them the priests. They taught in Judah, having the book of the law of the LORD with them; and they went throughout all the cities of Judah and taught among the people."*

Jehoshaphat's zeal for reform was obvious.  He was acting in obedience to God's Word (cf. Deuteronomy 17:18-20), and demonstrating his concern for a knowledge of the truth and the will to carry out the teaching of Scripture.[4]

---

[3] Thiele, *Mysterious Numbers* (1983), 96f.

[4] The teaching ministry of the descendents of Aaron is to be found in passages like Deuteronomy 33:10; Leviticus 10:11; Jeremiah 18:18; Hosea 4:6; and Malachi 2:7.

The basis of Jehoshaphat's reform was centered in the Word of God. Those whom the king sent out were to instruct the inhabitants of Judah in the Book of the Law (cf. 34:14).

It has been held by liberal Bible scholars that the "Book of the Law" mentioned in this passage is *not* our Deuteronomy because Deuteronomy was not written until the time of Josiah (622 B.C.). Later studies have shown such negative biblical criticism to be incorrect, for this book by Moses was in use around 869 B.C., nearly 250 years before the critics claim it was written. This has forced those who find fault with the Bible to revise their opinion. They now claim that those who were sent out by Jehoshaphat took with them only portions of the Law[5] (viz., Exodus 20:22-23:33), but not the Book of Deuteronomy. What is achieved by this concession is unclear. It seems to be a deceptive device to redirect the attention of modern Bible students away from the obvious fallacy of holding a late date for the writing of Deuteronomy.

The blessing of the Lord upon Jehoshaphat and Judah is seen in a number of ways: (1) God protects His people by filling their enemies with fear; (2) former enemies begin to bring tribute; (3) and Jehoshaphat increases, materially and numerically, in strength.

*Now the dread of the LORD was on all the kingdoms of the lands that were around Judah, so that they did not make war against Jehoshaphat. Some of the Philistines brought gifts and silver as tribute to Jehoshaphat; the Arabians also brought him flocks, 7,700 rams and 7,700 male goats. So*

---

[5] See the comments of Dillard, *I & II Chronicles*, 179.

*Jehoshaphat grew greater and greater, and he built fortresses and store cities in Judah. He had large supplies in the cities of Judah, and warriors, valiant men, in Jerusalem. This was their muster according to their fathers' households: of Judah, commanders of thousands, Adnah was the commander, and with him 300,000 valiant warriors; and next to him was Johanan the commander, and with him 280,000; and next to him Amasiah the son of Zichri, who volunteered for the LORD, and with him 200,000 valiant warriors; and of Benjamin, Eliada a valiant warrior, and with him 200,000 armed with bow and shield; and next to him Jehozabad, and with him 180,000 equipped for war. These are they who served the king, apart from those whom the king put in the fortified cities through all Judah.*

Jehoshaphat's army is in two parts: (a) his standing army (those counted by families or fathers' houses, cf. 17:14, 19), and (b) those who volunteered for service (cf. 17:16). The experienced fighting men were stationed in Jerusalem and in the fortified cities where they were well provisioned and well equipped.

### Unwise Alliance with an Ungodly Leader (18:1-19:1)

Believing himself to be in a powerful (and superior) position, Jehoshaphat made overtures of peace and mutual cooperation to King Ahab of Israel. He did not propose a reunion of the tribes as Abijah had done, but instead suggested an alliance between their two houses. His son would marry Ahab's daughter, and the two countries would enter into a mutually acceptable and binding treaty (cf.

18:3). The biblical information is very brief. All we are told is that *"Jehoshaphat ... allied himself by marriage with Ahab."* The result was an immediate cessation of the internecine wars that had been waged ever since the kingdom was divided in 931 B.C.

We cannot be sure of Jehoshaphat's reaction to the successful completion of the negotiations with King Ahab, but it is in keeping with human nature for a person to quietly congratulate himself/herself on the success of such diplomacy. Jehoshaphat had secured what he believed to be an honorable peace. Each nation retained its sovereignty and maintained its own religious beliefs. What could possibly be fairer? The Chronicler, however, implies that such a treaty was not necessary. The Lord had blessed Jehoshaphat in every way, and should there be an unprovoked invasion along any of Judah's borders, He could be relied upon to turn back their enemies. The alliance did pave the way, however, for an unwise and costly venture that nearly ended in disaster. We read:

> *Some years later he [Jehoshaphat] went down to visit Ahab at Samaria. And Ahab slaughtered many sheep and oxen for him and the people who were with him, and induced him to go up against Ramoth-gilead. Ahab king of Israel said to Jehoshaphat king of Judah, "Will you go with me against Ramoth-gilead?" And he said to him, "I am as you are, and my people as your people, and we will be with you in the battle." Moreover, Jehoshaphat said to the king of Israel, "Please inquire first for the word of the LORD." Then the king of Israel assembled the prophets, four hundred men, and said to them, "Shall we go against Ramoth-gilead to battle, or shall I*

*refrain?" And they said, "Go up, for God will give
it into the hand of the king." But Jehoshaphat
said, "Is there not yet a prophet of the LORD here
that we may inquire of him?" The king of Israel
said to Jehoshaphat, "There is yet one man by
whom we may inquire of the LORD, but I hate
him, for he never prophesies good concerning me
but always evil. He is Micaiah, son of Imla." But
Jehoshaphat said, "Let not the king say so."*

We have dealt with this story at length in our study
of I Kings. Sufficient to say that Jehoshaphat did not
realize that the cunning and wily Ahab was drawing him
into a trap. And this, I believe, shows Jehoshaphat's
gullibility. He was honest in his dealings with others, and
he expected them to be honest in their dealings with him.
He did not expect Ahab to be devious and deceitful.
Having been royally treated in Samaria, and possibly on the
day before his departure for Jerusalem, he was unprepared
for his host's subtle request. Ahab said in effect, "You
know that Ramoth-gilead[6] at one time belonged to Israel.
It's a strategic city and in our hands could protect our two
nations against any hostile incursions on the part of the
Syrians. Will you join with me so that we can recover this
city ... for our mutual benefit, of course?" And
Jehoshaphat readily agreed.

But Jehoshaphat's conscience bothered him. He felt
uneasy. It was his practice to seek God's will, and he
sensed inwardly that he had too hastily consented to
something without consulting the Lord. To allay his
misgivings, he suggested that they inquire of the Lord in

---

[6] *Macmillan Bible Atlas*, 131, 135. See also the *New
International Dictionary of Biblical Archaeology*, 384.

order to ascertain His will. And Ahab readily agreed. He could not do otherwise. However, he was a crafty monarch with four hundred prophets on his payroll. He knew that they would say and do exactly what he wanted. So, while their thrones were being set up in the open area before the gate, the prophets were summoned and primed so that they could support Ahab's plans. When asked about the viability of going to Ramoth-gilead, they responded with one voice predicting great success.

When their leader, Zedekiah, sensed that King Jehoshaphat remained unconvinced, he went to elaborate lengths to win him over (18:10). This, too, failed. With growing misgivings, Jehoshaphat asked if there was a (real) prophet of the Lord in the land. This forced Ahab to admit that there was. Then in a childish attempt at humor, he stated that he did not like him because he never predicted any good concerning him.

Jehoshaphat requested that he be brought before them.

> *Then the king of Israel called an officer and said, "Bring quickly Micaiah, Imla's son." Now the king of Israel and Jehoshaphat the king of Judah were sitting each on his throne, arrayed in their robes, and they were sitting at the threshing floor at the entrance of the gate of Samaria; and all the prophets were prophesying before them. Zedekiah the son of Chenaanah made horns of iron for himself and said, "Thus says the LORD, 'With these you shall gore the Arameans [Syrians] until they are consumed.'" All the prophets were prophesying thus, saying, "Go up to Ramoth-gilead and succeed, for the LORD will give it into the hand of the king."*

*Then the messenger who went to summon
Micaiah spoke to him saying, "Behold, the words
of the prophets are uniformly favorable to the
king. So please let your word be like one of them
and speak favorably." But Micaiah said, "As the
LORD lives, what my God says, that I will speak."
When he came to the king, the king said to him,
"Micaiah, shall we go to Ramoth-gilead to battle,
or shall I refrain?" He said, "Go up and succeed,
for they will be given into your hand." Then the
king said to him, "How many times must I adjure
you to speak to me nothing but the truth in the
name of the LORD?" So he said, "I saw all Israel
scattered on the mountains, Like sheep which have
no shepherd; And the LORD said, 'These have no
master. Let each of them return to his house in
peace.'" Then the king of Israel said to
Jehoshaphat, "Did I not tell you that he would not
prophesy good concerning me, but evil?"*

It would appear as if Micaiah, with obsequious
acquiescence, at first agreed with Ahab's prophets. He
knew that Ahab would not be deceived by his demeanor,
and so was ready when Ahab admonished him to tell the
truth. And Micaiah did so. Far from encouraging Ahab, he
told the king that he would die in the engagement: *"I see
Israel as sheep without a shepherd,"* he said. In other
words, the venture will end in disaster.

Ahab viewed Micaiah's prediction as evil—the
product of one who was prepared to misuse his office in
order to spite those with whom he disagreed—and
remanded the prophet into the custody of Amon the
governor of the city.

Sensing that his warning was being disregarded, Micaiah gave the two kings a second message. He had either received two visions earlier that day or they were given to him while he was standing before the gate of the city. His second vision was of a heavenly court. In this vision God is portrayed as inviting angelic beings to suggest ways by which Ahab could be enticed to go to Ramoth-gilead (18:19). None of their suggestions are feasible. Then another spirit, a lying spirit, comes before Him (cf. Job 1:6-12; 2:1-7) and suggests that he go and deceive Ahab's prophets (cf. I Kings 22:20-25). He is given permission to do so. This brief incident confirms that everything in heaven and earth, and even things under the earth, is under God's control (Philippians 2:10); and if He so desires He can use evil to accomplish His purpose. Let it also be noted that even though an evil spirit misled Ahab's prophets, Ahab had been warned and was responsible for the choice he made.

Zedekiah is incensed by Micaiah's words and strikes him forcefully on the cheek. This is one of the highest forms of insult. God's prophet then utters a third prediction: Zedekiah will know how wrong he has been on the day he seeks to hide himself from the Syrians by fleeing from one room to another in an endeavor to evade capture.

> So the king of Israel and Jehoshaphat king of Judah went up against Ramoth-gilead. The king of Israel said to Jehoshaphat, "I will disguise myself and go into battle, but you put on your robes." So the king of Israel disguised himself, and they went into battle. Now the king of Aram [Syria] had commanded the captains of his chariots, saying, "Do not fight with small or great, but with the king of Israel alone." So when

*the captains of the chariots saw Jehoshaphat, they*
*said, "It is the king of Israel," and they turned*
*aside to fight against him. But Jehoshaphat cried*
*out, and the LORD helped him, and God diverted*
*them from him. When the captains of the chariots*
*saw that it was not the king of Israel, they turned*
*back from pursuing him. A certain man drew his*
*bow at random and struck the king of Israel in a*
*joint of the armor. So he said to the driver of the*
*chariot, "Turn around and take me out of the*
*fight, for I am severely wounded." The battle*
*raged that day, and the king of Israel propped*
*himself up in his chariot in front of the Arameans*
*[Syrians] until the evening; and at sunset he died.*

Though Ahab attempted to nullify the word of the
Lord, and even disguised himself so as to be less
conspicuous, he was wounded when a soldier randomly
shot an arrow into the melee of soldiers. The king bravely
remained standing until evening, when he died. As news of
the king's death spread through the camp, the men of Israel
rolled up their blankets and began to walk back to their
own land. And the people of Judah did the same. What
Micaiah had predicted came to pass.

*"And Jehoshaphat the king of Judah returned in*
*safety to his house in Jerusalem"* (19:1).

The incidents recorded in this chapter were of the
utmost importance to the people for whom the Chronicler
wrote. The voice of the prophets had been neglected and
few were prepared to acknowledge their authority in Israel.
The fulfillment of Micaiah's predictions would reinforce
the role of those who were truly God's representatives.

We face a similar problem in our day.  Some men and women, who occupy our most influential pulpits, fail to declare to us the Word of the Lord.[7]  They may think they do, and may even make loud protests if their entrance into the ministry is ever questioned, but the fact remains that some are deluded into thinking the pulpit is the right (and perhaps *only*) place for them.  In reality they are in the same position as Zedekiah and his associates.

### *Stern Rebuke of a Godly Prophet (19:2-3)*

En route to his palace, Jehoshaphat is accosted by the prophet Jehu.

> *Jehu the son of Hanani the seer went out to meet him and said to King Jehoshaphat, "Should you help the wicked and love those who hate[8] the LORD and so bring wrath on yourself from the LORD?  But there is some good in you, for you have removed the Asheroth from the land and you have set your heart to seek God."*

Though Jehu is spoken of as *"the son of Hanani the seer,"* we are not sure if he was himself a *"seer."*  We do

---

[7] Some today have so listened to the voices of these false teachers (who pretend to teach God's Word or receive messages directly from Him) that they have even gone back on their faith (cf. Galatians 3:1-5; II Timothy 3:1-5; II Peter 2:1-3; I John 4:1-3).  And when someone arises who does tell us the truth, he or she is all too often scorned and maligned and silenced as a sower of discord and out of step with the times.

[8] For an explanation of "love" and "hate" in this context, see J. A. Thompson, *Vetus Testamentum* 29 (1979), 200-05.

not read that the words he spoke came from the Lord (cf. I Kings 16:1, which explicitly states that what was prophesied was from the Lord). Much of what Jehu said was true. Jehoshaphat had attempted to help the ungodly. He had been led into this compromise by his own good nature and desire for the peace of his people. But part of Jehu's rebuke did *not* come to pass. Jehoshaphat's actions did *not* bring down on himself the wrath of the Lord. This leads us to compare Jehu's stern rebuke with his father's denunciation of King Asa (16:7-9). Hanani, it will be remembered, also predicted dire judgment (16:9*b*) that never came to pass.

From this, it may be deduced that Jehu's father, Hanani, was the kind of person who saw everything in black and white (with lots of black and very little white). And being narrow-minded, he had taught his sons that any deviation from what was right (as he saw it) was always severely punished. And his sons grew up to be like him.

Whereas Hanani had predicted judgment on Asa, now Jehu predicted that judgment would come down on the head of Jehoshaphat. Both men erred. They exceeded the bounds of their office. They overlooked the fact that God has other ways of dealing with sin, and one of them is the central theme of the Chronicler who quotes the Lord as saying,

> *"[When] My people who are called by My name humble themselves and pray and seek My face and turn from their wicked ways, then I will hear from heaven, will forgive their sin and will heal their land" (7:14).*

Our God is a God of grace.

We have preachers today who are so afraid of offending people that they compromise the Word of God for the sake of popularity and the position they hold. They value more highly the income they receive and their acceptance by the leaders in their denomination than they do the approval of the Lord. They are like the prophets of Ahab who told him to go to Ramoth-gilead for victory awaited him there. And we have preachers like Jehu whose message is stern and devoid of grace. Such individuals frighten people into compliance by predicting that awful consequences will accompany their disobedience. Neither approach serves God's purpose. *"Speaking the truth in love"* (i.e., with respect for the individual and without compromise) was recommended by the apostle Paul and remains the best approach.

### *Wise Reforms of a Godly Leader (19:4-11)*

We have before stated that Jehoshaphat was a good and godly king. This may be seen once again in his desire to have his people instructed in the ways of the Lord. He not only sent out civil and religious leaders among the people, but even went around himself and personally encouraged them to follow the Lord (19:5-11). Many of his subjects had never seen their king in person, and to have him visit their small city or village must have had an impact on them. Jehoshaphat also took seriously the importance of governing his people righteously. To do this he appointed judges and other officials to administer justice in the fortified cities. The Levites, priests and heads of fathers' houses were to serve in Jerusalem as a court of appeal with Amariah and Zebadiah as chief officials.

*So Jehoshaphat lived in Jerusalem and
went out again among the people from Beersheba
to the hill country of Ephraim and brought them
back to the LORD, the God of their fathers... he
appointed judges in the land in all the fortified
cities of Judah, city by city. He said to the judges,
"Consider what you are doing, for you do not
judge for man but for the LORD who is with you
when you render judgment. Now then let the fear
of the LORD be upon you; be very careful what
you do, for the LORD our God will have no part in
unrighteousness or partiality or the taking of a
bribe."*

*In Jerusalem also Jehoshaphat appointed
some of the Levites and priests, and some of the
heads of the fathers' households of Israel, for the
judgment of the LORD and to judge disputes
among the inhabitants of Jerusalem. Then he
charged them saying, "Thus you shall do in the
fear of the LORD, faithfully and wholeheartedly.
Whenever any dispute comes to you from your
brethren who live in their cities, between blood
and blood, between law and commandment,
statutes and ordinances, you shall warn them so
that they may not be guilty before the LORD, and
wrath may not come on you and your brethren.
Thus you shall do and you will not be guilty.
Behold, Amariah the chief priest[9] will be over
you in all that pertains to the LORD, and
Zebadiah the son of Ishmael, the ruler of the house*

---

[9] For a discussion of the possible judicial significance of this
title, see J. R. Bartlett, *Vetus Testamentum* 19 (1969), 6.

*of Judah, in all that pertains to the king. Also the*
*Levites shall be officers before you. Act*
*resolutely, and the LORD be with the upright."*

None of Jehoshaphat's subjects were neglected.
From Beersheba in the south to Ephraim in the north, all
had adequate representation.[10]

This happy state of affairs continued for many
years. Then, without warning, Judah was invaded by
hostile nations who had grown envious of its prosperity and
were no longer overawed by the God whom the people of
Judah worshiped. Without warning, they formed a
coalition and invaded the land.

### Coalition of Ungodly Nations (20:1-30)

Jehoshaphat was taken completely by surprise. At
first we find it difficult to understand how this vast
coalition could penetrate so far into Judah without being
detected. A little reflection on recent events, however, will
temper our criticism of Jehoshaphat with a little humility.
In 1991, a defecting Cuban pilot, flying a Russian MIG-21
fighter, not only outwitted Cuban reconnaissance but also
slipped into Florida undetected. He avoided our radar
detection by flying 518 miles per hour at a scant fifty feet
above the ocean. And needless to say our defense system
was taken completely by surprise! This gives us less

---

[10] S. Mendelsohn, *Criminal Jurisprudence of the Ancient
Hebrews* (New York: Hermon, 1968), 270pp.; K. W. Whitelam, *The
Just King* (Sheffield, UK: University of Sheffield Press, 1979), 185-
206.

reason to criticize Jehoshaphat and a greater understanding of the fact that even the best defenses may grow lax.

All this reminds us that the events the Bible describes are true to life. Just when we begin to think that everything is going well, the unexpected happens.

> *Now it came about after this that the sons of Moab and the sons of Ammon, together with some of the Meunites, came to make war against Jehoshaphat. Then some came and reported to Jehoshaphat, saying, "A great multitude is coming against you from beyond the sea, out of Aram[11] and behold, they are in Hazazon-tamar (that is Engedi)." Jehoshaphat was afraid and turned his attention to seek the LORD, and proclaimed a fast throughout all Judah. So Judah gathered together to seek help from the LORD; they even came from all the cities of Judah to seek the LORD.*

The Moabites,[12] were probably the instigators of the attack on God's people, and were aided by the Ammonites[13] and the Meunites (possibly Edomites). At this period of history, each nation worshipped local (or tribal) deities. The people of Moab were at one time fearful of attacking Judah, but after a while they perhaps reasoned that if their gods were aided by the gods of Ammon and

---

[11] In Hebrew "Aram" (Syria), mra, and "Edom," mda, are very similar, and a copyist could easily confuse the one for the other.

[12] D. J. Wiseman, ed., *Peoples of Old Testament Times* (1973), 229-58.

[13] N. Glueck, *The Other Side of the Jordan* (1940), 208pp.; G. M. Landes, *Biblical Archaeologist* 24 (1961), 66-95.

Edom, then their combined strength could possibly overpower the God of Judah.[14]

It is evident that Jehoshaphat was taken completely by surprise, for this *"great multitude"* had reached Engedi,[15] half way up the western shore of the Dead Sea, before word was brought to him. The news caused Jehoshaphat to summon all Judah to prayer. In this respect, his action set a precedent that was followed in World War II. Hitler's army was only a week or two away from crossing the British Channel and invading England when King George called the nation to prayer. The people were fearful, but had resolved to defend their tiny island to the bitter end. Churches were left open 24 hours a day so that people could enter them and pray. Some stayed for a long while whereas others could spend only a few minutes in intercession. God, however, heard their prayers and, using the forces of nature as well as Hitler's unstable personality, turned the tide of war and miraculously delivered His people.[16]

*When the people had gathered together,*
*Jehoshaphat stood in the assembly of Judah and*
*Jerusalem, in the house of the LORD before the*

---

[14] This basic attitude is confirmed in sections of the famous "Moabite Stone" where Chemosh, the principal deity of Moab, is credited with either giving victory or else showing his displeasure by allowing the people of Moab to be defeated by their enemies (cf. G. A. Cooke, *A Text-Book of North-Semitic Inscriptions* [1903]), 1-14.

[15] *New International Dictionary of Biblical Archaeology*, 180.

[16] This story has finally been told by J. Lukas in *Five Days in London, May 1940* (New Haven, CT: Yale University Press, 1999), 236pp.

*new court, and he said, "O LORD, the God of our
fathers, are You not God in the heavens? And are
You not ruler over all the kingdoms of the
nations? Power and might are in Your hand so
that no one can stand against You. Did You not,
O our God, drive out the inhabitants of this land
before Your people Israel and give it to the
descendants of Abraham Your friend forever?
They have lived in it, and have built You a
sanctuary there for Your name, saying, 'Should
evil come upon us, the sword, or judgment, or
pestilence, or famine, we will stand before this
house and before You (for Your name is in this
house) and cry to You in our distress, and You will
hear and deliver us.' Now behold, the sons of
Ammon and Moab and Mount Seir, whom You did
not let Israel invade when they came out of the
land of Egypt (they turned aside from them and
did not destroy them), see how they are rewarding
us by coming to drive us out from Your possession
which You have given us as an inheritance. O our
God, will You not judge them? For we are
powerless before this great multitude who are
coming against us; nor do we know what to do,
but our eyes are on You."*

All Judah was standing before the LORD, with their
infants, their wives and their children. Note the
Chronicler's emphasis on *"all Judah"* (20:3, 13, 15, 18)
and *"every town"* (20:4). The response of the people to
Jehoshaphat was widespread. When they had assembled,
Jehoshaphat did not delegate the prayer for the people to
the high priest. He led the people in prayer himself, and his
prayer incorporated a realization of God's sovereignty,
praise for His gift of the land and the Temple, recognition

of His covenant with David, a reminder of the history of his people, and an entreaty for Him to show forth His power and deliver them.

> *Then in the midst of the assembly the Spirit of the LORD came upon Jahaziel the son of Zechariah, the son of Benaiah, the son of Jeiel, the son of Mattaniah, the Levite of the sons of Asaph; and he said, "Listen, all Judah and the inhabitants of Jerusalem and King Jehoshaphat: thus says the LORD to you, 'Do not fear or be dismayed because of this great multitude, for the battle is not yours but God's. Tomorrow go down against them. Behold, they will come up by the ascent of Ziz, and you will find them at the end of the valley in front of the wilderness of Jeruel. You need not fight in this battle; station yourselves, stand and see the salvation of the LORD on your behalf, O Judah and Jerusalem.' Do not fear or be dismayed; tomorrow go out to face them, for the LORD is with you."*

God's answer to Jehoshaphat came unexpectedly. Jahaziel, whose ancestry is traced with unerring precision, spoke to encourage the assembled throng. We are specifically told that the *"Spirit of the Lord"* came upon him. The prediction he uttered was enough to boggle the minds of those who heard him. They were not to be afraid. The very next morning they were to go out to battle, but they would not have to fight, for the Lord was going to give them the victory.

On hearing this, Jehoshaphat accepted by faith what he could not understand.

*He then bowed his head with his face to
the ground, and all Judah and the inhabitants of
Jerusalem fell down before the LORD,
worshipping the LORD. The Levites, from the
sons of the Kohathites and of the sons of the
Korahites, stood up to praise the LORD God of
Israel, with a very loud voice.*

The writer of Hebrews reminds us that, *"Faith is
the assurance of things hoped for, the conviction of things
not seen.... And [that] without faith it is impossible to
please Him, for he who comes to God must believe that He
is and that He is a rewarder of those who seek Him"*
(Hebrews 11:1, 6).

The army complies with God's instructions. The
soldiers rise early in the morning. As they are about to
leave Jerusalem, Jehoshaphat stands and addresses the
people. *"Listen to me, O Judah and inhabitants of
Jerusalem, put your trust in the LORD your God and you
will be established. Put your trust in His prophets and
succeed."* He then appoints those who sing to the Lord and
those who praise Him to lead the way, saying, *"Give thanks
to the LORD, for His lovingkindness is everlasting."* And
when they begin singing and praising God, the Lord sets
ambushes against the sons of Ammon, Moab and Mount
Seir.

Just how this is done we do not know. Many able
commentators are of the opinion that the ambushes were
part of the heavenly host who took on human form.
Whatever means the Lord used, Judah's enemies are
routed. Those in ambush have the effect of causing the
sons of Ammon and Moab to rise up against the inhabitants
of Mount Seir destroying them completely; and when they
have finished with them they begin to destroy one another.

When Judah arrives at a lookout point all they see are corpses lying on the ground. No one has escaped.

When Jehoshaphat and his people came to take their spoil, they found goods, clothing and valuable things. These they took for themselves. So great was the spoil that they could not carry it away. The Chronicler then concludes by saying, *"And they were three days taking the spoil because there was so much."*

All of this highlights for us the importance of prayer and a complete trust in the Lord. But can we expect the Lord to do the same today?

God still answers prayer. To properly understand the teaching of Scripture, we need to keep clearly in mind God's distinct relationship with His people Israel and His special relationship with believers in Christ. God had given Israel the land. He had also entered into what some have called a "suzerainty treaty" with them. If they obeyed His laws, He would bless and protect them. Jehoshaphat, therefore, had every right to appeal to the Lord for His special intervention. He was also correct in his appeal to the Lord to fulfill His plan and purpose for Israel.

We have a very definite but different relationship with the Lord. We share many of the blessings of the Abrahamic Covenant (cf. Romans 11:17-24). As we read through the New Testament, however, we find that our battles are with the temptations that arise out of our inordinate desires for what we want to have, what we want to do, and what we want to be (cf. I John 2:15-17). (Medieval writers condensed the struggles of Christians into three areas: the world, the flesh, and the devil.) We may certainly pray for God's intervention and help with our many and varied trials, but in our situation, He helps us progress through the trials and difficulties we face (cf. I Corinthians 10:13).

Our ordeals, of course, are as real to us as the threat facing Jehoshaphat and the people of Judah. However, when we pray, we do not have to pray toward the Temple (cf. Solomon's prayer in I Kings 8:28-53). As the people of Judah cast themselves on God's love and mercy, so do we (I Peter 5:7), and we have the witness of the Holy Spirit in our hearts so that we know that the Lord hears us. As the people of Judah trusted implicitly in the Lord, so must we. God may not help us in the same miraculous way, but His care and protection of us is as sure as it was in Jehoshaphat's time.

On the fourth day the men of Judah assembled in the valley of *Beracah* (meaning "blessing"), and there they blessed the Lord for His goodness to them. After this the place became known as "The Valley of Beracah." Their thanksgiving over, every man returned to Jerusalem with Jehoshaphat at their head. What a testimony this must have been to their wives and children. The Lord had not only kept them safe, He had made them to rejoice over their enemies. The procession came up the road toward Jerusalem with the people marching to the sound of harps, lyres and trumpets. They converged on the house of the Lord for further praise and thanksgiving.

*"And the dread of God was on all the kingdoms of the lands when they heard that the LORD had fought against the enemies of Israel."*

This interlude over, the kingdom of Jehoshaphat once again enjoys peace, for God gives them rest from all their enemies.

### Conclusion (20:31-21:1)

The Chronicler ends this portion of his narrative with a summary:

> *Now Jehoshaphat reigned over Judah. He was thirty-five years old when he became king, and he reigned in Jerusalem twenty-five years. And his mother's name was Azubah the daughter of Shilhi. He walked in the way of his father Asa and did not depart from it, doing right in the sight of the LORD. The high places, however, were not removed; the people had not yet directed their hearts to the God of their fathers. Now the rest of the acts of Jehoshaphat, first to last, behold, they are written in the annals of Jehu the son of Hanani, which is recorded in the Book of the Kings of Israel.*

Jehoshaphat's reign probably included a two-year co-regency during Asa's final illness. He was one of Judah's godly kings and lived on in the memory of his people as a leader who instructed them in the *"law of the Lord."* The people, however, were wedded to their *"high places,"* and Jehoshaphat was unable to remove these sacred sites from the land. In all probability, as soon as those commissioned to destroy them had departed, the people gathered the stones together and rebuilt them. And so while the king had set his heart on serving the Lord, his example was not widely followed.

One stain mars Jehoshaphat's closing years. He entered into an alliance with King Ahaziah of Israel (I Kings 22:48-49). The goal was to build sea-worthy ships (referred to as *"ships of Tarshish"*) to go to Ophir for gold. The expedition met with disaster, for the ships were broken

at the port of Ezion-geber (20:20-26).[17]  Because Solomon
had engaged in maritime trade with Ophir, it did not mean
that Jehoshaphat should do the same.  The alliance between
Solomon and Hiram was between two believers.  There is
no indication that Ahaziah had embraced the worship of
Yahweh.

So when should we follow a precedent and when
should we allow the opportunity to pass us by?  First and
foremost, we should always seek God's will.  Then,
depending on the nature of the alliance, we should limit our
involvement to those believers who can be trusted.  Finally,
there are times in life when we should be content with the
things the Lord has given us.  Having more does not make
us better (cf. Philippians 4:11; I Timothy 6:6; Hebrews
13:5).

## IN RETROSPECT

Of the many lessons to be learned from the life of
Jehoshaphat, one of the most important is that of security.
When I was in seminary, we would often sing the hymn
written by Lina Sandell, "More Secure is No One Ever."  It
goes like this:

> More secure is no one ever
> Than the loved ones of the Savior;
> Not yon star, on high abiding,
> Nor the bird in home-nest hiding.

> God His own doth tend and nourish,
> In His holy courts they flourish;
> Like a father kind He spares them,
> In His loving arms He bears them.

---

[17] Cf. Glueck, *The Other Side of Jordan*, 50-113; idem, *Rivers
in the Desert* (New York:  Farrar, Strauss and Cudahy, 1959), 153-68.

> Neither life nor death can ever
> From the Lord His children sever;
> For His love and deep compassion
> Comfort them in tribulation.
>
> Little flock, to joy then yield thee!
> Jacob's God will ever shield thee;
> Rest secure with this Defender,
> At His will all foes surrender.
>
> What He takes or what He gives us
> Shows the Father's love so precious;
> We may trust His purpose wholly—
> 'Tis His children's welfare solely.

God gave Jehoshaphat every token of His love and blessing. He lived in peace and prosperity. The Lord built a hedge around him, and even when his own folly backfired, the Lord kept him safe. We may not occupy positions of great influence, but we can follow Jehosha-phat's footsteps and seek to implement justice, to love kindness, and to walk humbly with our God (cf. Micah 6:8).

When our trials overwhelm us, we can remember what the Lord did for Jehoshaphat and receive encouragement from the words of Annie Johnson Flynt ...

> God has not promised Skies always blue,
> Flower strewn pathways All our lives through;
> God has not promised Sun without rain
> Joy without sorrow, Peace without pain.
> But God has promised Strength for the day,
> Rest for the labor, Light for the way,
> Grace for the trials, Help from above,
> Unfailing sympathy, Undying love.

Chapter Nine

# REAPING THE WHIRLWIND

II Chronicles 21:1-23:15

Who were the most evil women of history?
Obviously opinions will differ. Just about everyone will
agree, however, that Jezebel and her daughter, Athaliah,
should be somewhere near the top of the list. As queens,
they had a powerful influence over their husbands and in
time, each of them proved the correctness of Bernard L.
Montgomery's observation that "leadership which is evil,
though it may succeed for a time, in the end sows the seeds
of its own destruction" (cf. Hosea 8:7; Proverbs 10:25).

## SOURCE OF EVIL

Omri (885-874 B.C.) was an evil king of Israel.
Before ascending the throne, he served as general of the
Northern Kingdom's army. When the king died, a civil war
ensued. After four years, Omri emerged as the undisputed
master of the northern tribes (I Kings 16:21-22). He built
Samaria and made it his capital, and he strengthened his
dynasty by treaties and alliances with foreign countries.
History remembers him, however, as the one who
introduced the worship of Baal into Israel. He did this by
uniting in marriage his son Ahab, to Jezebel, daughter of
Ethbaal, king of Sidon.

Omri's legacy has been accurately described by the biblical historian: He *"did evil in the sight of the Lord, and acted more wickedly than all who were before him"* (I Kings 16:25f.). His worldly and irreligious policies were denounced centuries later by the prophet Micah who referred to them as *"the statutes of Omri"* (Micah 6:16). He died in 874 B.C.

Ahab and Jezebel probably had several children, but the most infamous was their daughter, Athaliah. She was later married to Jehoram, heir apparent to the throne of Judah. At the time of her marriage, Athaliah came to the southern kingdom filled with "missionary" zeal. She was determined to establish Baal worship in Judah as soon as a suitable opportunity presented itself. This happened when her father-in-law, Jehoshaphat, died in 848 B.C. To accomplish her ends, she brought into Judah priests and priestesses of Baal, and together with her husband, seduced the people by causing them to commit all sorts of sensual acts in the name of religion.

## OUTLINE

It is a constant surprise to us to observe how quickly the lessons of history are forgotten. We read in Scripture that God does not take pleasure in wickedness; that no evil dwells with Him; that the boastful shall not stand before Him, and that He will destroy those who speak falsehood and shed innocent blood (cf. Psalm 5:4-6; Isaiah 59:12); yet individuals who habitually do these things do so with a complete disregard for the fact that one day they will give an account to God for their deeds.

The Chronicler was aware of this and, in recounting this era of history, he did so by reminding his readers of the faithfulness of God (21:7; cf. Ezra 9:13; Psalm 99:8; Zechariah 1:4). The Lord remembered His covenant with the house of David and spared the nation because of the promise He had made (cf. 21:6 with 21:7).

The material the Chronicler included in his history was intended to encourage the returned exiles. He wanted to stimulate them in the way of righteousness and also to warn them of the fate of the wicked (note 21:6; 22:3-4, 7-8). The biblical text may be outlined as follows:

## THE PUNISHMENT OF THE WICKED

- God's Faithfulness in Preserving the House of David (21:1-7)

- God's Punishment of the Faithlessness of Jehoram (21:8-20)

- God's Judgment on the House of Ahab (22:1-23:15)

### *God's Faithfulness in Preserving the House of David (21:1-7)*

God had long ago promised David that he would always have a descendant to sit on his throne. Ultimately, this promise will be fulfilled in the Lord Jesus Christ (Luke 1:30-33). But centuries intervened during which several attempts were made to exterminate David's royal line. If this had been accomplished, God's plan of salvation would have been thwarted.[1]

---

[1] These attempts to eliminate the royal line did not take God by surprise. He foreknew what would happen and sovereignly

### The Division of the King's Estate (21:1-3).

Before his death, Jehoshaphat divided his estate among his sons. He gave each one fortified cities and great wealth. However, he appointed his oldest son, Jehoram,[2] to succeed him. We read:

> *Then Jehoshaphat slept with his fathers and was buried with his fathers in the city of David, and Jehoram his son became king in his place. He had brothers, the sons of Jehoshaphat: Azariah, Jehiel, Zechariah, Azaryahu, Michael and Shephatiah. All these were the sons of Jehoshaphat king of Israel. Their father gave them many gifts of silver, gold and precious things, with fortified cities in Judah, but he gave the kingdom to Jehoram because he was the firstborn.*

These verses raise questions in our minds. For example, why did Jehoshaphat appoint Jehoram his successor? Was it only because he was the firstborn? Surely Jehoshaphat knew that Jehoram was not well-liked by the people (cf. 21:20), and he must have known that he was not as honorable as his brothers (21:13*b*). Why then did Jehoshaphat appoint him his successor? And why did he give his sons fortified cities to live in and great wealth? Did he know of Athaliah's control over Jehoram, and was this his attempt to limit Jehoram's power (while also effectively limiting hers)? And did he divide up the realm

---

orchestrated events so that there would always be a descendant of David's line to sit on David's throne.

[2] Jehoram had served as co-regent with Jehoshaphat for several years prior to his father's death (853-848 B.C.).

in order to minimize the discontent of the people that he felt sure would accompany Jehoram's reign?[3]

Whatever answers we give to these questions, it must be admitted that Jehoshaphat faced the issues squarely and sought to do all he could to achieve the stability of the kingdom. When he died, the Chronicler states that he *"rested with his fathers"* (21:1) and was buried in the city of David. Though not without fault, Jehoshaphat did fear the Lord and attempted to bring peace to the people of Judah. As a result of his life and deeds, he has gone down in the annals of God's people as a good and wise king (I Kings 22:43).

**The Elimination of the New King's Rivals (21:4-7).** The opening words of verse 4 send a chill down our spines. They seem to confirm our worst suspicions. Apparently several months after his coronation, during which time he sought to make his position secure, Jehoram had his brothers killed. Verse 4*b* would seem to imply that he (or Athaliah) wanted absolute rule. Is it also possible that his brothers were opposed to the introduction of Baal worship into Judah? Jehoram knew of only one thing to do in order to feel secure, *viz.*, eliminate the opposition. And inasmuch as Athaliah was the person exercising power in the land, there is the distinct likelihood that she instigated the assassination of her brothers-in-law.

---

[3] Though the general principal of primogenetre was practiced in other lands, it was not the accepted standard in Judah. It is possible that Jehoshaphat make Jehoram king over Judah because it was part of the treaty (to insure peace with the Northern Kingdom) that he had made with Ahab and Jezebel at the time of Jehoram's marriage to their daughter, Athaliah.

*Now when Jehoram had taken over the kingdom of his father and made himself secure[4], he killed all his brothers with the sword[5], and some of the rulers of Israel also. Jehoram was thirty-two years old when he became king, and he reigned eight years in Jerusalem [848-841 B.C.]. He walked in the way of the kings of Israel, just as the **house of Ahab** did (**for Ahab's daughter was his wife**), and he did evil in the sight of the LORD. Yet the LORD was not willing to destroy the **house of David** because of the covenant which He had made with David, and since He had promised to give a lamp[6] to him and his sons forever (emphasis added).*

Jehoram's sin is based on the theory that life and security can be obtained by human means. He was not the first to believe that "might is right." The pages of history are filled with incidents of those who justified all sorts of atrocities by following a Machiavellian approach to ruling the masses. In this Jehoram erred. And not to be overlooked is the brief statement *"for Ahab's daughter was his wife."* She was the power behind the throne. Her influence neutralized all the good Jehoram might have derived from the example of his father. After the elimination of the princes and leaders of Judah, we are not surprised to find that Jehoram furthered the gross idolatries of Baalism so that they were now openly practiced in Judah. None dared stand against him, for one word from

---

[4] Dillard, *2 Chronicles*, 165.

[5] Williamson, *1 and 2 Chronicles*, 304.

[6] A "burning lamp" would imply that the house was occupied.

Athaliah would have soldier-priests of Baal executing yet another protester.

It is important to note that the Chronicler does not exonerate Jehoram for his crimes by blaming them on his wife. His idolatrous practices and faulty leadership brought about his demise.

### *God's Punishment of the Faithlessness of Jehoram (21:8-20)*

God's chastening of Judah's king took several forms. They were designed to give him the opportunity to turn from his evil ways. First, there was a revolt against the kingdom (21:8-11), followed by an invasion on the part of Judah's enemies (21:16-17). In between these events, Jehoram received a stern letter of reproof from the prophet Elijah (21:12-15).

#### The Revolt of Judah's Allies (21:8-11).

*In his days Edom revolted against the rule of Judah and set up a king over themselves. Then Jehoram crossed over with his commanders and all his chariots with him. And he arose by night and struck down the Edomites who were surrounding him and the commanders of the chariots. So Edom revolted against Judah to this day. Then Libnah revolted at the same time against his rule, because he had forsaken the LORD God of his fathers. Moreover, he made high places in the mountains of Judah, and caused the inhabitants of Jerusalem to play the harlot and led Judah astray.*

The Edomites were the first to revolt (cf. Genesis 27:40). They had been ruled by a deputy (I Kings 22:47), but now asserted their sovereignty. Jehoram tried to bring them under his control once more and took to the field of battle. It seems as if he placed great confidence in his chariots (instead of in the Lord). The Edomites encircled his camp, and he barely escaped with his life.

Next Libnah,[7] a city of the priests (Joshua 21:13), and one of the strongest fortified cities in Judah (II Kings 19:8), broke away from Judah. It is possible that this city had been given by Jehoshaphat to one of Jehoram's brothers. The people of Libnah quite possibly renounced allegiance to Jehoram because he had forsaken Yahweh, the God of his fathers. But this seems only to have stimulated him to greater evil. Instead of allowing all of his subjects freedom of worship, we now read that they were compelled to practice idolatry. Such legislated conformity indicates a dangerous willfulness that is further evidence of Jehoram's stubbornness in spite of all attempts to turn him from the path of sin.

**The Reproof of the Prophet (21:12-15).** At some point in his reign (possibly at the beginning[8]), the wayward king received a letter[9] from Elijah. This is remarkable, for

---

[7] *Macmillan Bible Atlas*, 108, 130.

[8] The beginning would be more likely if Elijah were still alive.

[9] Elijah's letter has aroused considerable controversy for, depending on which chronology is followed, Elijah may have already been taken up into heaven. Some writers try to ease their way out of the difficulty by emending the text to read "Elisha." For a discussion of the different views, see Dillard, *2 Chronicles*, 167; Myers, *II Chronicles*, 121-22; Williamson, *1 and 2 Chronicles*, 306-07.

Elijah was a prophet to the Northern Kingdom (not the Southern) and quite possibly penned this letter shortly before his miraculous ascension into heaven. The contents of the letter indicate a change in God's dealings with Jehoram. The Lord is now moving from chastisement to punishment. We read:

> *Then a letter came to him from Elijah the prophet saying, "Thus says the LORD God of your father David, 'Because you have not walked in the ways of Jehoshaphat your father and the ways of Asa king of Judah, but have walked in the way of the kings of Israel, and have caused Judah and the inhabitants of Jerusalem to play the harlot as the house of Ahab played the harlot, and you have also killed your brothers, your own family, who were better than you, behold[10], the LORD is going to strike your people, your sons, your wives and all your possessions with a great calamity; and you will suffer severe sickness, a disease of your bowels, until your bowels come out because of the sickness, day by day.'"*

Jehoram must have known of Elijah's involvement with the kingdom of Ahab and Jezebel—of the three and a half years of drought, of the destruction of the priests of Baal at Mount Carmel, and of the judgment pronounced on Ahab when he went to take possession of Naboth's vineyard (I Kings 21:19-22), and of Micaiah's prophecy in which he foretold Ahab's death (I Kings 22:26-33), and yet he still remained wedded to the idols his wife worshipped.

---

[10] Sometimes translated "Look," but here having the force of "So now." Elijah has reached a climax. Dire consequences are to come upon the willfully disobedient.

Even a stern letter from Elijah did not turn him from the errors of his ways.

It should also be noted that Elijah refers to Jehoram's sin by its proper name.[11]  What is surprising is that fact that, at the time of the murder of Israel's princes, Jehoram's actions did not bring an outcry from among the people (note Proverbs 28:12*b*, 28).

Jehoram ignores Elijah's warning.  The Lord, however, has different ways of dealing with rebellious people, even if they have developed a hardened heart (Proverbs 29:1).  In time, the Holy Spirit no longer strives with them (Romans 1:24-32) and they are abandoned to their fate.

Two brief statements conclude our story.  The first (21:16-17) deals with judgment against the people for their sins (of idolatry accompanied by a failure to support the house of the Lord), and the second deals with Jehoram's final days (21:18-20).

**The Invasion of Judah's Neighbors (21:16-17).** God now moves to punish Jehoram and the people.  The Philistines attack from the west and the Arabians and Ethopians (or Cushites) invade Judah from the south and southeast.

> *Then the LORD stirred up against Jehoram the spirit of the Philistines and the Arabs who bordered the Ethiopians; and they came against Judah and invaded it, and carried away all the possessions found in the king's house together with his sons and his wives, so that no*

---

[11] Jehoram's actions, therefore, must have been widely known.

*son was left to him except Jehoahaz, the youngest of his sons.*

The newfound boldness of Judah's enemies is occasioned by the perceived weakness of Judah's king. God's hand, that had previously protected His people, has been removed and so, in a series of invasions, Israel's enemies rob them of their possessions and strip the land of its substance. They even plunder the royal palace, and murder Jehoram's wives and children. But they leave only the youngest son to succeed him, and Athaliah, who was from Sidon in Phoenicia, was not killed with the other members of the royal family.

These facts prompt us to ask for an explanation. First, the Philistines probably spared Athaliah because they did not want to cause unnecessary hostilities with the Phoenicians, who were their northern neighbors. But they did not spare Athaliah's sons (24:7) other than Ahaziah whom they may have allowed to live for a couple of reasons: (1) The youngest son in any family had the least honor, and by sparing Ahaziah they were in essence mocking Judah who (in their eyes) did not have an honorable man to place on the throne; and (2) they may have allowed Jehoram's youngest son to live so that he could provide some stability in the area.[12]

From a biblical point of view, however, we take note of the fact that once again the seed of David was almost extinguished.

---

[12] The United States and its allies did much the same in "Operation: Desert Storm." They liberated Kuwait, but did not go after Saddam Hussein because his death would leave Iraq leaderless and Iran might then topple the balance of power in the Middle East.

**The Death of the King (21:18-20).** Even now, Jehoram refuses to humble himself and turn from his evil ways.

> *So after all this the LORD smote him in his bowels with an incurable sickness. Now it came about in the course of time, at the end of two years, that his bowels came out because of his sickness and he died in great pain. And his people made no fire for him like the fire for his fathers. He was thirty-two years old when he became king, and he reigned in Jerusalem eight years; and he departed with no one's regret (lit. 'without desire'), and they buried him in the city of David, but not in the tombs of the kings."*

Various attempts have been made to identify Jehoram's illness. Sufficient to say that it was protracted and painful. In the end, he died in agony. He was an unpopular monarch, and no one regretted his passing. The usual honors accorded a deceased king were not given to him. Though he was buried *"in the City of David,"* he was deemed unworthy of being interred in the tombs of the kings. And the Chronicler, though he lived centuries later, evidently shared the disdain of the people for he did not make mention of any sources from which additional information about Jehoram could be gleaned. He was a king no one wanted.

Athaliah's influence on Jehoram must have been very great. Though he was held accountable for his actions, there can be little doubt that she was the one who incited him to engage in wicked and immoral acts. Instead of being a blessing to her husband, she cast a pall over the whole nation.

*God's Judgment on the House of Ahab (22:1-23:15)*

**The King Nobody Knew (22:1-9).** We now move to consider how the Lord brought to an end the evils of Ahab's house. Ahaziah, the son of Jehoram and Athaliah, and the grandson of Ahab and Jezebel, sat on the throne of Judah after his father's death. He was twenty-two years of age when Jehoram died, and was unknown to people outside Jerusalem. He reigned for only one year (841 B.C.), during which time he was guided by the wicked counsel of his mother and the *"ambassadors"* whom she invited to come to Judah to *"counsel"* the young king (II Kings 8:24-29).

> *Then the inhabitants of Jerusalem made Ahaziah, his youngest son, king in his place, for the band of men who came with the Arabs to the camp had slain all the older sons. So Ahaziah the son of Jehoram king of Judah began to reign. Ahaziah was twenty-two years old when he became king, and he reigned one year in Jerusalem. And his mother's name was Athaliah, the granddaughter of Omri. He also walked in the ways of the house of Ahab,* **for his mother was his counselor to do wickedly.** *He did evil in the sight of the LORD like the house of Ahab,* **for they were his counselors** *after the death of his father, to his destruction. He also walked according to their counsel[13], and went with Jehoram [sometimes shortened to Joram] the son of Ahab*

---

[13] It is obvious from these verses that Judah's borders were open to Phoenician diplomats who exerted an evil influence on the young king.

*king of Israel to wage war against Hazael king of
Aram (i.e., Syria) at Ramoth-gilead. But the
Arameans (Syrians) wounded Joram. So he
returned to be healed in Jezreel of the wounds
which they had inflicted on him at Ramah, when
he fought against Hazael king of Aram (i.e.,
Syria). And Ahaziah, the son of Jehoram king of
Judah, went down to see Jehoram the son of Ahab
in Jezreel, because he was sick.*

*Now the destruction of Ahaziah was from
God, in that he went to Joram [here the
Chronicler uses the shortened form of his name].
For when he came, he went out with Jehoram
against Jehu the son of Nimshi, whom the LORD
had anointed to cut off the house of Ahab. It came
about when Jehu was executing judgment on the
house of Ahab, he found the princes of Judah and
the sons of Ahaziah's brothers ministering to
Ahaziah, and slew them. He also sought Ahaziah,
and they caught him while he was hiding in
Samaria; they brought him to Jehu, who put him
to death (emphasis added).*

Once again we read of Athaliah's formidable
presence. She probably encouraged her son to join his
uncle Joram of Israel in an expedition against Hazael, king
of Syria. The goal was to try and recover Ramoth-gilead.[14]
Ahaziah's uncle had been wounded in the battle (but not
seriously) and he went to his palace in Jezreel to recover
from his wounds. It was there that Ahaziah visited him.

---

[14] This was the city Ahab had tried to recover. It was also the
place where he was fatally wounded. See *Macmillan Bible Atlas*, 142.

At this point, the Chronicler reminds his readers of Jehu. He presumes that they already know of him as a result of their familiarity with the Book of Kings. When he came to Jezreel, Joram and Ahaziah rode out in separate chariots to meet him. Jehu executed both kings in order to break the back of Baal worship in Israel. At the time of his death, Ahaziah had reigned for less than one full year.

It is hard to understand a woman such as Athaliah, whose evil influence on her husband and her son was so profound that no good was found in them. Apparently, she was so persuaded of the viability of Baalism that, in spite of strong evidence to the contrary, she placed implicit faith in what she had been taught. And when Jehu killed her mother and all her relatives, she knew that she was the last surviving representative of the house of Ahab.

**The Queen Everyone Hated (22:10-23:15).** So far, we have considered the life of the king nobody wanted, and the short-lived reign of the king nobody knew, and now we read about Athaliah, the queen everybody hated.

Before the death of her husband, Jehoram, and her son, Ahaziah, Queen Athaliah had acquired much influence in public affairs (cf. I Kings 10:1), and she used her influence for evil. When tidings of her son's untimely death reached Jerusalem, she resolved to seat herself upon the throne of David (841 B.C.). Asserting her authority as Queen Mother, and most likely continuing the regal functions she had assumed during Ahaziah's absence at Jezreel (II Kings 9), she resolved to rule as queen. In order to remove all who might claim the right to sit on the throne, Athaliah caused all her grandchildren to be massacred (II Kings 11:1).

> *Now when Athaliah the mother of Ahaziah*
> *saw that her son was dead, she rose and destroyed*
> *all the royal offspring of the house of Judah.*

Two thoughts immediately come to mind:  (1) The
heartlessness of this grandmother (for grandmothers
invariably dote over their grandchildren), and (2) the fact
that once again the line of David came to within a hair's
breadth of being snuffed out.

"But how could a grandmother murder her innocent
grandchildren?" you ask.  The worship of Baal involved
human sacrifices (Psalm 106:36-38; Jeremiah 19:5), and
Athaliah had evidently become so callused that she was
beyond all natural feeling.  One infant of the royal house, a
baby named Joash, the youngest son of Ahaziah, was
rescued by his aunt Jehoshabeath, daughter of Jehoram
(probably by a wife other than Athaliah).

Consider the drama as this scene unfolds.
Jehoshabeath overhears the queen give orders to kill all
Ahaziah's children.  They are all young and are probably
playing in a room of the palace.  She hurries ahead of
Athaliah and the soldiers, enters the room, sees Joash and
his nurse, and hurriedly hides them in a room filled with
beds and bedding.  Take note of the Chronicler's account of
the events.

> *But Jehoshabeath the king's daughter took*
> *Joash the son of Ahaziah, and stole him from*
> *among the king's sons who were being put to*
> *death, and placed him and his nurse in the*
> *bedroom. So Jehoshabeath, the daughter of King*
> *Jehoram, the wife of Jehoiada the priest[15] (for*

---

[15] Jehoiada was considerably older than Jehoshabeath, for he
had grown sons from another marriage (cf. 23:15).

*she was the sister of Ahaziah), hid him from*
*Athaliah so that she would not put him to death.*
*He was hidden with them in the house of God six*
*years [841-835 B.C.] while Athaliah reigned over*
*the land.*

Jehoshabeath had married Jehoiada (22:11), the
high priest (24:6). He was a godly man who tried to
preserve the truth amid strong opposition and spiritual
decline. The majority of the people had forsaken the
worship of the Lord for the more sensual ceremonies
associated with the festivals honoring Baal. Now, in a
remarkable act of courage, Jehoiada's wife conceals the
baby Joash in the palace until it is safe to move him to the
Temple. There, under her care, and with Jehoiada
vigilantly attending to his safety, the young prince is kept
unharmed for the next six years. Though the flame of
God's promise to David flickered and seemed in danger of
going out, the Lord and this godly couple kept Joash alive
and nurtured him so that one day he would ascend the
throne of David. So secretive was the priest and his
princess-wife that Joash's existence was not suspected by
Athaliah.

In Joash's seventh year the bloodstained and evil
reign of Athaliah comes to a sudden end. Jehoiada, the
high priest, believing that the time has arrived to show the
lawful king to the nation, calls to him the five *"captains of
hundreds"* (23:1)—men whom he can trust. Then, after
also securing the co-operation of the Levites and chief men
in the towns, he brings the young heir into the Temple court
to receive the pledge of allegiance of the soldiers of the
guard. This is how it happened.

*[The soldiers of the guard] went
throughout Judah and gathered the Levites from
all the cities of Judah, and the heads of the
fathers' households of Israel, and they came to
Jerusalem. Then all the assembly made a
covenant with the king in the House of God. And
Jehoiada said to them, "Behold, the king's son
shall reign, as the LORD has spoken concerning
the sons of David. This is the thing which you
shall do: one third of you, of the priests and
Levites who come in on the sabbath, shall be
gatekeepers, and one third shall be at the king's
house, and a third at the Gate of the Foundation;
and all the people shall be in the courts of the
house of the LORD. But let no one enter the house
of the LORD except the priests and the ministering
Levites; they may enter, for they are holy. And let
all the people keep the charge of the LORD. The
Levites will surround the king, each man with his
weapons in his hand; and whoever enters the
house, let him be killed. Thus be with the king
when he comes in and when he goes out." So the
Levites and all Judah did according to all that
Jehoiada the priest commanded. And each one of
them took his men who were to come in on the
sabbath, with those who were to go out on the
sabbath, for Jehoiada the priest did not dismiss
any of the divisions. Then Jehoiada the priest
gave to the captains of hundreds the spears and
the large and small shields which had been King
David's, which were in the house of God. He
stationed all the people, each man with his
weapon in his hand, from the right side of the
house to the left side of the house, by the altar and*

*by the house, around the king. Then they brought
out the king's son and put the crown on him, and
gave him the testimony and made him king. And
Jehoiada and his sons anointed him and said,
"Long live the king!"*

On the day set apart for Joash's coronation, every
precaution is taken not to arouse any suspicion. Even
Athaliah's regular guard is on duty at the palace. The
remainder of the soldiers are commissioned to protect the
young king by forming a long and closely serried line
across the Temple. They are also instructed to kill anyone
who should approach within certain limits. And they are
furnished with David's spears and shields that the work of
restoring his descendant might take on added symbolic
significance.

When the guard has taken up their position, the
young prince is brought out. He is then anointed, crowned,
and presented with the Testimony or Law. The people are
overawed by the knowledge that a legitimate king had been
spared the massacre of Ahaziah's other sons, and they give
expression to their joy with loud shouts of praise.

Athaliah hears the commotion, and hurries to the
Temple to find out what is going on. There she sees Joash
standing by a pillar with a crown on his head, receiving the
acclamations of the assembled multitude.

*When Athaliah heard the noise of the
people running and praising the king, she came
into the house of the LORD to the people. She
looked, and behold, the king was standing by his
pillar at the entrance, and the captains and the
trumpeters were beside the king. And all the
people of the land rejoiced and blew trumpets, the*

*singers with their musical instruments leading the
praise. Then Athaliah tore her clothes and said,
"Treason! Treason!" Jehoiada the priest
brought out the captains of hundreds who were
appointed over the army and said to them, "Bring
her out between the ranks; and whoever follows
her, put to death with the sword." For the priest
said, "Let her not be put to death in the house of
the LORD." So they seized her, and when she
arrived at the entrance of the Horse Gate of the
king's house, they put her to death there.*

Picture for yourself Athaliah's hasty walk to the
Temple where she sees a young lad wearing a crown. She
knows intuitively what has happened. She is furious. Her
cries of *"Treason! Treason!"* fail to excite any movement
in her favor, and Jehoiada, the high-priest, without allowing
time for pause, orders the Levitical guards to remove her
from the sacred precincts. Once away from the Temple,
she is executed (21:6; 22:10-12; 23). The only other person
killed in this virtually bloodless revolution is Mattan, the
priest of Baal, whom Athaliah had brought to Judah. Other
priests of Baal probably flee back to Phoenicia as fast as
they can.

It is significant that the Chronicler does not
conclude Athaliah's reign in the usual way. No sources of
information are cited where data about her may be found.
She had usurped the throne and, in the mind of the biblical
historian, is considered unworthy of remembrance.

*"So all of the people of the land rejoiced
and the city was quiet. For they had put Athaliah
to death with the sword" (23:21).*

## THE FAITHFULNESS OF GOD

Many pertinent lessons can be drawn from these chapters. Some of them are obvious, but others are less so. First, we are reminded of God's promise to chasten any of David's "sons" for their disobedience. Speaking to David, the Lord said: *"When your days are complete and you lie down with your fathers, I will raise up your descendant after you, who will come forth from you, and I will establish his kingdom ... I will be a father to him and he will be a son to Me; when he commits iniquity, I will correct him with the rod of men and the strokes of the sons of men, but My lovingkindness shall not depart from him ... your house and your kingdom shall endure before Me forever; your throne shall be established forever"* (II Samuel 7:12, 14, 16). God's faithfulness is seen in that He acted in accordance with His word.

Second, the sovereign power of God is borne out in the preservation of the Davidic line. Time and again, it was threatened with extinction, but the Lord's promise to David was not broken.

Third, as we read the text carefully, we note the paired judgments (21:8-11 and 16-17) that came upon Jehoram. These testify to the political failure of his reign. God's retributive justice is illustrated in the way in which his sons were killed (cf. 21:2 with 17 and 22:1).

Fourth, when judgment came upon the family of Ahab, Ahaziah, who had identified himself with the house of Ahab, suffered the same fate as the house of Ahab. And Athaliah, who represented the final link in the dynasty begun by her grandfather, Omri, was cut off in accordance with the will of the Lord. Her influence on those about her was entirely negative. Her infamy is contrasted with the

courage and resourcefulness of Jehoshabeath who risked
her life to save the youngest of her brother's sons.

Finally, we need to remember that these were dark
days in Judah. The righteous preferred to hide rather than
take a bold stand for the truth. One man attempted to fill
the spiritual vacuum in Judah: Jehoiada. Many among the
people believed that no heir to the throne of David had
survived Athaliah's massacre, and so for a six-year period
their faith floundered. Jehoiada and his wife cared for the
child of Ahaziah and prepared him as best they could for
the day when he would take his rightful place on the throne
of Judah.

Of encouragement to each one of us as we review
this chapter is the fact that God's promises are sure! What
He has promised will come to pass. And though He may
patiently endure those who are evil, in the end His
retributive justice will overtake them.

# Chapter Ten

# THE NEED FOR MATURITY

II Chronicles 23:18-24:27

As parents, we all desire to see our children grow into confident, mature adults. But how may we achieve this goal? What is involved in maturity, and how do we aid them in their preparation for life?

It would appear that there are three basic types of parents: Authoritarian, authoritative and permissive. These can be placed on a continuum and, of course, there are degrees within each group. Furthermore, in a home a child's father and mother may represent different parenting styles. The authoritarian model is controlling and establishes hard-and-fast rules by which to govern virtually every aspect of a child's life. Those who are permissive are lassiz faire and are inclined to allow the child unlimited freedom. Experience has shown that the authoritative style is the best, and greatest success is achieved in those homes where children are given responsibility in keeping with their abilities, and their independence is increased as they grow older.

It helps if father and mother stand united in their approach to parenting and discuss any disagreements they may have in private. They also need to have a goal and to ask themselves, "What characteristics do we desire to see our sons and daughters develop as they progress toward maturity?"

Maturity involves growth in the following areas: Personal autonomy; mature sexuality; an internalized sense of morality; career choice; and the ability to make long-range and short-range goals.

Fortunately for us, the Bible gives us examples of healthy and unhealthy models of child rearing. As we have pointed out earlier in our studies of the historical books of the Old Testament, an appropriate model for the rearing of our children requires that both parents engage in a continuous process of *involvement, modeling* and *instruction.* Results are not achieved overnight, and frequently parents suffer from disappointment. The Bible, however, serves as a continuous source of enlightenment.

In the early years of a child's life, there is the need for nurture (cf. I Thessalonians 2:7)—the kind provided by a nursing mother when she creates an atmosphere of tender affection accompanied by unconditional love and acceptance. Later on, a need arises for parents (and particularly the father) to teach their children discipline, to give them a sense of direction, and to encourage them in the performance of different tasks so that they develop a positive, proactive approach to life (cf. I Thessalonians 2:11).

*Autonomy* is not a synonym for irresponsibility. As a child grows, it is important for him or her to develop the personal and interpersonal traits that will enable him/her to be appropriately independent, and make wise choices regardless of external pressures. Initially this may take the form of encouraging a son or daughter to choose what clothes they wish to wear, to dress himself/herself, and take responsibility for his/her personal hygiene (e.g. clean teeth, washed hands before meals, etc.). In the course of time, these areas of responsibility will be enlarged to include handling money responsibly, learning how to read, write and drive a car. Much later, mature autonomy will involve living outside the home, paying one's own bills and living within one's means.

Then there is the need for a child to develop a *mature sexual identity*. As children watch their parents, they learn from them how to act and how to relate to others. Early in life, a child will begin to identify with his or her same-sex parent. From a father a young boy learns what men are like, and in the relationship of his parents with one another he learns how men treat women and vice versa. In time these observations will be carried over into his dating relationships and culminate in the one whom he will marry. And the same is true of girls. From her mother, a young girl learns what women are like and how they relate to men. In time what she learns will be reproduced in her relationship with her husband.

Vitally related to a mature sexual identity is the cultivation of an *internalized morality*. As our children grow through the different stages of their development, they begin to develop a sense of right and wrong. In our social milieu, many contrary forces bring pressure to bear upon a developing boy or girl. These include television, peer pressure, movies, books, magazines and even classroom instruction. Each of these can have a detrimental effect on a young person's system of values. Parents obviously wish to avoid falling into the trap of being legalistic or, on the other hand, abdicating their role and letting each child go his or her own way. And this is where Bible reading and discussion come in. By using the

Bible as an objective source of wisdom, lessons can be
learned that will be of enduring value.

In the course of time, each of our children will be
faced with a *career choice*. This should be in keeping with
the gifts God has given to him or her. And whatever their
line of work, they should be taught that all honorable
professions and occupations are worthy of respect (cf.
Colossians 2:17). Our children should also be encouraged
with the importance of lifelong learning so that they can
keep pace with social changes as well as with changes
within their chosen vocation.

Finally, parents should teach each child how to
make *short-range* and *long-range goals*. Initially this may
involve keeping a calendar of their commitments (e.g.,
when certain homework assignments are due), or
participating with other family members in preparing for a
vacation. Parents can encourage this kind of planning in
such a way that confidence grows and the process becomes
habitual. In the course of time the goals each child sets
should include spiritual and eternal realities.

As we consider the passage before us we will find
that it illustrates the success and failure of the parenting
process.

## OUTLINE

The story contained in these chapters is pivotal in
the history of God's people. For six years, those living in
Judah believed that the covenant God made with David (II
Samuel 7:14) had failed. All they knew was that the
rightful descendants of David's line had been killed, and
that the wicked Athaliah had seized the throne. Unknown
to them, an infant named Joash had been rescued and God's

promise of an enduring Davidic dynasty had not been thwarted.

During Athaliah's six-year usurpation of the throne, a moral and spiritual decline was evident and the worship of Baal reigned supreme. In the Temple, however, Joash was secretly being reared by the aged high priest, Jehoiada, and his young wife, Jehoshabeath—sister of the late king. Then, when Joash was seven, Jehoiada called together all the people to Jerusalem where he anointed Joash king over Judah. And Joash reigned from 835-796 B.C.

Here is a brief outline of this section. It continues the era of the history of Israel and Judah when they shared an uneasy peace.

## CONTINUATION OF DAVID'S DYNASTY (23:18-24:27)

The Commencement of the Boy-King's Reign (23:16-21)

The Early Years of the Boy-King's Reign (24:1-14)

The Later Reign of the King (24:15-27)

Many important truths lie latent in the text (e.g., cause and effect relationships, as well as incidents that underscore the ways in which God honors those who honor Him, et cetera). Our primary objective, however, will be to highlight the ways in which we may lead our sons and daughters to maturity.

## CONTINUATION OF DAVID'S DYNASTY
(23:18-14:27)

### *Commencement of the Boy-King's Reign (23:16-21)*

**The Reforms of the High Priest (23:16-19).**
Following the coronation of the young Joash, Jehoiada
immediately institutes some important reforms.

> *Then Jehoiada made a covenant between*
> *himself and all the people and the king, that they*
> *would be the LORD'S people.  And all the people*
> *went to the house of Baal and tore it down, and*
> *they broke in pieces his altars and his images, and*
> *killed Mattan the priest of Baal before the altars.*

> *Moreover, Jehoiada placed the offices of*
> *the House of the LORD under the authority of the*
> *Levitical priests, whom David had assigned over*
> *the House of the LORD, to offer the burnt*
> *offerings of the LORD, as it is written in the Law*
> *of Moses—with rejoicing and singing according to*
> *the order of David.  He stationed the gatekeepers*
> *of the House of the LORD, so that no one would*
> *enter who was in any way unclean.*

Let us visualize the scene.  As Athaliah's blood
seeps into the ground at the place where she was killed,[1]

---

[1] Athaliah's body was probably dragged through the streets to
the Valley of Hinnom (which served as the city's refuse dump) or else
taken there on an open cart.  Once the soldiers had passed through the
Dung Gate, her corpse was probably dumped out with the other
garbage.  A slow burning fire would gradually have consumed her
remains.  Athaliah's body was not interred with the kings of Judah
because she had usurped the throne.

Jehoiada calls on the people to enter into a covenant with the Lord. He knows that only as they commit themselves to walk in the paths of righteousness can they expect His blessing. In doing so, he leads by example. And the king, as his first official act, joins in.

In God's administration of human affairs there are three groups of people specifically designated to be His theocratic representatives: viz., the prophet, the priest, and civil leaders (including the king).[2] In the covenant entered into at Joash's coronation, both priest and king act in unison.

But what is the purpose of this covenant? God's Word called upon His people to be holy and worship Him alone (cf. Deuteronomy 4:23-24; 7:6). The temple of Baal that had been erected under Athaliah's supervision was an abomination in His sight and an impediment to His worship. On entering into the covenant the people (perhaps reminded of the teaching of the Law by Jehoiada or else prompted by an inner urge to make good their commitment to the Lord) hasten to the temple of Baal and begin breaking it down. They do not possess heavy equipment such as would be used today, and each stone has to be pried loose and thrown to the ground. While some take delight in dismantling the walls and throwing the large stones to the ground, others cart the rubbish away (for otherwise the accumulation of broken stones would have hindered the complete destruction of the temple).

At some point Mattan, the priest of Baal, perhaps unaware of Athaliah's demise, either protests the action being taken or else is discovered in hiding. He is

---

[2] See my Introduction to *Judges*.

unceremoniously brought between the altars on which he had offered animal and human sacrifices, and executed. Other priests and priestesses may have shared a similar fate (though this is not a part of the biblical record) or else, when they saw the angry crowd coming toward Baal's temple, sensed danger and hid. Then, when it was safe to do so, they took off for Phoenicia.

Meanwhile back in Jerusalem Jehoiada is busy. Ever since the death of Jehoshaphat the Temple and its worship had been neglected. As high priest he now takes prompt action to restore its services. Everything is done according to the teaching of Moses and David. In addition, to maintain the purity of those entering the Temple, he appoints gatekeepers to turn away all that are ceremonially unclean.

And so a day that had started out not knowing what might happen ends with the Lord once again at the center of His people's lives.

## The Enthronement of the Boy-King (23:20-21).

> *"He [Jehoiada] took the captains of hundreds, the nobles, the rulers of the people and all the people of the land, and brought the king down from the house of the LORD, and came through the upper gate to the king's house. And they placed the king upon the royal throne."*

Jehoiada may justly be regarded as a "king-maker." At no time, however, did he covet the crown, though he probably served as Joash's advisor (particularly during his early years). If this is true, then it is easy for us to understand how the king and the people maintained an unsullied loyalty to the Lord.

Joash had grown up in the Temple where he looked upon Jehoshabeath as his mother. But what of his real mother, Zibiah? There are many respected writers who believe that Joash's mother was murdered by Athaliah when the king's children were killed. However, it is just possible that she escaped the queen mother's "purge" and returned to Beersheba. If so, then it is comforting to think that, after believing her son dead, she may have been invited to Jerusalem to see him crowned.[3]

**The Satisfaction of the People (23:21).** *"So all of the people of the land rejoiced and the city was quiet. For they had put Athaliah to death with the sword."* This statement is included by the Chronicler as evidence of God's blessing, for to live a quiet and peaceable life is one of His blessings (I Timothy 2:2).

## *Early Years of the Boy-King's Reign (24:1-14)*

**Summary of the Boy-King's Reign (24:1-3).** *"Joash was seven years old when he became king, and he reigned forty years in Jerusalem .... He did what was right in the sight of the LORD all the days of Jehoiada the priest. Jehoiada took two wives for him, and he became the father of sons and daughters."[4]*

---

[3] If Zibiah had remarried, then obviously her permanent place would be with her second husband.

[4] I am a strong believer in monogamy. My wife and I have been married for forty-five years. It must be admitted, however, that in Bible times (as well as in different cultures around the world today) bigamy or polygamy was accepted. Though we view such practices with opprobrium, those in Africa and elsewhere who are involved in these unions do not share our disdain. To them it is system of birth control, provides "babysitters" within the family circle, and makes it

**Repair of the House of the Lord (24:4-14).** These verses are divided into two broad sections: (1) the plan that failed (24:4-7), and (2) the plan that succeeded (24:8-14).

The Plan That Failed (24:4-7).

> *Now it came about after this that Joash decided to restore the house of the LORD. He gathered the priests and Levites and said to them, 'Go out to the cities of Judah and collect money from all Israel to repair the house of your God annually, and you shall do the matter quickly.' But the Levites did not act quickly. So the king summoned Jehoiada the chief priest and said to him, 'Why have you not required the Levites to bring in from Judah and from Jerusalem the levy fixed by Moses the servant of the LORD on the congregation of Israel for the tent of the testimony?' For the sons of the wicked Athaliah had broken into the house of God and even used the holy things of the house of the LORD for the Baals.*

Joash, having been reared in the Temple, has a special concern for the buildings that at one time comprised his home. The years since Solomon had built the House of the Lord had seen some deterioration caused by wind and weather, and willful destruction on the part of those who are described as Athaliah's "sons" (i.e., her "servants," 24:7). Our TV news makes it easy for us to imagine such

---

possible for the work of the household to be shared among a greater number of people. Though I am content with having only one wife, the fact that Jehoiada, as God's high priest, took two wives for Joash should not occasion our censure.

malicious destruction, for we frequently see on the screen acts of wanton violence against places of worship.

Verse 4 brings before us one of the Chronicler's contrasts. Joash determines to *"restore"* the House of the Lord. The word really means *"renewal."* It is used of personal restoration (cf. Psalms 51:10; 103:5) as well as the repair of buildings or things (cf. 15:8; Isaiah 61:4). In order to repair the Temple, Joash gathers the priests and Levites together and instructs them to raise money for the needed renovations. In this we see him taking appropriate action. In times past this work had been paid for out of the king's treasury, but it would appear that the crown is no longer able to sustain such expense, so Joash institutes a plan whereby the people will contribute the needed money.[5]

Verse 5b, however, tells us that the Levites did not carry out the king's orders. Did they despise his youth and so treat his words lightly? Had they grown accustomed to Jehoiada making all decisions pertaining to the Temple? We do not know. All we do know is that twenty-three years elapse with nothing done to restore the Temple to its original condition (cf. II Kings 12:6).

It is not uncommon for older people to treat lightly the wishes of those who are young. Timothy faced this problem when the apostle Paul commissioned him to pastor a church (I Timothy 4:12. See also the requirements of an elder or a deacon, I Timothy 3:1-15). Wisdom (that comes with maturity) and godly independence are essential elements in leadership.

---

[5] Cf. V. Hurowitz, *Journal of Near Eastern Studies* 45 (1986), 289-94.

After twenty-three years, when the negligence of the Levites comes to Joash's attention, he summons Jehoiada to the palace and demands to know why his original order has not been carried out. Was he embarrassed over the fact that his earlier instructions had been ignored? Did he feel a certain chagrin over his failure to follow up on his order? Perhaps on account of his youth and desire to impress Jehoiada, in his zeal he had omitted to involve the high priest in his plan so that there was inadequate supervision.

In this connection Joash's well-meaning plans serve to illustrate how the well-meaning plans of the young may fail on account of their inexperience.

**The Plan That Succeeded (24:8-14).** With Jehoiada before him, the king cites the precedent for collecting money that had been established by Moses when the sons of Israel came out of Egypt (Exodus 38:21, 26). He had apparently assumed that the priests and Levites would be familiar with this principle and would have acted accordingly. If so, he was mistaken. Those involved in ministry are not always knowledgeable of God's Word.

Joash realizes that nothing can be done about the past, and so institutes a new plan (24:8). He gives instructions for a large wooden chest is to be built. It is to have a hole bored in the lid, and it is to be placed in a prominent place[6] at the entrance to the Temple. A proclamation is then issued instructing the people to place their contributions in the box.

---

[6] Cf. Dillard's explanation of the difference between the Chronicler's account and that of the compiler of I Kings in his *2 Chronicles*, 191.

*So the king commanded, and they made a
chest and set it outside by the gate of the house of
the LORD.  They made a proclamation in Judah
and Jerusalem to bring to the LORD the levy fixed
by Moses the servant of God on Israel in the
wilderness.  All the officers and all the people
rejoiced and brought in their levies and dropped
them into the chest until they had finished.  It
came about whenever the chest was brought in to
the king's officer by the Levites, and when they
saw that there was much money, then the king's
scribe and the chief priest's officer would come,
empty the chest, take it, and return it to its place.
Thus they did daily and collected much money.
The king and Jehoiada gave it to those who did the
work of the service of the House of the LORD; and
they hired masons and carpenters to restore the
House of the LORD, and also workers in iron and
bronze to repair the House of the LORD.  So the
workmen labored, and the repair work progressed
in their hands, and they restored the House of God
according to its specifications and strengthened it.
When they had finished, they brought the rest of
the money before the king and Jehoiada; and it
was made into utensils for the house of the LORD,
utensils for the service and the burnt offering, and
pans and utensils of gold and silver. And they
offered burnt offerings in the House of the LORD
continually all the days of Jehoiada.*

This time Joash's plan works. The people respond, and before long there is enough money[7] for the hiring of masons and carpenters as well as workers in iron and bronze. As a result the Temple is restored to its original design, and the money left over is devoted to making various utensils used in daily worship. The utensils made by Solomon had been stolen by Athaliah's accomplices and profaned by being used in the house of Baal.

### Later Reign of the King (24:15- 27)

#### Death of the King's Mentor (24:15-16).

*"Now when Jehoiada reached a ripe old age he died; he was one hundred and thirty years old at his death. They buried him in the city of David among the kings, because he had done well in Israel and to God and His house."*

The Chronicler pauses to mention the passing of the good and godly high priest. His age at the time of his death is remarkable, for not since patriarchal times had people lived that long.[8] Because Jehoiada had lived an exemplary life, he is buried in the city of David among the kings. This is unique in the annals of God's people and the honor bestowed on Jehoiada shows the esteem in which he was held by the people. It is to his eternal credit that he had

---

[7] We use the term "money," but in reality metal of different kinds was contributed and its value ascertained by its weight.

[8] Longevity in Old Testament times was a sign of God's special favor. Among those who lived a long time was Abraham-175 years (Genesis 25:7); Isaac-180 (Genesis 35:28), Jacob-147 (Genesis 47:9, 28); Joseph-110 (Genesis 50:22); and Moses-120 (Deuteronomy 34:7).

held fast to his integrity during the evil reigns of Jehoram, Ahaziah and Athaliah.

**Counsel of His New Advisors (24:17-19).** The Chronicler then continues his history of the tribe of Judah with an ominous *"but."*

> *"But after the death of Jehoiada the officials of Judah came and bowed down to the king, and the king listened to them. They abandoned the house of the LORD, the God of their fathers, and served the Asherim and the idols; so wrath came upon Judah and Jerusalem for this their guilt."*

These leaders of the people had probably chafed under the seemingly rigid policies of Jehoiada. With the priest's death they come to King Joash and, with every form of flattery and with a feigned interest in the welfare of the people, they request Joash to relax some of the religious requirements. And Joash goes along with their request.

The king's decision forces us to ask why he was so easily influenced by the officials of Judah. Being swayed by their toadyism and acceding to their request indicates that he, even though he was about forty years of age, lacked a sense of right and wrong. And then we must ask, "Is it possible that having lived under Jehoiada's shadow for so long he was overawed by authority figures? Did Jehoiada's brand of righteousness keep at bay obsequious individuals so that Joash had grown to manhood lacking the discernment necessary to recognize different forms of guile? And had Jehoiada's training been so strong and controlling that Joash lacked independence of thought and so was unaccustomed to making hard decisions?" In the final analysis it seems evident that Joash was also swayed by externals (e.g., a significant number of people and their positions of importance).

As we bring this story closer to home, we need to remember that people who advocate change (like the leaders of Judah) often approach those in power with honeyed speech, stressing the value of toleration and the benefits in popularity that will accrue to the leader who grants the people certain latitude. Sycophants are skilled in the art of manipulation and will not hesitate to hint at the fact that not everyone is in favor of the established policies. Such hypocritical reasoning makes it easy for someone lacking maturity to go along with a proposed compromise.

In the case they brought before Joash, the leaders made it easy for him to see how valuable moderation would be. The reasonableness of their proposal would also have been given the *coup de grace* when they pointed out how inconvenient it was for all the people to travel long distances to come to Jerusalem three times a year for the appointed feasts (Exodus 23:14-16). Their suggestion that the people be allowed to worship at the ancient sites (i.e., the high places) seemed most reasonable. In the back of the minds of the officials of Judah, however, there is the desire to return to the sensual worship of Baal and the Ashtoreth.

Scripture presents matters in a clear light. However plausible the petition of the officials may have been, their suggestion and the king's decision are viewed by God as the abandonment (*'azab*) of the covenant. As we shall see, their abandonment of the Lord will lead to His abandonment of them. And He will tailor their punishment to fit their crime.

**Reproof of the King by the Prophets (24:19-22).**
God is unwilling that any should perish and though He
could have dealt with Joash and the leaders of the people in
anger, He graciously sent prophets to them. One of these
prophets is Joel. The sad fact is that though the prophets
testify against them, they will not listen. They did not
realize that through the ministry of the prophets the Lord
was giving His people a second chance. These men of God
stood in the line of the theocracy, and the people should
have heeded their warning (cf. Numbers 14:41; I Chronicles 28:9). Instead of repenting of their departure from the
Lord, they cling to their idols.

The apostasy of the people was made easy because
many of the priests, who were charged with the
responsibility of teaching the people the Word, did not
know the Lord. Most of them lived in the cities and
villages of Judah and came to Jerusalem only when they
were required to officiate in the Temple. Zechariah, the
son of Jehoiada, of course, was an exception.

After the reproof of the prophets had been ignored,
the Spirit of God came upon Zechariah. We read:

> *Then the Spirit of God came on Zechariah
> the son of Jehoiada the priest; and he stood above
> the people and said to them, "Thus God has said,
> 'Why do you transgress the commandments of the
> LORD and do not prosper? Because you have
> forsaken the LORD, He has also forsaken you.'"
> So they conspired against him and at the
> command of the king they stoned him to death in
> the court of the house of the LORD. Thus Joash
> the king did not remember the kindness that his
> father Jehoiada had shown him, but he murdered*

*his son. And as he died he said, "May the LORD
see and avenge!"*

The officials were probably intimidated by the
forceful preaching of Zechariah and began plotting against
him.  Then, perhaps accusing him of treason (i.e., speaking
against the king's express command) they make Joash an
accomplice to their crime by having him authorize
Zechariah's murder.

This was a heinous act, for as Scripture points out
Joash completely ignored the benefit he had received from
Jehoiada! (who is referred to as *"his father"* in v. 22).  And
though he was not present when the one who had been like
a brother to him was stoned to death, Zechariah's murder
took place on the exact spot where he (Joash) had been
anointed king over God's people.

Joash may have thought that his participation in
Zechariah's murder would soon be forgotten.  Not so!
Centuries later the Lord Jesus will speak of Zechariah's
death when He will refer to the martyrs of the Old
Testament (cf. Luke 11:51).  Retribution, however, will be
in kind.  As Joash had conspired against Zechariah, so his
servants will conspire against him.

Zechariah's dying words have been used by some in
an attempt to drive a wedge between the teaching of the
Old Testament and that of the New.  What he said as he
was dying is contrasted with the words of the Lord Jesus
(Luke 23:34) and Stephen (Acts 7:60).  Those who
propagate such false teaching attempt to show that grace is
a New Testament phenomenon.  It is not. The context
exposes their error.  The Chronicler mentions the
"kindness" (*hesed*) shown Joash by Jehoiada, and *hesed* is

the Old Testament counterpart of the New Testament *charis*, "grace."

It is always dangerous to misinterpret any portion of God's Word, and a significant number of commentators and preachers have made much of Zechariah's usage of the word *"avenge."* The word *daras* has in some Old Testament contexts been translated either "inquire" and "require." Its root is to "ask" or "seek," and it does not necessarily look at revenge. In reality, Zechariah may have been asking God to seek out the evildoers with a view to bringing them to repentance.

In Joash's actions we see signs of immaturity. He possessed a follower mentality, lacked an internalized sense of right and wrong, and failed to take independent action.

**Reproof of the King by the Lord (24:23-24).** God's response to Joash's actions takes the form of a Syrian invasion.

> *Now it happened at the turn of the year [i.e., Spring] that the army of the Arameans [Syrians] came up against him; and they came to Judah and Jerusalem, destroyed all the officials of the people from among the people, and sent all their spoil to the king of Damascus. Indeed the army of the Arameans [Syrians] came with a small number of men; yet the LORD delivered a very great army into their hands, because they had forsaken the LORD, the God of their fathers. Thus they executed judgment on Joash.*

Several important ironies are to be found in these verses. The people of Judah and Jerusalem had been worshipping Astarte (i.e., Ashtaroth, identified as the goddess of love and war[9]). When the Syrians invaded the land, the people of Judah would have expected Astarte to protect them and give them success in battle. Obviously, being only the creation of human minds, she could not. Judah suffered a resounding defeat, and the "leaders," who had persuaded Joash to grant latitude to the people thus paving the way for their apostasy, were themselves killed.

**Assassination of the King (24:25-27).** Those who seek God find Him; those who abandon Him are themselves abandoned; those who conspire to do evil are conspired against; and those who kill are themselves killed.

> *When they [the Syrians] had departed from him [Joash], for they left him very sick, his own servants conspired against him because of the blood of the son of Jehoiada the priest, and murdered him on his bed. So he died, and they buried him in the city of David, but they did not bury him in the tombs of the kings."*

The murder of Joash is a form of retribution in kind. But the writer is not finished. Whereas the righteous Jehoiada was honored by being buried with the kings of Judah, this honor was withheld from Joash. The very people whose favor he desired to win disapproved of his actions.

> *Now these are those who conspired against him: Zabad the son of Shimeath the Ammonitess, and Jehozabad the son of Shimrith the Moabitess. As to his sons and the many oracles against him*

---

[9] An abbreviated form of her name is Anat or Anath. See A. S. Kapelrud, *The Violent Goddess: Anat in the Ras Shamra Texts* ( Oslo: Universitetsforlaget, 1969), 48-109.

*and the rebuilding of the house of God, behold,*
*they are written in the treatise of the Book of the*
*Kings. Then Amaziah his son became king in his*
*place.*

## BALANCED GROWTH

Both Peter and Paul spoke of the need for growth
toward maturity. Peter likened it to the insatiable desire of
a newborn baby for nourishing milk (I Peter 2:1-2). Paul,
however, lamented the fact that some converts who should
have grown to the point where he could have fed them with
the *"meat"* of the Word of God were too infantile to be
able to digest it (I Corinthians 3:1-2; cf. II Corinthians
13:11 where he encourages them to *"become complete"*).
Growth toward maturity is a process, and Paul stated more
than once that it was his desire to present every believer
*"perfect"* (i.e., complete, mature) in Christ (Colossians
1:28).

But how is this attained? The answer lies in
Hebrews 5:13-6:1. *" For everyone who partakes only of*
*milk is not accustomed to the word of righteousness, for he*
*is an infant. But solid food is for the mature, who because*
*of practice have their senses trained to discern good and*
*evil. Therefore ... let us press on to maturity ...."* Notice
that it is achieved through the practice of the things
contained in *"the word of righteousness"* (i.e., God's
Word) that our senses are developed so that we are able to
discern between good and evil.

As we have noticed in the writings of both Peter and
Paul, the figure of a *"baby"* describes an immature
Christian. An infant is unable to digest solid food and is
compelled to subsist on milk. And as long as believers

remain baby Christians, they are without the skills necessary to progress in the way of righteousness and they cannot understand or enter into the truths that God has revealed in the Scriptures (cf. I Corinthians 2:6-8; 14:20; Ephesians 4:13-14).

But notice how Hebrews 6:1 begins: The word *pherometha* means *"let us press on."* It is used to encourage readers who have the goal of reaching true maturity. And such is within the grasp of each one of us. As God's Word is studied and its message made a part of our life, the goal that at one time seemed so elusive becomes attainable.

Some, however, will say that they are the product of a dysfunctional family and that the trials (and perhaps trauma) of their early years has left them weakened in one way or another. I can empathize with people in such a position. However, by meditating on some portion of Scripture every day, an inner change takes place and progress toward true spiritual maturity is made. And so, without resorting to questionable religious experiences, and by relying on the teaching ministry of the Holy Spirit, the past can be corrected and the *"fullness"* spoken of in the New Testament can become a part of your experience.

## Chapter Eleven

# THE DOWNWARD PATH

II Chronicles 25:1-26:2

For many years, my wife and I hosted a Bible study in our home. We invited our business friends to these discussions, most of whom had not darkened the door of a church in years. In the course of time, many of them accepted Christ as their Savior. One who didn't was a young man named Hector. At first, Hector showed great interest in spiritual matters. He was the kind of person, however, who told everyone what was going on in his life and, unfortunately, he took up the time of the people in the office where he worked, talking of spiritual matters. His employer became annoyed at Hector's lack of production and when he could tolerate it no longer, he called him into his office. The interview was brief. Hector had to make a choice between "this religious binge" he was on and his career. He chose the latter. He stopped coming to our home and to my knowledge never again came close to receiving God's gift of salvation through Christ.

Hector reminds me of Turnaway in John Bunyan's *Pilgrim's Progress*. Those who are familiar with this beautiful allegory of the spiritual pilgrimage we all are making will remember that two men, Christian and

Hopeful, were journeying from the City of Destruction to the Celestial City. En route, they entered a dark lane where they came across a frightening scene. Seven demons were carrying a man toward a black door whom they had bound with seven strong cords. The man resembled someone whom Christian and Hopeful had seen before—Turnaway, a resident in the town of Apostasy. At the sight, both Christian and Hopeful began to tremble, for the awful fate of the man filled them with fear.[1]

## OUTLINE

Many of us know someone like Turnaway, for there are many who once took an interest in spiritual matters, but following some trial or testing, have taken *"the broad way that leads to destruction"* (cf. Matthew 7:13-14). In this chapter, we will read of the tragic story of Amaziah who turned away from the Lord (cf. 25:27) and ended up missing the best of this world and the next.

## THE TRAGEDY OF HALF-HEARTEDNESS (25:1-28)

. A Salutary Beginning (25:1-13)

. A Foolish Decision (25:14-16)

. An Unnecessary War (25:17-28)

Before we can properly assess the events of Amaziah's reign, we need to clear up as best we can a small chronological problem. Establishing a viable

---

[1] *The Works of John Bunyan*, ed. G. Offor. 3 vols. (Edinburgh: Banner of Truth, 1991), III:146-47.

timeline by which to assess the period of the kings has always presented Bible students with difficulties. For centuries, it became a battleground with those defending the integrity of God's Word taking a beating at the hands of critics. Just when Bible-believers appeared to have exhausted every possible means of maintaining a belief in the reliability of Scripture, along came Dr. Edwin R. Thiele who convincingly demonstrated that co-regencies (with a father and his son reigning simultaneously) solved nearly all of the chronological problems.

Did Amaziah (796-767 B.C.) reign conjointly with his son, Uzziah (790-739 B.C.). The answer is most likely, yes. It would appear as if, when the uneasy peace between Israel and Judah (that had prevailed since the time of Jehoshaphat) ended in a war between the North and the South, Amaziah was one of the hostages taken captive to Samaria. This was probably in the fifth year of his reign. The people then appointed his sixteen-year-old son, Uzziah, as their king. While Amaziah remained the titular king of Judah, his captivity in Israel guaranteed the South's "good behavior." When Israel's king died in 782 B.C., Amaziah was released and returned to Judah. He possibly took up residence in Jerusalem, but he was never popular. Somehow trouble arose and he fled to the well-fortified city of Lachish, where he was assassinated.[2]

---

[2] Thiele, *Mysterious Numbers of the Hebrew Kings* (1982), 63-64, 113-16.

## THE TRAGEDY OF HALFHEARTEDNESS (25:1-28)

### *A Salutary Beginning (25:1-13)*

#### Respect for the Law (25:1-4).

> *"Amaziah was twenty-five years old when he became king, and he reigned twenty-nine years in Jerusalem. And his mother's name was Jehoaddan of Jerusalem. He did right in the sight of the LORD, yet not with a whole heart. Now it came about as soon as the kingdom was firmly in his grasp, that he killed his servants who had slain his father the king. However, he did not put their children to death, but did as it is written in the law in the book of Moses, which the LORD commanded, saying, 'Fathers shall not be put to death for sons, nor sons be put to death for fathers, but each shall be put to death for his own sin.'"*

From the life of Joash, Amaziah's father, we learned of the importance of adhering faithfully to the truth. When Joash abandoned the Lord, the Lord abandoned him. In the end, he was murdered by two of his servants. Now we read that as soon as his son had the kingdom firmly under his control, he had his father's murderers executed. He was knowledgeable of the Mosaic Law and did not follow the precedent set in other Near Eastern countries where one's entire family would be exterminated for the sins of one member (Deuteronomy 24:16; cf. Jeremiah 31:29-31; Ezekiel 18:1-20).

**Recovery of the Land (25:5-13).** The people of Edom were constantly fighting against the people of

Judah.[3]  Soon after Amaziah's ascension to the throne, the new king found it necessary to number the fighting men of Judah.

> *Moreover, Amaziah assembled Judah and appointed them according to their fathers' households under commanders of thousands and commanders of hundreds throughout Judah and Benjamin; and he took a census of those from twenty years old and upward and found them to be 300,000 choice men, able to go to war and handle spear and shield.*
>
> *He hired also 100,000 valiant warriors out of Israel for one hundred talents of silver.[4]  But a man of God came to him saying, "O king, do not let the army of Israel go with you, for the LORD is not with Israel nor with any of the sons of Ephraim.  But if you do go, do it, be strong for the battle; yet God will bring you down before the enemy, for God has power to help and to bring down."*
>
> *Amaziah said to the man of God, "But what shall we do for the hundred talents which I have given to the troops of Israel?" And the man of God answered, "The LORD has much more to give you than this."*

---

[3] Cf. J. Bartlett, *Journal of Theological Studies* 20 (1967), 1-20; C. Bennett, *Palestine Exploration Quarterly* (1966), 123-26.

[4] The amount paid the mercenaries would have amounted to one talent per 1,000 men.  There are three shekels in each talent, and so each man would have received three shekels (or a little more than an ounce).

*Then Amaziah dismissed them, the troops that came to him from Ephraim, to go home; so their anger burned against Judah and they returned home in fierce anger.*

*Now Amaziah strengthened himself and led his people forth, and went to the Valley of Salt and struck down 10,000 of the sons of Seir. The sons of Judah also captured 10,000 alive and brought them to the top of the cliff and threw them down from the top of the cliff, so that they were all dashed to pieces.*

*But the troops whom Amaziah sent back from going with him to battle, raided the cities of Judah, from Samaria to Beth-horon, and struck down 3,000 of them and plundered much spoil.*

From what is revealed in the text it is possible that the Edomites took the offensive.[5] Amaziah assembled the fighting men of Judah and found that they numbered only 300,000 (compared with Asa's 580,000 and Jehoshaphat's 1.16 million). Perhaps this fact motivated him to hire mercenaries from Israel, whose services he paid for in advance. This action brought the rebuke of an unnamed prophet who told the king that the Lord was not with Israel. Their apostasy had caused Him to withdraw His hand from them. As a nation they were now under judgment. And so we come to one of the emphases of this book, *viz.*, the need to trust the Lord without reservation.

---

[5] We reach this conclusion because the battle was fought within Judah's territory. *Macmillan Bible Atlas*, 103, 137. Cf. A. P. Stanley, *Sinai and Palestine* (London: Murray, 1889), 88-92; Abel, *Geographie de la Palestine*, II:407; *New Unger's Bible Dictionary* (1988), 1114.

Verse 8*a* is difficult to translate, and the best we can do is attempt a literal paraphrase: "But if with them you are about to act strongly in war, God will bring you down before the enemy." Amaziah, however, was concerned about the money he had already paid for the mercenaries' services. It is probable that the one hundred talents of silver seriously depleted Judah's resources. His response to the man of God reveals the shallowness of his faith in the Lord. His question brings a quick response. He is told that the Lord is able to give him infinitely more than he has invested in the mercenaries.

When the Israelite soldiers are told to return to their homes, they respond in anger, and plunder the towns and villages of Judah from *"Samaria to Beth Horon"* (25:10). But where were they when word reached them to turn back? Either they had returned to their homes and then decided to attack the unprotected towns of Judah; or they were still in Samaria and had not yet marched south to join Amaziah's army; or the reference to Samaria includes the section of land previously captured by Asa (15:8-9) and occupied by the people of Judah during the reign of Jehoshaphat (17:2; 19:4-5). The incursion of Israel finally ended at Beth-Horon, about ten miles northwest of Jerusalem.[6] By keeping to the west they avoided all entanglements with Judah's forces that were engaged in battle southeast of Jerusalem. They plundered and pillaged each town and village at will. This was a cruel and unnecessary act of aggression against the members of their own extended family.

---

[6] *Macmillan Bible Atlas*, 71, 73.

As we turn our attention to the war with Edom, we come across another interpretative problem. There is confusion over the identity of Seir from whence the attacking Edomites came. Older commentators accepted that this was the "rose-red city of Petra." Recent scholars believe that it was the Wadi el-Milh, east of Beersheba (cf. I:18:12), and some have concluded that it was es-Sela two and a half miles northwest of Bozrah.

The Lord gave Amaziah a significant victory. His army killed 10,000 Edomites and captured an equal number. The latter were taken to the top of a high hill and thrown to their deaths. To us, this sounds like a barbaric way of dealing with prisoners taken in war. In the ancient Near East, however, it was looked upon as one way to insure that a defeated enemy could not mount a counter-attack for at least a generation.

Amaziah then went to Sela (Petra) and forced it into submission (II Kings 14:7).

### A Foolish Decision (25:14-16)

The aftermath of the victory the Lord had given Amaziah finds him burning incense to the gods of the Edomites.

> *Now after Amaziah came from slaughtering the Edomites, he brought the gods of the sons of Seir, set them up as his gods, bowed down before them and burned incense to them. Then the anger of the LORD burned against Amaziah, and He sent him a prophet who said to him, "Why have you sought the gods of the people who have not delivered their own people from your hand?" As he was talking with him, the king said to him, "Have we appointed you a royal counselor? Stop!*

*Why should you be struck down?" Then the
prophet stopped and said, "I know that God has
planned to destroy you, because you have done
this and have not listened to my counsel."*

But why did Amaziah worship the Edomite gods
after the battle? It was a well-established practice in the
ancient Near East that the conqueror took the idols of a
subjected kingdom so as to leave the vanquished feeling
helpless (for their gods were no longer among them). In
addition, there is evidence that the kings of pagan lands did
offer sacrifices to these foreign deities to honor them for
having allowed the invading army to vanquish their
people.[7] And then there is the belief that if they suitably
placated these deities, they would not turn on their
conquerors.

Whatever Amaziah's motivation may have been, it
was an act of blatant idolatry. It was the Lord of glory who
had given him the victory, and to bow the knee to any god
was to pay homage to that deity. The Lord was justifiably
angry, and He sent a messenger to the king. The prophet's
words were unmistakably clear (25:8-10). The king,
however, became angry on hearing them and commanded
the prophet to "Stop! Stop!" He then asked haughtily who
had elected him to the King's Cabinet so that he presumed
to speak to the king? The prophet did stop, but concluded
that the Lord had determined to destroy Amaziah.

Before we proceed on to the next section, we need
to pause and analyze Amaziah's attitude as it has been
revealed to us thus far. Though he began well, he operated
on a horizontal dimension of reality, and was easily filled

---

[7] One example being Ashurbanipal.

with fear. He was fearful of Edom's strength and so hired
mercenaries. When he was told to send the mercenaries
back to their homes, he feared the loss of the money he had
paid for their services. He did listen to the prophet the Lord
sent to him, but after being given a significant victory, he
acted in a way typical of other pagan monarchs. His fear
now turned to pride, and when he was rebuked he refused
to listen to the word of the Lord.

### An Unnecessary War (25:17-28)

It might appear as if Amaziah's next action was
designed to redress the wrongs done his people. In reality,
it was a selfish move and may have been aimed at
reimbursing himself for the ten thousand talents paid to the
mercenaries.[8]

#### A Humiliating Defeat (25:17-24).

*"Then Amaziah king of Judah took counsel
and sent to Joash [also known as Jehoash] the son
of Jehoahaz the son of Jehu, the king of Israel,
saying, "Come, let us face each other."*

*Joash the king of Israel sent to Amaziah
king of Judah, saying, "The thorn bush that was in
Lebanon sent to the cedar that was in Lebanon,
saying, 'Give your daughter to my son in
marriage.' But there passed by a wild beast that*

---

[8] Some Bible scholars are of the opinion that Amaziah's
message to Jehoash, the king of Israel, was in effect to propose
marriage between their royal houses. This would seem to garner
support from Jehoash's reply. In reality the terminology "come let us
face each other" was akin to action portrayed in Western movies when
someone "called out" another person for a showdown in the street.

*was in Lebanon and trampled the thorn bush.
You said, 'Behold, you have defeated Edom.' And
your heart has become proud in boasting. Now
stay at home; for why should you provoke trouble
so that you, even you, would fall and Judah with
you?"*

*But Amaziah would not listen, for it was
from God, that He might deliver him and his
people into the hand of Joash because they had
sought the gods of Edom. So Joash king of Israel
went up, and he and Amaziah king of Judah faced
each other at Beth-shemesh, which belonged to
Judah. Judah was defeated by Israel, and they
fled each to his tent. Then Joash king of Israel
captured Amaziah king of Judah, the son of Joash
the son of Jehoahaz, at Beth-shemesh, and
brought him to Jerusalem and tore down the wall
of Jerusalem from the Gate of Ephraim to the
Corner Gate, 400 cubits. He took all the gold and
silver and all the utensils which were found in the
house of God with Obed-edom, and the treasures
of the king's house, the hostages also, and
returned to Samaria.*

Amaziah's pride was exposed by Jehoash of Israel.
In much the same way as he would not listen to the man of
God whom the Lord sent to him, so now he did not listen to
Israel's king. North and South met in a battle that was
fought within Judah's borders. The Lord had turned
against Amaziah and he suffered a humiliating defeat at
Beth-Shemesh.[9] This was more than a tacit victory.

---

[9] About 15 miles west of Jerusalem. Cf. *Macmillan Bible
Atlas*, 108, 112-13.

Jehoash now controlled the trade routes along the coast. He also captured Amaziah,[10] took other hostages, stripped Jerusalem and the Temple of all riches, and broke down about six hundred feet of the wall of Jerusalem (most likely the northwest section). Dr. J. A. Thompson has accurately pointed out that no reference is made to the length of time Amaziah was held in captivity, although we are told that he outlived Jehoash by fifteen years. Often when a reigning monarch died, his political prisoners were released. If that is what happened on this occasion, then it would provide a reasonable explanation for the release of Judah's king."[11]

This leaves us to conclude that all of the activities about which we have read probably took place in the first five years of Amaziah's reign. His deportation to Samaria most likely accounted for Uzziah being made king by the people at the early age of sixteen.

**Untimely End (25:25-28).** When King Jehoash of Israel died, he was succeeded by Jeroboam II—one of Israel's most powerful kings. He brought unparalleled prosperity to the Northern Kingdom. Jeroboam II may have thought it an act of goodwill to release Amaziah. During the reign of his father, Jehoash, Assyria had been gaining in strength. Though Assyria did not at this time constitute a severe threat, Jeroboam II may have believed it to be the better part of wisdom to have a grateful ally to the south should war with Assyria become inevitable. And so Amaziah was returned to Judah to reign jointly with his son, Uzziah.

---

[10] This is implied for chronological reasons.

[11] Thompson, *2 Chronicles*, 325.

At what point Amaziah turned away from following Yahweh is not told us. This act of apostasy may have been set in motion much earlier when two events occurred one after another: (1) his burning of incense to Edom's idols, and (2) his rebuke by the man of God. The final hardening of heart did not occur until after his release from captivity. Is it possible that the catalyst was the popularity and/or godliness of Uzziah? If so, this would have dealt a serious blow to his pride, and this may have led to some treasonable act.

> *And Amaziah, the son of Joash king of Judah, lived fifteen years after the death of Joash, son of Jehoahaz, king of Israel. Now the rest of the acts of Amaziah, from first to last, behold, are they not written in the Book of the Kings of Judah and Israel? From the time that Amaziah turned away from following the LORD they conspired against him in Jerusalem, and he fled to Lachish; but they sent after him to Lachish and killed him there. Then they brought him on horses and buried him with his fathers in the city of Judah.*

The conspiracy that ended Amaziah's life did not occur the moment he turned his back on God. As Dr. M. J. Selman has pointed out, divine judgment in Chronicles often took place years later (cf. chs 21-23).[12] It was as if God, in His infinite mercy, gave each offender time to repent. In the case of Amaziah, his own officials conspired against him. When he learned of this, he fled to Lachish. They follow him there and killed him in cold blood.

---

[12] Selman, *2 Chronicles*, 464.

## TYING UP LOOSE ENDS

The Bible has a great deal to say about pride. Perhaps one of the best-remembered texts is in Proverbs 16:18-19, *"Pride goes before destruction, and a haughty spirit before stumbling. It is better to be humble in spirit with the lowly than to divide the spoil with the proud."* Pride manifests itself in many ways (cf. I Peter 5:5; James 4:6; Daniel 4; Esther 5; Matthew 23:12). In this chapter, we see it in the contempt Amaziah showed to God's spokesman when he refused to listen to him, in his attitude toward Jehoram, and the assumed superiority that caused him to be confident of an easy victory over Israel. Pride is also evident in rage when one is slighted; or becomes impatient when contradicted; and in its most blatant form, when one willfully turns one's back on God Himself. A byproduct of pride may be seen in the fact that it alienates others so that in the end the proud person finds himself/herself alone and friendless.

We do not hear or read much about pride today. A lot of attention is focused on feelings of inferiority, but pride is either glossed over or masked by an emphasis on self-assertion, self-realization, et cetera. Defining pride in understandable terms is difficult, for we, as Occidentals, see less wrong with pride than with inferiority complexes. And pride is deemed to be less offensive than self-effacement. As a result, our culture tends to hold in high esteem the crafty politician, the vainglorious entertainer, the haughty academician, the charismatic preacher, or the cavalier valedictorian, and heap scorn on or ignore the genuinely humble.

The evil effects of pride are beyond calculation, for pride is not confined to Western civilization. It has spread itself universally across all nations and among all individuals. It was the sin of pride that caused Satan's downfall (cf. Isaiah 14:12-15; Ezekiel 28:17*a*), and pride has been "the parent of discontent, ingratitude, covetousness, poverty, presumption, passion, extravagance, bigotry, war, and persecution" ever since. It brought about Amaziah's overthrow.

*Most assuredly, therefore, we should be on our guard against all manifestations of pride and follow the example of the Lord Jesus* (Philippians 2:5-8). Though we as believers are indeed "exalted" by our union with Christ, we should never exalt ourselves. Whatever we have, we owe to the love of God, to the grace of the Lord Jesus Christ, and to the indwelling ministry of the Holy Spirit. We can rejoice in the possession of our God-given virtues (I Corinthians 4:7), and consider at the same time the gifts and abilities given to others by the same Spirit (cf. Romans 12:3).

Conscious of God's goodness to us, we can praise God for having given a variety of gifts to us (cf. Romans 15:17-18; II Corinthians 3:5), which we use in His service.

# Chapter Twelve

# THE IMPORTANCE OF SINGLENESS
# OF PURPOSE

II Chronicles 26:1-27:9

We have all watched ball games in which a team does well in the first and second periods, only to falter in the third and then fall apart in the final quarter. In the beginning, it seemed impossible for them to lose. Their failure (perhaps repeated more and more often as the season draws to a close) leaves their fans feeling disillusioned. Lay analyses of the game seek to determine the cause of each debacle, but in reality such criticisms reveal more about the disillusioned fan than the coach or the team.

Failure after a good beginning leaves us disappointed; and as distressing as these events may be in sports, there are times when they parallel our experience of life. The Chronicler has illustrated this for us in the lives of three kings: Joash, who abandoned the Lord only to have the Lord abandon him (24:20); Amaziah, who turned away from following the Lord to find that the Lord turned away from him (25:16); and now in Uzziah who, when he became strong, acted corruptly and was cut off from the House of the Lord (26:16, 21). In each case, a reign that had begun well finished poorly.

Because we share a common humanity, each of us faces the challenge of finishing well. This does not mean that our eternal salvation is in jeopardy (Philippians 1:6). It does mean that we should heed the repeated admonitions of the apostle Paul to be watchful and persevere to the end. And vigilance is needed, for pride sneaks up on us when we least expect it. It hides our faults from us while magnifying them to everyone else.

Pride is defensive in nature. It prevents us from coming to a fair and true estimate of ourselves. Because of pride, we tend to overestimate our skills or abilities and hide our shortcomings. This causes us to look down on others and either ignore their contribution or diminish their worth. Pride thrives on attention and is often used as a defense mechanism to compensate for our personal insecurities. G. K. Chesterton wrote:

O God of earth and altar, Bow down and hear our cry,

Our earthly rulers falter, Our people drift and die;

The walls of God entomb us, The swords of scorn divide:

Take not Thy thunder[1] from us, But take away our pride.

Uzziah is the third king of Judah who became proud, and his pride led to his downfall.

## THE WEB OF TIME

Before we can study Uzziah's life, we need to understand the events that led to his enthronement as well as the difficulties he faced. Amaziah, Uzziah's father, was taken captive by Jehoash of Israel when Uzziah was only

---

[1] The Bible.

sixteen years of age. Though nominally king of Judah,
Amaziah spent the best years of his life in captivity. When
Jehoash of Israel died, Amaziah was allowed to return to
Judah and presumably reigned jointly with Uzziah until his
death. Meanwhile in Israel, Jeroboam II (794-753 B.C.)
succeeded Jehoash. His reign was a long one and brought
prosperity to Israel. When he died, he was succeeded in
turn by Zechariah (753 B.C.), Shallum (752 B.C.) and
Menahem (752-742 B.C.). The reign of all of these kings
paralleled the reign of Uzziah (790-739 B.C.).

Whereas Uzziah shared the early part of his reign
with his father, Amaziah, from 750 B.C. onwards, his son,
Jotham, occupied the throne of Judah. During the half-
century or more when Uzziah sat on the throne of Judah,
Assyria continued to gain in strength. With the ascendancy
of Tiglath-Pileser III (745-727 B.C.), Assyria threatened
the sovereignty of Syria as well as the independence of
Israel and Judah.

## OUTLINE

We will follow this simple outline as we seek to
understand the text:

UZZIAH'S TAINTED RECORD (26:1-23)

The People's Choice (26:1-5)

The King's External Affairs (26:6-8)

The King's Internal Affairs (26:9-15)

The King's Personal Affairs (26:16-23)

JOTHAM'S UNSULLIED TESTIMONY (27:1-9)

## *Uzziah's Tainted Record (26:1-23)*

**The People's Choice (26:1-5).** We have already noted that when Amaziah was taken captive by the king of Israel, the people decided to make his sixteen-year-old son, Uzziah, king. This fact is mentioned twice in the Bible for emphasis. Initially, it concludes the writer's account of the reign of Amaziah; then it introduces the reign of Uzziah.

> *And all the people of Judah took Uzziah,*
> *who was sixteen years old, and made him king in*
> *the place of his father Amaziah.  He built Elath*
> *and restored it to Judah after the king slept with*
> *his fathers.  Uzziah was sixteen years old when he*
> *became king, and he reigned fifty-two years in*
> *Jerusalem; and his mother's name was Jechiliah*
> *of Jerusalem.  He did right in the sight of the*
> *LORD according to all that his father Amaziah*
> *had done.  He continued to seek God in the days*
> *of Zechariah, who had understanding through the*
> *vision of God;* **and as long as he sought the**
> **LORD, God prospered him** *(emphasis added).*

Uzziah ("the Lord is strong") is called "Azariah" ("the Lord helps") in the Book of Kings. On occasion, the two names are used interchangeably. Uzziah provides us with an example of strong leadership and the Chronicler records that the single-most important accomplishment of his life, following the death of his father, was to reclaim and rebuild the port of Elath at the head of the Gulf of Aqaba.[2] This seaport gave access to trade to and from the

---

[2] *Macmillan Bible Atlas*, 104-05, 112. See the *New International Dictionary of Biblical Archaeology*, eds. Blaiklock and Harrison, 175-77 (see bibliography).

East. It had been used by Solomon (cf. 8:17-18), but in the reign of Jehoram of Judah its control had been lost (21:8-10). Now under Uzziah, valuable imports once again land there and the import taxes increase Judah's wealth.

In his early years, Uzziah did what was right in the eyes of the Lord (26:4). Like Joash who had Jehoiada as his mentor (24:2), Uzziah had as his skilled adviser a man of God named Zechariah. Nothing is known of Zechariah apart from what is recorded here, and that is sufficient. The focal point of his teaching was the need to hold the Lord in supreme reverence, and as long as Uzziah did so God granted him one success after another.

We should not pass from this introductory paragraph without noting once again the Chronicler's favorite emphasis on God's blessing as a result of *"seeking Him"* and *"doing what is right in His eyes."* Without question these are truths the Chronicler wanted the returned exiles to remember.

**The King's External Affairs (26:6-8).** As soon as Uzziah was seated on his father's throne, he undertook to defend Judah's borders. The surrounding nations had heard of Amaziah's defeat by Joash and of Uzziah's coronation, and may have concluded that Judah was in a weakened military position and lacked seasoned leadership. This latter thought may have been given credence because Uzziah was made king by *"the people"* (the implication being that the officials and leaders of Judah may not have been behind the new king). And so they concluded that Judah was now vulnerable to attack.

Uzziah's first course of action is to disabuse Judah's enemies of their erroneous ideas.

*"Now he [Uzziah] went out and warred
against the Philistines, and broke down the wall of
Gath and the wall of Jabneh and the wall of
Ashdod; and he built cities in the area of Ashdod
and among the Philistines.  God helped him
against the Philistines, and against the Arabs who
lived in Gur-baal, and the Meunites.  The
Ammonites also gave tribute to Uzziah, and his
fame extended to the border of Egypt, for he
became very strong."*

Here, in three verses, is a record of God's blessing
of Uzziah.  It is significant that his initial conquests are
directed against the Philistines and Arabs who live along
Judah's western and southwestern borders.[3]  These nations
had been a threat to the people of Judah for centuries.  Gath
and Ashdod had been part of the Philistine pentapolis in the
days of Samson, Saul and David; and Jabneh[4] was so
strategically situated that it gave the Philistines easy access
into the interior of Judah (cf. 25:21). Uzziah conquered
these fortresses-cities, broke down a portion of the wall of
each one, and then populated the area with people from his
own tribe.

The Lord also helped Uzziah against the Meunites[5]
who lived near Kadesh Barnea.  With these victories behind
him, the Ammonites to the west did not want to go to war

---

[3] *Macmillan Bible Atlas*, 133-34, 144-45.

[4] Possibly the Jabneel of Joshua 15:11, and the place later
called Jamnia where the Jewish scholars met following the fall of
Jerusalem (A.D. 70) and discussed the Old Testament canon.

[5] Williamson, *1 and 2 Chronicles*, 335.

with Judah and so gave Uzziah gifts (probably accompanied by a pledge to be his vassals). And his fame spread all the way to the border of Egypt.

These military successes are evidence of God's blessing. Judah was now secure.

**The King's Internal Affairs (26:9-15).** But there's more: The Lord prospered Uzziah in domestic affairs as well.

> *Moreover, Uzziah built towers in Jerusalem at the Corner Gate and at the Valley Gate and at the corner buttress and fortified them. He built towers in the wilderness and hewed many cisterns,[6] for he had much livestock, both in the lowland and in the plain. He also had plowmen and vinedressers[7] in the hill country and the fertile fields, for he loved the soil. Moreover, Uzziah had an army ready for battle, which entered combat by divisions according to the number of their muster, prepared by Jeiel the scribe and Maaseiah the official, under the direction of Hananiah, one of the king's officers. The total number of the heads of the households, of valiant warriors, was 2,600. Under their direction was an elite army of 307,500, who could wage war with great power, to help the king against the enemy. Moreover, Uzziah prepared for all the army shields, spears, helmets, body*

---

[6] *Zondervan Pictorial Encyclopedia of the Bible*, V:925.

[7] J. Graham, *Biblical Archaeologist* 47 (1984), 55-58; A. Rainey, *Bulletin of the American Schools of Oriental Research* 245 (1982), 57-62.

*armor, bows and sling stones.  In Jerusalem he*
*made engines of war invented by skillful men to be*
*on the towers and on the corners for the purpose*
*of shooting arrows and great stones.[8] Hence his*
*fame spread afar, for he was marvelously helped*
*until he was strong.*

There was an earthquake[9] sometime during
Uzziah's reign (cf. Amos 1:1; Zechariah 14:5), and some of
his building activities may have been restorative in nature.
Regardless of when the earthquake occurred, building
projects in the Bible are frequently signs of prosperity, and
by implication, are evidences of God's favor.  The
refortification of Jerusalem, as well as the erection of new
buildings, was in all probability completed while the wars
were being fought.[10]

The towers Uzziah built in the desert were for
defense (although they may also have been for the royal
shepherds), and the numerous wells that were dug provided
an ample water supply for his animals as well as his
servants.  Then, in a unique verse we are told that Uzziah
*"loved the soil."*  He was a farmer at heart and he
cultivated the fertile lands (*karmel*) to the south of
Jerusalem.  (This area is not to be confused with Mount
Carmel in the Northern Kingdom overlooking the
Mediterranean Sea).

Further evidence of God's blessing is to be found in
Uzziah's well-trained and well-equipped army that is of

---

[8] Yadin, *Art of Warfare in Bible Lands*, II:325-27.

[9] J. Morgenstern, *Hebrew Union College Annual 12-13 (1937-38), 1-54;* E. J. Ariel, *Geological Survey of Israel* 43 (1967), 1-14.

[10] Ibid., 336-37.

sufficient significance to be mentioned in the annals of Tiglath-Pileser III of Assyria. He records a campaign against a coalition of kings, one of whom is "Azriau" from "Iuda" (*viz.*, Uzziah from Judah).[11] That the other kings are not mentioned by name in the Assyrian king's annals is important for it shows Uzziah's unquestioned prominence as the leader of the western alliance.

The size of Uzziah's standing army has occasioned considerable debate. Numbers in the Bible are frequently called into question as being too large. Inasmuch as there is no real consensus among Bible scholars, we will accept the biblical account as it has come down to us.

Uzziah also provided his soldiers with weapons. This is an important statement for, in addition to reflecting his prosperity, it sets a new precedent. In the past, each soldier was expected to provide his own weapons.

**The King's Personal Affairs (26:16-23).** After Uzziah became powerful there was a change. He became proud. Perhaps he looked down on the priesthood because they were not performing their duties with sufficient zeal and believed that he could infuse some life into the routine of the Temple services. But where should he begin? The simplest function was to offer incense on the altar inside the Temple.

> *But when he became strong, his heart was*
> *so proud that he acted corruptly, and he was*
> *unfaithful [*ma'al[12]*] to the LORD his God, for he*

---

[11] *Ancient Near Eastern Tests*, 282-83.

[12] For a discussion of Ma'al, see F. H. W. Gesenius, *A Hebrew and English Lexicon of the Old Testament*, trans. E. Robinson,

*entered the Temple of the LORD to burn incense
on the altar of incense. Then Azariah the priest
entered after him and with him eighty priests of
the LORD, valiant men. They opposed Uzziah the
king and said to him, "It is not for you, Uzziah, to
burn incense to the LORD, but for the priests, the
sons of Aaron who are consecrated to burn
incense. Get out of the sanctuary, for you have
been unfaithful and will have no honor from the
LORD God."*

For centuries, people had been burning incense at
the high places (cf. I Kings 3:3; 22:43; II Kings 12:3; 14:4;
etc.) and the kings of the nations regularly performed such
duties. This may have led Uzziah to believe that he could
do the same. In actual fact, he was wrong. He presumed
that he could perform such an act with impunity, while his
real motivation came from his pride.

Let us note that it was *"when he became powerful"*
that he succumbed to the kind of temptation that faces
strong leaders. He became headstrong and thought himself
incapable of failure. His opinion of himself blinded him to
any consequences of his action. He did not pause to think
of what God's Word might teach. If the kings of the
surrounding nations could burn incense to their gods,[13] why
should he not show the same honor to the one true God? It

---

eds. F. Brown, S. R. Driver, and C. A. Briggs (Oxford: Clarendon,
1952), 591.

[13] Cf. M. Haran, *Temples and Temple Service* (Oxford:
Clarendon, 1978), 230-45; Idem, *Vetus Testamentum* 10 (1960), 113-
25; K. Nielsen, *Vetus Testamentum Supplement 38* (Leiden: Brill,
1986), 147pp.

is always a dangerous precedent to take one's cue from what others are doing. God's Word is our guide. Uzziah's neglect of its teaching led to his usurpation of the place of the priest. The Chronicler describes his actions as *ma'al*, "unfaithful" (i.e., a violation of the Law, cf. Exodus 30:1-10; Numbers 16:40; 18:1-7) which he was obliged to uphold.

When Uzziah was confronted by the high priest, Azariah, he was told to desist. At this, he became very angry for he could not imagine anyone having the audacity to challenge his authority. We read:

> *But Uzziah, with a censer in his hand for burning incense, was enraged; and while he was enraged with the priests, the leprosy broke out on his forehead before the priests in the house of the LORD, beside the altar of incense.*

Leprosy immediately made him unclean. This was not Hansen's Disease, but can refer to any number of skin disorders.[14] It caused the king to be unfit for human company.

> *Azariah the chief priest and all the priests looked at him, and behold, he was leprous on his forehead; and they hurried him out of there, and he himself also hastened to get out because the LORD had smitten him. King Uzziah was a leper to the day of his death; and he lived in a separate house, being a leper, for he was cut off from the house of the LORD. And Jotham his son was over the king's house judging the people of the land.*

---

[14] E. Hulse, *Palestine Exploration Quarterly* 107 (1975), 87-105.

*Now the rest of the acts of Uzziah, first to
last, the prophet Isaiah, the son of Amoz, has
written.  So Uzziah slept with his fathers, and they
buried him with his fathers in the field of the grave
that belonged to the kings, for they said, "He is a
leper." And Jotham his son became king in his
place.*

Though Uzziah had many noble qualities and
greatly blessed his nation, his pride led to his downfall.
The root form of the word translated "pride" means "to be
high."  Its usage is often linked to parts of the body (Isaiah
2:11, 17), as, for example, the eyes (Psalm 101:5; Isaiah
5:15), the heart (Ezekiel 28:2, 5, 17), the spirit (Proverbs
16:18; Ecclesiastes 7:8), and one's speech (I Samuel 2:3).
From these and other references, we conclude that pride
manifests itself in arrogance, conceit and haughtiness (cf.
Jeremiah 48:29).

The essence of pride comes about when we shift
confidence from God to self.  That is why in the writings of
Job through Ecclesiastes *"the proud"* are distinguished
from *"the righteous"* and *"the humble."*  And this basic
attitude is manifested in insolence, scoffing, presumption,
stubbornness, willfulness and hardness of heart.  As a
result, a person does not seek God, becomes quarrelsome
and his or her life ends in loneliness and isolation.

### Jotham's Unsullied Testimony (27:1-9)

Jotham (750-739 B.C.) profited from the experience
of his father, and of the kings who preceded him.  He ruled
in the fear of God.  Although he was unable to correct all
the corrupt practices into which the people had fallen, his
sincere intentions were rewarded with a prosperous reign.

He was successful in his wars. The Ammonites, who had *"given gifts"* as a sort of tribute to Uzziah, ceased to do so after his leprosy incapacitated him from governing. This changed when Jotham became settled as sole ruler of his people. They were constrained by Jotham to pay a heavy tribute in silver, wheat, and barley.

Jotham also engaged in many important public works. The principal gate of the Temple was rebuilt by him; Ophel in Jerusalem was also strengthened with new fortifications; various towns were built or rebuilt in the mountains of Judah; and castles and towers of defense were erected in the wilderness.

Jotham died greatly lamented by his people, and was buried in the sepulchre of the kings. His reign was supported by the ministry of the prophets Isaiah, Hosea, and Micah.[15]

## THE FOUR CARDINAL VIRTUES OF GOOD LEADERSHIP

It is easy to see reasons for success in the life of someone like Jotham, but what will give our lives lasting significance? To come to the end of our life and to be able to look back on it with gratitude and satisfaction should be every believer's goal. Such satisfaction is dependent upon internal and external criteria.

Some knowledgeable individuals have proposed the four cardinal virtues of prudence, justice, self-control and

---

[15] The words of Micah (6:8) "What does the LORD require of you but to do justice, to love kindness, and to walk humbly with your God?" have often been applied to those assuming public office.

perseverance as the *sine quo non* of personal and professional success. There is much to be gained from a consideration of these traits. And we find evidence of them in the short account of Jotham's life. For example, we know that Jotham ruled in reverential awe of God. He did what was right in the sight of the Lord. As a result, the Lord blessed him; his people lived in peace, and the nation prospered.

*Prudence* is found in people who take their Godward relationship seriously. Discretion will characterize their thoughts and actions (cf. Hebrews 5:14, noting the words *"by reason of use"*). This trait involves the habit of submitting all decisions to the Lord for His direction, and living life under the authority of the Scriptures. On this practice hinge one's practical wisdom, impartiality, and tact.

The Bible informs us that God is righteous, and He expects His followers to live righteous lives. Jotham *"did what was right"* in the eyes of the Lord. It was an outgrowth of his respect for the Lord and his observance of His Law. Consequently, his rule was characterized by *justice*. He was a man of integrity and diligently carried out his religious and civic duties. His people found him equitable and grew to love him.

An outgrowth of living one's life in reverential awe of God is *self-control*. Jotham did not enrich himself at the expense of his subjects. Even when he became mighty *"he prepared his ways before the Lord his God."* His reign was marked by singleness of purpose, purity of heart and mind, genuine humility, and patience.

Finally, there was his *perseverance*. As Jotham systematically set about building his nation's defenses, he found it necessary to subdue Judah's enemies. And such was his influence that other nations (e.g., the Ammonites) sought his favor. In addition, throughout his reign, he consistently did what was right. He resisted the pressures to conform to the practices of those about him, endured opposition, and showed the kind of determination that eventually triumphs over the vicissitudes of life.

These internal traits are seen in the things that a person is able to accomplish. Fundamentally, what God requires of us is to keep our major purpose clear, lay aside all that hinders bringing this goal to a successful conclusion, and then press toward the mark with a clear conscience, courage, sincerity and a spirit of selflessness.[16]

---

[16] Adapted from B. L. Montgomery, *The Path to Leadership* (London: Collins, 1961), 13.

Chapter Thirteen

# A HIGHLY FAVORED FAILURE

## II Chronicles 28:1-27

Several years ago my wife and I revisited the famous Yosemite Valley. The majestic mountains, impressive waterfalls and crystal clear rivers have always held us in awe. This valley is truly one of the most beautiful we have ever seen. As we headed home, we consulted some travel brochures and a map and found that we could return to southern California via an old, abandoned mining town named Bodie. This now-deserted town is, according to the brochure, one of the "best preserved ghost towns in the West." We took the bumpy road to Bodie—the same road formerly used by horse-drawn carts taking ore to a depot for smelting—and upon our arrival, we found scores of empty buildings that once bustled with activity. All are now discreetly maintained in a condition of "arrested decay," while weeds grow freely around the many discarded mining implements.

In its heyday, Bodie had a reputation for every form of violence and depravity. Its sixty-five saloons were the chief centers of corruption. A solitary church still stands, but it is small when compared with other buildings. It is best remembered for one preacher who lashed out against the "tempests of lust and passion ... on Maiden Lane and Virgin Alley." Immorality was commonplace, and the richest people were the "ladies of the night." Such was the godless atmosphere of this frontier town that when one little New England girl learned that her parents were selling up everything to seek their fortune in Bodie, she went to church to pray. The preacher overheard her say, "Goodbye God, I'm going to Bodie." Needless to say he reported this in the church's newsletter.[1]

The circumstances facing this little girl were much the same as those of pious families in Israel that chose to flee south to Judah to escape the growing Assyrian menace ... and with good reason. Though they sought a better life, Judah, under King Ahaz, was as evil a place as could be found anywhere (cf. 28:19).

But how are we to define evil? Theologians are prone to think of evil in the sense that we all are sinners and have inherited a sin nature from Adam and so cannot help but commit evil deeds. In this they are correct, but when we consider a person such as Ahaz, we must of necessity think of someone who was so incorrigibly corrupt that his malignant wickedness permeated everything he did. Such evil goes beyond being disingenuous, adulterous or having a pathological tendency to manipulate every situation (and especially the truth) to suit oneself. It implies the absence of all goodness.

---

[1] W. Carter, *Ghost Towns of the West* (Menlo Park, CA: Lane, 1971), 88-93. It is a pity that this little girl was ignorant of Psalm 139 and other Scriptures that could have encouraged her to hold fast to her faith.

But some are sure to question if such a condition is possible. It is. Those who follow current affairs know that within the last one hundred years numerous individuals who fit this description have risen to power in different parts of the world. Their lives have blighted all who have come into contact with them. Mass graves, sadistic torture, "ethnic cleansing" and the suppression of all that is decent and honorable are their legacy.

Ahaz of Judah (735-715 B.C.)—who is not to be confused with Ahab of Israel (874-853 B.C.)—is presented on the pages of Scripture as a person without redeeming qualities. The great commentator, Matthew Henry, wrote:

> "Never surely had a man greater opportunity of doing well than Ahaz had, finding things in good posture, the kingdom rich and strong and religion established; and yet here we have him in these few verses ... wickedly corrupt and debauched. He had a good education given him and a good example set him: but parents cannot give grace to their children. All the instructions he had were lost upon him: *He did that which was evil in the sight of the Lord*"[2]

Before we begin a survey of King Ahaz's life, there are some pertinent issues that we need to discuss.

---

[2] Henry, *Commentary on the Whole Bible*, II:765. Emphasis in the original.

## PERTINENT ISSUES

### Early Training

The Chronicler often mentions the name of a king's mother when he records the passing of the torch from one monarch to the next. He could have done so here, but he did not and we must ask, "Why?" In the harems of Judah's kings, a mother played a very important role in the rearing of her son or sons, sometimes influencing them for good and sometimes for evil.

But why has Ahaz's mother been omitted from the biblical record? It is possible that she died while he was in his infancy. If so, then the young prince may have been reared by a near relative. Whatever the domestic situation, his instruction (which lasted throughout his formative years) could have included a tutor who subtly undermined the good Jotham was doing. Such subversion begins by creating doubt in the mind of the young or by making assertions that appear reasonable. Then as time passes a trusted mentor can say something like, "The people are growing restless under the strict religious policies of the current administration." And later on, "There are many religions, and each one serves a distinct purpose" or, "There are many roads to God, and no one belief system possesses all the truth." In time, young Ahaz may have been told, "When you take the throne, be more tolerant of other religions than your father. Test the different religions and hold on to the best." All of this would sound very sophisticated to a young lad.

Regardless of how it happened, Ahaz grew to adulthood without a strong God-consciousness.

Does this scenario seem farfetched? It's not. It takes place daily in our public schools where our children are taught things that deliberately contradict what is taught in the home. And such teaching has a corrosive effect on the child as well as society.

## A Chronological Difficulty

As in the case of several of the kings of Judah, the dates of Ahaz's reign present us with a chronological difficulty. (Some critics have even called this the most difficult problem in the Bible, for Ahaz's age at death coupled with his son's age when he ascended the throne would seem to indicate that Ahaz became a father at age eleven.) The most plausible explanation is a co-regency between Ahaz and his father, Jotham. This could have added significantly to his age, though he only reigned independently for twenty years (735-715 B.C.).

## A Serious Indictment

In the course of time, Ahaz became king. The most serious indictment of him is his total departure from the worship of the Lord and the involvement of the people of Judah in his apostasy (28:11-4, 19). The Lord chastened him by allowing the surrounding nations to attack Judah, kill their finest warriors and carry into slavery large portions of the population (28:5-19). To assure Ahaz of God's help, Isaiah met with him. The king vacillated in his response to Isaiah's message. He was told that he could ask for any sign from the Lord God (Isaiah 7:11)—the more difficult the better. With hypocrisy that makes our flesh crawl, the faithless king replied: "I will not ask, nor

will I test the LORD!"[3]  He lacked the honesty to put God
to the test even when invited to do so.  Isaiah then gave the
king the prophecy of the virginal conception of the Messiah
(Isaiah 7:14).[4]

   We encounter the same kind of hypocrisy today.  It
is designed to mask the rejection of the truth.


## The Demise of Israel

   Toward the end of Ahaz's reign, the Assyrians
conquered the Northern Kingdom and carried away into
captivity most of the people (722 B.C.).  These displaced
individuals were resettled in other countries.  Knowing this,
one would have expected King Ahaz to turn from his sins
and lead the Southern Kingdom in repentance (cf. 7:14).
Instead, he intensified his wickedness.


## OUTLINE

AHAB:  KING OF JUDAH (28:1-27)

   A.  His Unbridled Wickedness (28:1-4)

   B.  His Humiliating Defeats (28:5-19)

   C.  His Unending Quest (28:22-27)

---

   [3] Let it be noted that, all-too-often, *hypocrisy is the homage
vice pays to virtue.*

   [4] W. Graham, *American Journal of Semitic Languages and
Literature*  (1934), 201-16; J. Gray, *Expository Times* 63 (1951-52),
263-65.

Ahaz was *the last king of the divided kingdom.* As we study his life we note initially his unbridled wickedness.

### *His Unbridled Wickedness (28:1-4)*

> *Ahaz was twenty years old when he became king and he reigned sixteen years in Jerusalem; and he did not do right in the sight of the LORD as David his father had done. But he walked in the ways of the kings of Israel; he also made molten images for the Baals. Moreover, he burned incense in the valley of Ben-hinnom and burned his sons in fire, according to the abominations of the nations whom the LORD had driven out before the sons of Israel. He sacrificed and burned incense on the high places, on the hills and under every green tree.*

Ahaz is the only king of Judah of whom it was said that he did not do what was right in the eyes of the Lord. Others *"did evil in the eyes of the Lord,"* but here the criticism is much more pointed. Instead of patterning himself after the example of his father, or Jehoshaphat, or David, he chose as his model the kings of Israel. In this, he turned a blind eye and a deaf ear to the testimony of history and the ministries of Elijah and Elisha who had spoken to those in the Northern Kingdom in the name of the Lord. And he ignored the fate of Ahab, Jezebel, Athaliah and the rest of their line. Instead, he hardened his heart against God's reproofs and spurned all evidence of God's righteous judgments.

Ahaz's rejection of the Lord could not be described in general terms. For the sake of the returned exiles who might be unfamiliar with his penchant for idolatry, the Chronicler specifies his sins: He burned incense to pagan deities in the Valley of Ben-Hinnom just south of Jerusalem,[5] sacrificed his sons by burning them with fire (cf. Leviticus 20:1-5; II Kings 3:26-27; 23:10; Jeremiah 7:31-32; 19:4-5; Ezekiel 16:20-21; Micah 6:7), and practiced the same kind of sensual wickedness that had led the Lord to expel the Canaanites from the land centuries before (Leviticus 18:28; 20:23; Deuteronomy 7:22-26; 12:2-4; 18:9-14).

It is no wonder that the Chronicler saw Judah plunging ever deeper into a cesspool of iniquity that robbed the people of their joy and placed the nation in imminent danger of God's righteous judgment.

### His Humiliating Defeats (28:5-19)

God's chastening takes the form of a series of invasions. First, Syria and then Israel attack Judah.[6]

> Wherefore, the LORD his God delivered
> him into the hand of the king of Aram [Syria]; and
> they defeated him and carried away from him a
> great number of captives and brought them to
> Damascus. And he was also delivered into the
> hand of the king of Israel, who inflicted him with
> heavy casualties. For Pekah the son of Remaliah
> slew in Judah 120,000 in one day, all valiant men,
> because they had forsaken the LORD God of their
> fathers. And Zichri, a mighty man of Ephraim,
> slew Maaseiah the king's son and Azrikam the
> ruler of the house and Elkanah the second to the

---

[5] *Macmillan Bible Atlas*, 205.

[6] B. Oded, *Catholic Biblical Quarterly* 34 (1972), 153-64.

> *king. The sons of Israel carried away captive of*
> *their brethren 200,000 women, sons and*
> *daughters; and they took also a great deal of spoil*
> *from them, and brought the spoil to Samaria*
> *(28:5-8)*

Ahaz's corrosive leadership negates all the good his father had done and brings the wrath of God down on the nation. A careful reading of the text highlights the defeats from which the people of Judah suffered. After decimating the Judean army, the Syrians carried away captive a significant portion of the population (cf. 28:5, 8, 11, 13-15). They were destined to either serve their captors as slaves or else be sold into slavery. Such depopulation seriously weakened the nation.

Israel also attacked Judah, with the same result. The king's son (and presumably heir apparent to the throne) was killed along with Ahaz's closest advisors. And a very large number of people were taken captive (28:7).

> *But a prophet of the LORD was there,*
> *whose name was Oded; and he went out to meet*
> *the army which came to Samaria and said to them,*
> *"Behold, because the LORD, the God of your*
> *fathers, was angry with Judah, He has delivered*
> *them into your hand, and you have slain them in a*
> *rage which has even reached heaven. Now you*
> *are proposing to subjugate for yourselves the*
> *people of Judah and Jerusalem for male and*
> *female slaves. Surely, do you not have*
> *transgressions of your own against the LORD*
> *your God? Now therefore, listen to me and*
> *return the captives whom you captured from your*
> *brothers, for the burning anger of the LORD is*
> *against you."*

*Then some of the heads of the sons of
Ephraim—Azariah the son of Johanan, Berechiah
the son of Meshillemoth, Jehizkiah the son of
Shallum, and Amasa the son of Hadlai—arose
against those who were coming from the battle,
and said to them, "You must not bring the captives
in here, for you are proposing to bring upon us
guilt against the LORD adding to our sins and our
guilt; for our guilt is great so that His burning
anger is against Israel." So the armed men left
the captives and the spoil before the officers and
all the assembly.*

*Then the men who were designated by
name arose, took the captives, and they clothed all
their naked ones from the spoil; and they gave
them clothes and sandals, fed them and gave them
drink, anointed them with oil, led all their feeble
ones on donkeys, and brought them to Jericho, the
city of palm trees, to their brothers; then they
returned to Samaria (28:6-15).*

The Chronicler gives the reason for these
misfortunes. The king and his people *"had forsaken the
Lord God of their fathers"* (28:6b). God, however, is more
gracious than the Judahites deserve. As the men of Israel
return to their homes, Oded, a prophet of the Lord, meets
the army and challenges them with the propriety of what
they are doing. The people of Judah are their relatives.
They come from the same family. Oded then challenges
them to let their captives go, reminding them that they
sinned in their attitude toward those in Judah and have
incurred God's wrath.

The men of Israel listen to him and, in a magnani-
mous way, they do as he has instructed. They clothe all

their naked captives from the spoil; give them all clothes and sandals, feed them and give them something to drink, anoint them with oil, lead all their feeble ones on donkeys, and bring them to Jericho. Then they return to Samaria (28:15).

Some writers see in this incident, the Old Testament counterpart of the story of the "Good Samaritan" (Luke 10:25-37).[7]

In spite of such unexpected goodness, Ahaz does not acknowledge the hand of God in these events. As with people today, he believes that there is a simplistic explanation for such a dramatic turn of events. But fearing further hostilities from either the north or the south, he determines to get help from Assyria. Of importance to us in our study of this passage is the stress laid by the Chronicler on the word *'azar*, "help."

> *At that time King Ahaz sent to the kings[8] of Assyria for help. For again the Edomites had come and attacked Judah and carried away captives. The Philistines also had invaded the cities of the lowland and of the Negev of Judah, and had taken Beth-shemesh, Aijalon, Gederoth, and Soco with its villages, Timnah with its villages, and Gimzo with its villages, and they settled there. **For the LORD humbled Judah because of Ahaz king of Israel, for he had brought about a lack of restraint in Judah and***

---

[7] F. S. Spencer, *Westminster Theological Journal* 46 (1984), 317-49.

[8] The plural is unusual. It probably looks at the kings of city-states under Tiglath-pileser (d. 727 B.C.).

*was very unfaithful to the LORD. So Tilgath-pileser king of Assyria came against him and afflicted him instead of strengthening him. Although Ahaz took a portion out of the house of the LORD and out of the palace of the king and of the princes, and gave it to the king of Assyria, it did not help him (28:16-21, emphasis added).*

Ever the politician, and in defiance of the words of Isaiah (see Isaiah 7), Ahaz sent for help to Assyria. He intended to buy their favor by giving them a large present and agreeing to become one of the empire's vassals.[9]

Whether Ahaz expected opposition from the south (Edom) and southwest (Philistia) is not known. We do know that the Edomites, taking advantage of Judah's weakened condition, attack the Southland (or Negev).[10] And the Philistines, who want to recover their losses to Uzziah (26:6), attack from the west. Ahaz finds himself harassed on all sides. Of course, the reason why the Lord allows these attacks is to drive him to acknowledge his need of His help. Instead, Ahaz, who is now called *"king of Israel"* because the north has fallen to Tiglath-Pileser III of Assyria, is unable to unite the people and lead the people righteously. The net result is that he receives no help from Assyria.

As we summarize Ahaz's reign, we find that throughout his years on the throne, he constantly made the

---

[9] The historic accuracy of this piece of history has been confirmed by archaeologists. Cf. Williamson, *1 and 2 Chronicles*, 347-48.

[10] Cf. J. R. Bartlett, *Palestine Exploration Quarterly* 104 (1972), 26-37; J. A. Thompson, *Vetus Testamentum* 29 (1979), 200-05.

wrong decisions and relied on the wrong people for assistance. Like someone caught in a whirlpool, his waywardness constantly sucked him downward ... and he drew Judah down with him.

### His Unending Quest (28:22-27)

Ahaz was now the vassal of Assyria[11] and compelled along with his people to pay a heavy tribute every year. Isaiah continued to minister in Judah,[12] but we do not read of the king humbling himself and pleading with the Lord for His mercy. Instead, he intensifies his idolatrous practices out of the misguided belief that if all of the gods that he worshipped combine their strength, he would be given success. Unfortunately for him, he ignored the truth contained in the history and writings of his own people.[13]

Throughout his life, Ahaz was intent on manipulating his circumstances to serve his own ends. With twisted logic, he believed that his misfortunes stemmed from his toleration of the Temple of the Lord in Jerusalem. To show the gods whom he worshipped how sincere he was in his devotion to them, he went into the

---

[11] In *Ancient Near Eastern Texts* (282), Ahaz is mentioned under his full name *Ia-u-ha-zi* (Jehoahaz) of *Ia-u-da-a-a* (Judah).

[12] J. Gray, *Expository Times* 63 (1952), 263-65; H. W. F. Saggs, *Iraq* 17 (1955), 126-60.

[13] In this Ahaz is not alone. People today ignore the teaching of God's Word, preferring instead the theories of certain philosophers or the assurances of certain politicians or data that indicate sociological trends. The only sure guide is a thorough knowledge of the Scriptures.

Temple, broke up the furniture, put out the light and shut the doors. He continued to sacrifice on a pagan altar he had commissioned to be made, for it stood in the open court of the Temple. For the people, however, the shutting of the doors meant that incense (symbolic of prayer) was no longer burned before the Lord, the appointed feasts were no longer kept and they no longer brought their sacrifices to the Lord. And because the priests were no longer actively supported in the ministry, they had no option but to return to their ancestral homes.

The Chronicler's closing remarks tell of Ahaz's death. The people had long since lost respect for him. He was buried in Jerusalem, but not in the tombs of the kings. He was remembered as a king about whom nothing good could be said.

### SIN'S SPIRAL

Scripture informs us that it is *"a fearful thing to fall into the hands of the living God"* (Hebrews 10:31). Though God is a God of mercy (Exodus 34:6-7; Psalm 103:8; Romans 2:4), yet He is angry with the wicked every day (Psalm 7:11). Ahaz ignored all of the Lord's attempts to turn him from the path of evil and, in the end, succeeded in arousing His anger (28:25). Yet God was faithful to His covenant (II Samuel 7:14; cf. Deuteronomy 7:9-10; see also Psalm 25:10). In grace, He sent Isaiah the prophet to the king, but the king would not listen. Then He sent against him a succession of nations, but Ahaz would not repent.

Was repentance possible, or was Ahaz locked into a predetermined course of action? Speaking through Jeremiah, the Lord outlined His plan through the ages:

*"At one moment I might speak concerning
a nation or concerning a kingdom to uproot, to
pull down, or to destroy it; if that nation against
which I have spoken turns from its evil, I will
relent concerning the calamity I planned to bring
on it.*

*"Or at another moment I might speak
concerning a nation or concerning a kingdom to
build up or to plant it; if it does evil in My sight by
not obeying My voice, then I will think better of
the good with which I had promised to bless it. So
now then, speak to the men of Judah and against
the inhabitants of Jerusalem saying, 'Thus says
the LORD, "Behold, I am fashioning calamity
against you and devising a plan against you. Oh
turn back, each of you from his evil way, and
reform your ways and your deeds."'" But they
will say, "It's hopeless! For we are going to
follow our own plans, and each of us will act
according to the stubbornness of his evil heart."
… "My people have forgotten Me. They burn
incense to worthless gods …." (Jeremiah 18:7-
16).*

How could Ahaz and the people of Judah be so
blind? Sin is very seductive. When we embrace a
wrongful attitude about God and His Word, follow human
wisdom and fail to do what is right, we set ourselves up as
gods and look upon the fulfillment of our desires as the
means whereby we achieve our highest good. We wrongly
conclude that whatever is good for us is good for other
people as well. Then with ourselves as the center of our
universe, God is gradually excluded until we give no
thought to Him and His ways. When this happens, it isn't

long before the security we enjoyed, the peace and pleasure we took for granted, and the benefits of truth and justice are lost.

From the life of Ahaz, we observe that sin blinds the eye to all that is righteous and good; it hardens the heart so that all appeals to return to the Lord are ignored; the mind becomes warped so that one's own strategies for getting ahead are preferred to godly counsel and, in the end, the willful sinner can no longer recognize the truth (cf. 28:22). When we persist in sin, it also strips the sinner of all dignity and he becomes an object of contempt to those about him. Appeals to outside sources of help prove fruitless and, in the end, he dies friendless and forsaken.

Chapter Fourteen

# THE ROCKY ROAD TO RENEWAL

## II Chronicles 29:1-31:21

As everyone knows, California has its faults!

These fault lines crisscross the state and periodically remind residents of their presence. When an earthquake strikes, it often scares people into a hasty confession of their sins. My family and I have lived in California for more than thirty years and we have experienced several of these major tremors.

According to the U. S. Geological Survey, there are between thirty and forty quakes in California every day. Most of them scarcely register on the Richter Scale and pass unnoticed by people hastening to work or engaged in their favorite indoor or outdoor activity. It is only the big ones that rattle windows and send people diving under desks or retreating beneath the dining room table.

Hollywood has quickly latched on to the earthquake phenomenon and has made movies in which people in different places have been caught in the grip of a quake. In many cases, the moviemakers use actual footage of the disaster and are quick to show cracked buildings, toppled skyscrapers, the ground splitting open, and gas lines and water mains that have been ruptured. And to heighten spectator suspense, some have shown cars and even houses disappearing into open sinkholes or people being trapped in an elevator. And to maximize the drama of those who are watching, they show the electricity suddenly being cut off bringing those in the elevator to the brink of panic,[1] aftershocks that weaken the cables causing them to unravel, and one particularly violent aftershock that snaps the last steel threads of the cable so that the elevator plunges toward the basement accompanied by the shrieks of those who are trapped inside. Just before everyone is killed, emergency brakes come on and sparks are seen flying up the elevator shaft. After this there is a brief pause that gives the occupants time to pry open the door and make their escape with the last person exiting the elevator only a second or two before the brakes fail once again and the cage careens headlong to its destruction.

But what does this have to do with our study of II Chronicles? Judah had reached its nadir under King Ahaz. The shock waves of idolatry had prepared the nation for a free-fall that would end in disaster. Superstition had taken the place of convictions and indifference had become wedded to unbelief. It was at this critical stage in the nation's history that Hezekiah came to the throne. It seemed as if the brakes had been applied. Whatever happened next would spell the difference between escape from God's impending judgment or disaster. Would the new king be able to help his people to safety?

When we look for guidance on spiritual renewal, few passages of the Bible speak to us as clearly and as

---

[1] Of course, emergency lights quickly restore some visibility.

decisively as II Chronicles 29-32 (cf. Romans 15:4; 1 Corinthians 10:6-11).

Hezekiah (715-686 B.C.)[2] came to the throne of Judah at one of the lowest points in his nation's history. His father had closed the doors of the Temple and encouraged the worship of all the gods of the heathen whom the Lord had driven out of the land in order to make a place for His people (Deuteronomy 29:19, 28). The reigns of recent kings may be likened to the stomach-wrenching plunge of an elevator whose cables had broken. Under Ahaz, the foundations of the nation had been shaken and the gravitational pull of the people's apostasy was plunging them into oblivion. The aftershocks of his evil policies had merely increased the speed of their free-fall to destruction. Then, when Hezekiah came on the scene the "brakes" were applied and the judgment of God was temporarily averted.[3]

But why does the Chronicler devote more space to Hezekiah that to any other king (David and Solomon excepted)? What principles does he expect us to learn from his life?[4]

Like Father, Like Son?

---

[2] J. McHugh, *Vetus Testamentum* 14 (1964), 446-53.

[3] J. B. Payne, *Bibliotheca Sacra* 126 (1969), 40-52.

[4] F. Moriarty, *Catholic Biblical Quarterly* 27 (1965), 399-406.

Before we examine the events of Hezekiah's life we need to try and explain the difference between the young king and his father. The majority of writers find it convenient to ignore the dramatic difference between Ahaz and Hezekiah, and obliquely sidestep the issue of how Hezekiah could receive such unqualified praise. But such a sloppy handling of the text leaves us with unanswered questions. The most plausible explanation for Hezekiah's godly lifestyle would seem to be the things his mother taught him during the formative years of his life.

A godly mother's example is impossible to calculate. Hezekiah's mother's name was *"Abijah, the daughter of Zechariah,"* and it is possible that her formative influences led him to do *"right in the sight of the Lord, according to all that his father (i.e., ancestor) David had done."* Abijah was the daughter of a man named Zechariah. But who was he? There are several men of God who bore this name, two of the most likely ones being (a) the mentor of Uzziah (26:5) and (b) the descendent of Levi who assisted in cleansing the Temple (29:13). A third possibility, though one that is less likely, necessitates that we take the word "daughter" as descendent (i.e., great granddaughter) and links her with Zechariah the prophet-priest (24:20). Whichever view is preferred, it is evident that Abijah was reared in a godly home, and though it must have been difficult for her to be married to a man as depraved as Ahaz, she nonetheless devoted herself to instilling in their son a reverential awe of God.

In Praise of Mothers

Too little is said in praise of mothers. The late Sydney J. Harris pointed out that "the commonest fallacy among women is [the belief] that simply having children makes one a mother—which is as absurd as believing that having a piano makes one a musician." Billy Graham's admonition comes closer to hitting the mark. He said, "Let your home be your parish, your little brood your congregation, your living room a sanctuary, and your knee a sacred altar."

Hezekiah must have had a good mother, and though her marriage probably brought her continual grief, she instilled in her son those characteristics that would enable him to be a good king. With the death of her husband, Ahaz, Hezekiah ascended the throne. The Assyrians still posed a significant threat, and there were probably many in Judah who wondered if the new king could insure the safety of the nation. Would it be through compromise? Would he increase their taxes to placate an already greedy suzerain? Or would he raise an army and rebel against the power of Assyria? The last seemed out of the question when one considers the overwhelming might of the Assyrians. So how would he cope with the daunting burden of leadership so suddenly laid on his shoulders?

## OUTLINE

A study of the historic background must include the fact that the Northern Kingdom had finally succumbed to the Assyrians (722 B.). The nobles and leading citizens had been taken into captivity by Shalmaneser V (727-722 B.C.), and his army stripped the Northern Kingdom of everything of value. With the death of Ahaz of Judah, Hezekiah became the first king of the *Surviving Kingdom* (29:1-32:33). He was as good as his father had been evil. Assyria was still a significant threat even though, for a period of time, the army of this great nation was occupied elsewhere. This gave Hezekiah time to implement his reforms.

The following outline will give us a brief overview of the surviving kingdom of Judah.

### History of the Surviving Kingdom (29:1-36:23)

The Reign of Hezekiah (29:1-32:33)

Importance of His Reforms (29:1-31:21)

Events of His Reign (32:1-33)

The Reign of Manasseh (33:1-20)

The Reign of Amon (33:21-25)

The Reign of Josiah (34:1-36:1)

The Reign of Jehoahaz (36:2-4)

The Reign of Jehoiakim (36:4-8)

The Reign of Jehoiachin (36:9-10)

The Reign of Zedekiah (36:11-21)

Appendix (36:22-23)

Only Hezekiah and Josiah were good kings.[5] The rest were evil and in 606 B.C. brought on the nation the first of three deportations to Babylonia.

The accession of Hezekiah to the throne of Judah seemed to offer hope to people of Judah as well as to the remnant in Israel that had been left behind when the

---

[5] E. Todd, *Scottish Journal of Theology* 9 (1956), 288-93.

majority of the Northerners had been deported by Shalmaneser. The Chronicler even hints at the possibility of the North and South uniting and forming one kingdom again. Here is an outline of Hezekiah's reign:

THE REIGN OF HEZEKIAH, Part 1 (29:1-32:33)

A. The Importance of His Reforms (29:1-31:21)

    1. Renovation of the Temple (29:1-36)

    2. Celebration of the Passover (30:1-27)

    3. Reforms of the King (31:1-21)

B. Events of His Reign (32:1-33)

## *Importance of His Reforms (29:1-31:21)*

The importance of Hezekiah's reign can only be adequately explained in light of his Godward relationship,[6] for nothing is more central to the Chronicler's message than the proper worship of the Lord.

**Renovation of the Temple (29:1-36).** The Chronicler begins by providing us with a brief description of Hezekiah as a reformer (29:1-2), and then proceeds to tell us of his reform (29:3-36). *"Hezekiah became king*

---

[6] A negative assessment of Hezekiah's reign and reforms is to be found in L. K. Handy's article in *Zeitschrift fur die alttestamentliche Wissenschaft* 100 (1988), 111-15. See also J. Rosenbaum, *Harvard Theological Review* 72 (1979), 23-43; and H. H. Rowley, *Bulletin of the John Rylands Library* 44 (1961-62), 395-431.

*when he was twenty-five years old[7]; and he reigned twenty-nine years in Jerusalem."*

We may be quite confident that Hezekiah's initial actions were greeted with responses ranging from skepticism on the one hand to hostile criticism on the other. Such reactions are to be expected when a new leader takes over. In the case of Hezekiah, he immediately set about implementing religious reforms and this did more than raise a few eyebrows. From the very beginning of his reign, he set about righting the wrongs of his father, and his first order of business was to reopen the Temple.

But what of the political situation? Shouldn't his first move be to assure the king of Assyria of Judah's willing status as a vassal? And wouldn't it be prudent to quietly take a census to ascertain how many fighting men he could call on in a crisis?

Hezekiah was aware of the fact that wise, godly leadership was essential if God's people were to remain free, and so he began his reign by implementing God's revealed will. Both he and the people needed to reverse the course of action taken by his father and adopted with such

---

[7] As was noted in the previous chapter, the accession of Hezekiah is regarded as one of the most difficult chronological problems in the Bible. Critics are quick to point out that if Ahaz began his reign at age twenty, and reigned for only sixteen years, Hezekiah must have been born when his father was eleven years old. Various explanations have been offered to explain this problem. The most plausible is a co-regency with his father Jotham that is not a part of his sixteen-year reign as described by the Chronicler (see Thiele's *Mysterious Numbers of the Hebrew Kings* (1983), 64, 120, 133, 200-01.

enthusiasm by the nation. There was need for reform and repentance. He acted upon these beliefs.

> *"In the first year of his reign, in the first month, he opened the doors of the house of the LORD and repaired them. He brought in the priests and the Levites and gathered them into the square on the east. Then he said to them, 'Listen to me, O Levites. Consecrate yourselves now, and consecrate the house of the LORD, the God of your fathers, and carry the uncleanness out from the holy place. For our fathers have been unfaithful and have done evil in the sight of the LORD our God, and have forsaken Him and turned their faces away from the dwelling place of the LORD, and have turned their backs. They have also shut the doors of the porch and put out the lamps, and have not burned incense or offered burnt offerings in the holy place to the God of Israel. Therefore the wrath of the LORD is against Judah and Jerusalem, and He has made them an object of terror, of horror, and of hissing, as you see with your own eyes. For behold, our fathers have fallen by the sword, and our sons and our daughters and our wives are in captivity for this. Now it is in my heart to make a covenant with the LORD God of Israel, that His burning anger may turn away from us. My sons, do not be negligent now, for the LORD has chosen you to stand before Him, to minister to Him, and to be His ministers and burn incense'" (29:3-11).*

Before his counselors had time to advise him on the precarious state of affairs and suggest political ways to cope with the menacing power of Assyria, Hezekiah took prompt action to undo the damage done by his father (cf. 28:22-24). He opened the doors of the Temple. It is significant that the priests and Levites did not approach him with this request. Nor did they request that the Temple services be restored. Apparently many of them had suffered the fate of the fire that was supposed to burn continually before the Lord (Leviticus 6:13), for their passion for the work of the Lord had died out.

Next Hezekiah addressed all the members of the tribe of Levi (priests as well as Levites). He summoned them to Jerusalem and met with them in a large square to the east of the Temple. Without mincing words, he underscored the faithlessness of their fathers to the Lord and His work. They had done evil in His sight, forsaken His Word, turned their faces away from the Temple and turned their backs on all they knew to be right. They had also shut the doors of the porch and put out the lamps, and had not burned incense or offered burnt offerings. In place of true worship, they had allowed to be erected in the Temple court pagan altars to the gods of the heathen.

Hezekiah further illustrates the danger that faced all who lived in Judah. He reminded them of the fate that had befallen Israel. Then, he offered them some encouragement by telling those present of his desire to enter into a covenant with the Lord. The preposition *le* would seem to indicate that this was to be a one-sided covenant. The king and the people intend to implore God to be gracious to them and, in turn, promised to obey His Word.

Next, the king challenged the priests and Levites with the need for them to consecrate[8] themselves to the

---

[8] *Qadas*, "be holy."

Lord. His instructions were prefaced by the Hebrew word *'atta*, "now." The priests and Levites were to set themselves apart to the Lord for His service and then cleanse the Temple of all defilement so that it might once again be fit for the worship of God. From this command to the priests and Levites, it becomes evident that Hezekiah wanted nothing less than a pure priesthood.

As soon as those who minister in the sanctuary have consecrated themselves, Hezekiah leads the nation in seeking the Lord with all their heart (15:12). And because this matter is urgent, he concludes with a final exhortation to the priests and Levites not to be negligent in carrying out his instructions.

But what is involved in the priests and Levites *"consecrating"* themselves before they begin the task of cleansing and rededicating the Temple?

The word *"consecrate"* is well-known in ecclesiastical circles, but is not widely understood outside of the ministry. Basically, it means to *"make holy, set apart [for God's service], or hallow"* someone or something (cf. I Peter 1:15-16). This will involve confession of all known sin and a commitment of the individual or the consecrated thing to the Lord and His service.

Following the consecration of themselves to the Lord, the priests and Levites are to remove all *nidda*, *"defilement,"* so that both they and the Temple may be fit for God's praise.

Hezekiah did not issue orders without explaining the reason for them. In the past, their fathers had been unfaithful to the Lord. They had rejected the Lord in a most flagrant and persistent manner and followed pagan patterns of worship. The folly of such actions is now open for all to see. They have committed the same sins as the nations whom God thrust out of Canaan when He brought the Israelites out of Egypt and gave the land to His people. Such rebellion has aroused God's anger (29:8, 10), with the result that He has begun to punish them. Many of the brightest and best have been taken into captivity, their children have been torn from their homes to be sold as slaves, their wives have been led away to spend the rest of their days as slaves of the rich or unwilling occupants of some filthy brothel, while many of the leaders of the people have been killed in battle.

The Levites respond by setting themselves apart for the work of the Lord (29:12-15). Once they have purified themselves, they commence cleansing the Temple court. The priests follow their example and go into the inner part of the House of the Lord and bring out all the debris. They give it to the Levites, who take everything to the Brook Kidron. There, idols are broken and ground to powder, articles made of wood are burned and every trace of idolatry is thrown into the waters of the brook and washed away (29:16).

The work of the priests is just as thorough, and in addition to cleansing the Temple of all the debris that had gathered there, the utensils used by the priests are washed and rededicated to the worship of the Lord.

The cleansing of the Temple takes sixteen days (29:17). When the task has been completed, the priests report everything to King Hezekiah (29:18-19). The Passover should have been celebrated on the fourteenth day of the month (Numbers 9:1-11), but had to be delayed on account of the restoration of the Temple. It was determined, therefore, to consecrate the Temple and hold the Passover a month later.

> *Then King Hezekiah arose early and assembled the princes of the city and went up to the house of the LORD. They brought seven bulls, seven rams, seven lambs and seven male goats for a sin offering for the kingdom, the sanctuary, and Judah. And he ordered the priests, the sons of Aaron, to offer them on the altar of the LORD. So they slaughtered the bulls, and the priests took the blood and sprinkled it on the altar. They also slaughtered the rams and sprinkled the blood on the altar; they slaughtered the lambs also and sprinkled the blood on the altar.*

> *Then they brought the male goats of the sin offering before the king and the assembly, and they laid their hands on them. The priests slaughtered them and purged the altar with their blood to atone for all Israel, for the king ordered the burnt offering and the sin offering for all Israel.*

> *He then stationed the Levites in the house of the LORD with cymbals, with harps and with lyres, according to the command of David and of Gad the king's seer, and of Nathan the prophet; for the command was from the LORD through His prophets. The Levites stood with the musical instruments of David, and the priests with the trumpets.*

> *Then Hezekiah gave the order to offer the burnt offering on the altar. When the burnt*

*offering began, the song to the LORD also began
with the trumpets, accompanied by the instruments
of David, king of Israel. While the whole
assembly worshipped, the singers also sang and
the trumpets sounded; all this continued until the
burnt offering was finished.*

*Now at the completion of the burnt
offerings, the king and all who were present with
him bowed down and worshipped. Moreover,
King Hezekiah and the officials ordered the
Levites to sing praises to the LORD with the
words of David and Asaph the seer. So they sang
praises with joy, and bowed down and worshipped
(29:20-30).*

It would appear as if verses 20-24 and 25-30 take
place simultaneously. The focus of the first paragraph is on
the priests and the rededication of the Temple, while the
second paragraph directs the attention of readers to the
Levites, their music and the worship of all who gather in
the Temple court. Then, as we look ahead, verses 31-36
acquaint us with the offerings of the people.

It is of interest to us to note that King Hezekiah
arises early in the morning and, gathering together the
officials of the city, goes to the Temple to offer sacrifices
for the sin of the people. As leaders, they take with them
seven bulls, seven rams, seven male lambs and seven male
goats—all unblemished—to be burnt on the altar as a
sacrifice for the sin of the kingdom (perhaps a reference to
the royal house) of Judah, the sanctuary that had been
polluted by the presence of cultic priests and priestesses
and a variety of pagan altars, and the people of Judah who
had willingly frequented idolatrous shrines throughout the
land (Leviticus 4:1-5:13; 6:24-30; cf. Ezekiel 43:18-27).

In this book, we shall also read of whole burnt offerings (Leviticus 1:1-17; 6:8-13) that will be offered up for sin in general, thus enabling an unholy people to approach a holy God. The burnt offering symbolized the complete dedication of the individual or the nation to the Lord. Grain or thanksgiving offerings (Leviticus 2:1-16; 6:14-23) involved a general expression of thanksgiving and dedication. Peace (or fellowship) offerings (Leviticus 3:1-17; 7:11-38) were expressions of gratitude and a desire for fellowship with the Lord. And guilt or trespass offerings (Leviticus 5:14-6:7; 7:1-10) were intended to make atonement for specific sins, or compensate injured persons for their losses.

Verse 23 indicates that the goats were brought before the king and the assembled officials, who laid their hands on them (cf. Leviticus 1:4). Throughout Scripture the laying on of hands is used as a symbol of identification.

Verses 25-26 give tacit proof of Hezekiah's knowledge of God's Word. The role of the Levites, including their songs, is in accordance with Scripture and the divinely sanctioned service instituted by King David (followed by King Solomon, cf. 7:6). The music is designed to enhance the worship of the Lord.

Verse 27 is particularly significant and is worthy of a slight digression. We read that *"When the burnt offering began, the song of the Lord [also] began."* We have here the answer to the lack of joy experienced by a significant number of Christians today. When people get right with the Lord through confession of their sins, the payment of their vows, and the rededication of themselves to Him, they begin to experience the joy of the Lord in their hearts (Romans 12:1-2).

As we come to verse 29, we observe that the entire assembly bows and worships the Lord. This is not a once-and-then-forgotten experience. The musical ministry of the Levites continues from day to day. And as the people participate in the activities, the joy of the Lord becomes their strength (cf. Nehemiah 8:10).

This day began well, but Hezekiah is not satisfied. He moves to involve even more of the people.

> Then Hezekiah said, "Now that you have consecrated yourselves to the LORD, come near and bring sacrifices and thank offerings to the house of the LORD." And the assembly brought sacrifices and thank offerings, and all those who were willing brought burnt offerings. The number of the burnt offerings which the assembly brought was 70 bulls, 100 rams, and 200 lambs; all these were for a burnt offering to the LORD. The consecrated things were 600 bulls and 3,000 sheep.

> But the priests were too few, so that they were unable to skin all the burnt offerings; therefore their brothers the Levites helped them until the work was completed and until the other priests had consecrated themselves. For the Levites were more conscientious to consecrate themselves than the priests. There were also many burnt offerings with the fat of the peace offerings and with the libations for the burnt offerings.

> Thus the service of the house of the LORD was established again.

> *Then Hezekiah and all the people rejoiced*
> *over what God had prepared for the people,*
> *because the thing came about suddenly (29:31-*
> *36).*

Progress has been consistent. On this one day, the Temple has again been opened for worship, appropriate sacrifices have been offered to atone for the sins of the people, the services of the Levites have resounded with God's praise, and God has been honored. Now the people are invited to get right with the Lord by bringing their own sacrifices to the Temple. The Hebrew expression for *"dedicate yourselves"* is *"fill your hand."* It was originally used of priests.[9] The reference to *zebahim, "sacrifices,"* probably refers to thank offerings for the purpose of enjoying peace with the Lord and fellowship with Him.

The number of animals brought to the Temple for sacrifice is large (29:32ff.). An insufficient number of the priests have purified themselves for they had grown lax in the days of Ahaz, and are slow to obey the new king's command. This causes an unwarranted delay in serving the needs of the people. It then falls to the Levites who were more devout than the priests, to help with the sacrifices (29:34).

The king and the people rejoice, for what may have seemed like an impossible task has been accomplished in less than three weeks (29:17, 20). The Lord has honored

---

[9] In 13:9, it refers to people who entered the priestly office for what they could get out of it, but in I:29:5, the emphasis is on doing whatever you can for God's glory, cf. Ecclesiastes 9:10. Of course, the sense of this verse also stretches to receiving equitable compensation for services rendered, Luke 10:7; I Timothy 5:18).

Hezekiah's decision, and His blessings are now being experienced by all who are present.

## IS THERE HOPE?

And there's hope for us. Years ago, in my youth, we used to sing a song that went something like this:

"There's a way back to God from the dark paths of sin.

There's a door that is opened, and you may go in.

At Calvary's cross is where you begin,

When you come as a sinner to Jesus."[10]

There may have been other stanzas, but this is all I can remember.[11] As with Hezekiah, the process of renewal began with confession. Then steps were taken to give people an opportunity to dedicate themselves unreservedly to the Lord. And these services were concluded with singing. We learn that when this happens the "song of the Lord" begins again in our hearts.

---

[10] I've searched diligently for this song in a hundred hymnals. If I can locate it, I'll gladly give credit to the author and publisher.

# Chapter Fifteen

# INVITATION, CONSECRATION, WORSHIP

## II Chronicles 29:1-31:21

What is real worship, and what part should it play in our lives? Ask the majority of evangelical Christians who attend a "place of worship" Sunday by Sunday, and they will most likely answer that worship is the singing of choruses with a hymn or two thrown in to satisfy the needs of older members of the congregation. The emphasis in such settings is on the feelings that can be aroused and the mood that is created. Others, however, claim that worship involves their entire being—mind, emotions and will. They stress the importance of drawing aside from the world and, singing a few hymns and with open Bible before them, have a preacher exhort them from the Word. Then they conclude with silent prayer followed by the Benediction.

Writing at the outbreak of World War II, Anglican Archbishop, Dr. William Temple, wrote:

Worship is the submission of all our nature to God. It is the quickening of conscience by His holiness; the nourishment of mind with His truth; the purifying of imagination by His beauty; the opening of the heart to His love; the surrender of will to His purpose—and all of this gathered up in

adoration, the most selfless emotion of which our
nature is capable and therefore the chief remedy
for that self-centeredness which is our original sin
and the source of all actual sin.[1]

True worship is the response of all that we have to
all that God is,[2] or as Dr. Evelyn Underhill[3] said, "Worship
is the total adoring response of man to the one Eternal God
self-revealed in time."   But such an "adoring response"
requires commitment.  It often takes time to develop, and it
necessitates that we acknowledge who God is and bow
before Him "in spirit and in truth."  Anything less is a
carnal attempt to pay homage to God.  And let us never
forget that the most outwardly devout people at the time of
Christ were the Pharisees.  Of them the Lord Jesus said,
*"This people honors Me with their lips, but their heart is
far from Me.  In vain do they worship Me, teaching as
doctrines the precepts of men"* (Matthew 15:8-9).  And
where did their futile exercises lead?  To a kind of legalism
in which individuals go through motions that please the
flesh but whose spiritual introspection and outward
expression of love for the Lord seldom, if ever, touches on
the personhood of God, the reality of divine revelation, the
scope of God's will, the power of redemption (to which

---

[1] W. Temple, *Readings in St. John's Gospel*, First Series
(London:  Macmillan, 1939), 68.

[2] A brilliant and very wise treatment of this subject is by W.
W. Wiersbe, *Real Worship* (Nashville:  Oliver Nelson, 1986), 191pp.  I
readily acknowledge my indebtedness to Wiersbe for his numerous
valuable insights.

[3] E. Underhill, *Worship* (London:  Nisbet, 1936), 61.

they pay little more than lip service) and the authority of His Word.

How may we correct this trend? We must begin by realizing that true worship results in transformation. In this respect a study of the reestablishment of worship under the leadership of King Hezekiah can prove helpful. As we do so, we should take note of the principles by which true worship can embrace and transform all of life. However, because the events about which we will read took place in the Old Testament, we need to keep clearly in mind the distinction between Israel's worship at the Temple and the teaching of the New Testament. The Temple in Jerusalem must not to be confused with the church. The Temple was the place where God met with His ancient people. His glory filled the Holy of Holies. As we read the writings of the apostle Paul, we realize that each believer is the temple of God (I Corinthians 6:19) and that the Holy Spirit resides in us. It is His desire to transform us and make us like Christ (II Corinthians 3:18).

As we focus our attention on the renewal of worship under King Hezekiah, we find that worship is more than words; true communion with our eternal, unchanging Lord is more than conversation. Real worship should refresh the soul as sleep refreshes the body. It is the vital link between the creature and the Creator. To truly worship God requires the activity of our entire being. It is an expression of our adoration, reverence, trust, love, loyalty and dependence upon God. And this is a necessity for all of us lest we become consumed with views of our own importance and end up leading empty, profitless lives.

## OUTLINE

In our last chapter, we gave special consideration to the cleansing of the Temple and the sacrifices that were offered. These sacrifices were offered for the *whole nation*. They acknowledged the sin of *all the people* and had as their goal bringing the people back into a right relationship with the Lord. Now, in chapters 30-31, we take note of the way in which *individuals* repented of their sins and offered those sacrifices that would enable them to enjoy God's blessings.

THE REIGN OF HEZEKIAH, Part 2 (29:1-32:33)

A. The Importance of His Reforms (29:1-31:21)

> 1.      Renovation of the Temple (29:1-36)
>
> 2.      Celebration of the Passover (30:1-31:1)
>
> 3.      Reforms of the King (31:2-21)

B. Events of His Reign (32:1-33)

We begin with A. 2, the "Celebration of the Passover" and continue with A. 3, "Reforms of the King."

### *Celebration of the Passover (30:1-31:1)*

The passage before us falls into three sections:

(1) Preparation for the Passover (30:1-12);

(2) Celebration of the Feast of Unleavened Bread (30:13-22); and

(3) the Extended Period of Worship (30:23-31:1).

King Hezekiah took advantage of the renewed
spiritual fervor to try and reunite all Israel.

**Preparation for the Passover (30:1-12).** It was
fitting that the newly reopened Temple be the scene of a
special Passover accompanied by the Feast of Unleavened
Bread.

> *Now Hezekiah sent [couriers] to all
> Israel[4] and Judah and wrote letters also to
> Ephraim and Manasseh, that they should come to
> the house of the LORD at Jerusalem to celebrate
> the Passover to the LORD God of Israel. For the
> king and his princes and all the assembly in
> Jerusalem had decided to celebrate the Passover
> in the second month, since they could not
> celebrate it at that time, because the priests had
> not consecrated themselves in sufficient numbers,
> nor had the people been gathered to Jerusalem.
> Thus the thing was right in the sight of the king
> and all the assembly. So they established a decree
> to circulate a proclamation throughout all Israel
> from Beersheba even to Dan, that they should
> come to celebrate the Passover to the LORD God
> of Israel at Jerusalem. For they had not
> celebrated it in great numbers as it was
> prescribed.*
>
> *The couriers went throughout all Israel
> and Judah with the letters from the hand of the
> king and his princes, even according to the*

---

[4] Wiseman, *Peoples of Old Testament Times*, 182, points out
that the time for reunion was most opportune for the Assyrians were
preoccupied with events in other parts of their far-flung empire.

*command of the king, saying, "O sons of Israel,
return to the LORD God of Abraham, Isaac and
Israel, that He may return to those of you who
escaped and are left from the hand of the kings of
Assyria. Do not be like your fathers and your
brothers, who were unfaithful to the LORD God of
their fathers, so that He made them a horror, as
you see. Now do not stiffen your neck like your
fathers, but yield to the LORD and enter His
sanctuary, which He has consecrated forever, and
serve the LORD your God, that His burning anger
may turn away from you. For if you return to the
LORD, your brothers and your sons will find
compassion before those who led them captive and
will return to this land. For the LORD your God is
gracious and compassionate, and will not turn His
face away from you if you return to Him."*

*So the couriers passed from city to city
through the country of Ephraim and Manasseh,
and as far as Zebulun, but they laughed them to
scorn and mocked them. Nevertheless some men
of Asher, Manasseh and Zebulun humbled
themselves and came to Jerusalem. The hand of
God was also on Judah to give them one heart to
do what the king and the princes commanded by
the word of the LORD.*

These festivities take place one month later than
prescribed in the Law. And the reason? The consecration
of the priests and Levites, together with the cleaning of the
Temple, had taken longer than expected.[5] Moses had

----

[5] McConville (*I & II Chronicles*, 231) rightly observes that "It
was one thing to *be* a priest or Levite, but quite another to be fit, at any
given time, to *act* as such."

anticipated that there might be occasions when individuals would not be able to participate in the Passover either because of absence from Jerusalem or some form of defilement, and so he made provision for the celebration to take place one month later (cf. Numbers 9:9-13). Hezekiah takes this concession and applies it to the whole nation.

But why not omit these feasts until the next year?[6] Spiritual laxity had characterized the religious observances of both Israel and Judah in the past, and Hezekiah did not want this sad state of affairs to continue.[7] The Passover commemorated Israel's deliverance from bondage in Egypt and its inception as a nation (Exodus 12:27; Deuteronomy 16:1), and it was fitting that God's people keep the feast now to renew their covenant with their Suzerain and turn away the consequences of His wrath (cf. Exodus 12:13). Furthermore, the Feast of Unleavened Bread would remind them of the need for purity if they were to continue to enjoy God's good hand upon them.

Two points of emphasis are to be found in these verses: The Chronicler emphasizes Hezekiah's desire for *unity* between the north and the south, and he also stresses the importance of obedient *worship* as the means whereby God's blessings can be assured. Other kings had tried to unite the kingdoms, only to fail. Now, with the fall of the Northern Kingdom to the Assyrians in 722 B.C., Hezekiah hoped that the remnant in the north would be awakened to the seriousness of their predicament. He sent out

---

[6] Cf. S. Talman, *Vetus Testamentum* 8 (1958), 48-74.

[7] The Chronicler's repeated use of *sub*, "return," should not pass unnoticed. Cf. Dillard, *2 Chronicles*, 226.

invitations for them to come and join him in Jerusalem, but sin (in the form of the worship of false gods) had so hardened their hearts that the response to Hezekiah's invitation fell far short of his wishes (contra. 30:12). In the refusal of the majority of the Israelites to come to Jerusalem, they demonstrate their continued unfaithfulness to the Lord and show that they rightly deserve the judgment that has come upon them.

### Celebration of the Feast of Unleavened Bread (30:13-22).

In the Bible, the Feast of Unleavened Bread was always associated with the Passover. It was one of the three mandatory feasts that all Israelites were required to attend (Exodus 23:14-17; Deuteronomy 16:16-17). In the course of time, however, this requirement was only observed by the godly. And it is the godly that respond to Hezekiah's invitation.

> *Now many people were gathered at Jerusalem to celebrate the Feast of Unleavened Bread in the second month, a very large assembly. They arose and removed the altars that were in Jerusalem; they also removed all the incense altars and cast them into the brook Kidron. Then they slaughtered the Passover lambs on the fourteenth of the second month. And the priests and Levites were ashamed of themselves, and consecrated themselves and brought burnt offerings to the house of the LORD. They stood at their stations after their custom, according to the Law of Moses the man of God; the priests sprinkled the blood, which they received from the hand of the Levites.*
>
> *For there were many in the assembly who had not consecrated themselves; therefore, the*

*Levites were over the slaughter of the Passover
lambs for everyone who was unclean, in order to
consecrate them to the LORD.  For a multitude of
the people, including many from Ephraim and
Manasseh, Issachar and Zebulun, had not purified
themselves, yet they ate the Passover otherwise
than prescribed. For Hezekiah prayed for them,
saying, "May the good LORD pardon everyone
who prepares his heart to seek God, the LORD
God of his fathers, though not according to the
purification rules of the sanctuary."*

*So the LORD heard Hezekiah and healed
the people.*

*The sons of Israel present in Jerusalem
celebrated the Feast of Unleavened Bread for
seven days with great joy, and the Levites and the
priests praised the LORD day after day with loud
instruments to the LORD.*

*Then Hezekiah spoke encouragingly to all
the Levites who showed good insight in the things
of the LORD. So they ate for the appointed seven
days, sacrificing peace offerings and giving thanks
to the LORD God of their fathers.*

One of the first acts of the people is to remove (1)
the sacrificial altars erected to the false gods that Ahaz had
set up, and (2) the smaller altars upon which incense had
been burned to these pagan deities.  These are taken out of
Jerusalem to the Brook Kidron where they are smashed and
thrown into the river.  In this way, the people show their
singleness of heart.  They want to remove the causes of sin
and impurity from their lives.  After this, they consecrate
themselves and each family sacrifices a Passover lamb.

When this ritual was first instituted, the blood of the lamb was smeared on the doorposts and lintel of the homes of believing Israelites (Exodus 12:7, 22-23).  Now the blood is sprinkled on the altar (30:16).

A problem arises when it is found that some of the people from the northern tribes, perhaps on account of ignorance, are ceremonially unclean.  Apparently this comes to the attention of the leaders when these individuals become ill (30:17-20, noting esp. v. 20; cf. I Corinthians 11:27-30).  Hezekiah responds to this crisis by praying for the people.  The Lord hears his prayer and heals those who are sick.[8]  Hezekiah then has Levites assist them with their sacrifices.

It is interesting to note that Hezekiah is repeatedly referred to as a man of prayer.  The exiles, for whom these chronicles were written, would have been heartened by his example.  The inclusion of this incident in the narrative demonstrates that God hears and responds to prayers offered in sincerity, and pardons the offenses of those who trust in Him.

With sin and uncleanness removed, and the blood of the Passover lamb sprinkled on the altar, the people give expression to joyful praise.  Their spirits have been transformed from doubt and fear to gladness and peace.  And once again, the exiles who read the Chronicler's history will be motivated to follow the example of those of an earlier time and experience the joy of the Lord as their strength (cf. Nehemiah 8:11b).

**Extended Period of Worship (30:23-31:1).**  The people have experienced a special time of blessing (similar

---

[8] Thompson, *1, 2 Chronicles*, 355.

to young people at a summer camp or as a result of some special meetings) and they want to perpetuate the events that have brought such enrichment into their lives. And so it was with the people in Jerusalem.

> *Then the whole assembly decided to celebrate the feast another seven days, so they celebrated the seven days with joy. For Hezekiah king of Judah had contributed to the assembly 1,000 bulls and 7,000 sheep, and the princes had contributed to the assembly 1,000 bulls and 10,000 sheep; and a large number of priests consecrated themselves. All the assembly of Judah rejoiced, with the priests and the Levites and all the assembly that came from Israel, both the sojourners who came from the land of Israel and those living in Judah.*

> *So there was great joy in Jerusalem, because there was nothing like this in Jerusalem since the days of Solomon the son of David, king of Israel.*

> *Then the Levitical priests arose and blessed the people; and their voice was heard and their prayer came to His holy dwelling place, to heaven.*

> *Now when all this was finished, all Israel who were present went out to the cities of Judah, broke the pillars in pieces, cut down the Asherim and pulled down the high places and the altars throughout all Judah and Benjamin, as well as in Ephraim and Manasseh, until they had destroyed them all. Then all the sons of Israel returned to their cities, each to his possession.*

It has been noted that the emphasis in these verses is on the large number of offerings rather than the number of the people.  In addition to being a good leader, Hezekiah is a generous man.  He provides an adequate number of animals for the needs of the people, and the princes follow his example.  The result is that there is sufficient food for all who attend the feast.  As they eat, first with their families and then in larger groups, new friendships are formed; a common sense of purpose pervades the *"whole assembly,"* and a spirit of unity binds them together.

At the end of the second week, the Levitical priests lead in a prayer for the Lord to bless His people.  God, even though He is in heaven, hears their prayer.  Such knowledge would further reinforce the confidence of any dispirited exiles who may have begun to wonder if they could expect answers to their prayers.  As the people are dismissed to go to their homes, they spontaneously fan out and destroy the pagan centers of worship in both Israel and Judah.  They realize that purity and singleness of heart are the keys to God's continued blessing.

But why didn't those who refused Hezekiah's invitation and scorned and mocked his messengers (30:10) stop their countrymen from smashing their idols and destroying their centers of (pagan) worship (31:1)?  There seems to be only one answer:  They were cowards.  Those who had been to Jerusalem were possessed of a holy boldness[9] that intimidated all who bowed the knee to Baal and Astarte.

---

[9] The book by O. Harari, *The Leadership Secrets of Colin Powell* (New York:  McGraw, 2002), 278pp., though not dealing with this issue specifically, does portray former General Powell, and later

## *Reforms of the King (31:2-21)*

After the eradication of the many places of idolatrous worship, particularly in the Northern Kingdom of Israel, the enthusiasm of the people continues. They return to their homes in a jubilant mood, and among their leaders there is a determination to build upon the gains that have been made.

*And Hezekiah appointed the divisions of the priests and the Levites by their divisions, each according to his service, both the priests and the Levites, for burnt offerings and for peace offerings, to minister and to give thanks and to praise in the gates of the camp of the LORD. He also appointed the king's portion of his goods for the burnt offerings, namely, for the morning and evening burnt offerings, and the burnt offerings for the sabbaths and for the new moons and for the fixed festivals, as it is written in the law of the LORD.*

*Also he commanded the people who lived in Jerusalem to give the portion due to the priests and the Levites, that they might devote themselves to the law of the LORD. As soon as the order spread, the sons of Israel provided in abundance the first fruits of grain, new wine, oil, honey and of all the produce of the field; and they brought in abundantly the tithe of all.*

Secretary of State, as a man who followed the course of action he deemed to be right without regard for the clamor of his carping critics.

*The sons of Israel and Judah who lived in the cities of Judah also brought in the tithe of oxen and sheep, and the tithe of sacred gifts which were consecrated to the LORD their God, and placed them in heaps.*

*In the third month they began to make the heaps, and finished them by the seventh month. When Hezekiah and the rulers came and saw the heaps, they blessed the LORD and His people Israel. Then Hezekiah questioned the priests and the Levites concerning the heaps. Azariah the chief priest of the house of Zadok said to him, "Since the contributions began to be brought into the house of the LORD, we have had enough to eat with plenty left over, for the LORD has blessed His people, and this great quantity is left over."*

*Then Hezekiah commanded them to prepare rooms in the house of the LORD, and they prepared them. They faithfully brought in the contributions and the tithes and the consecrated things ... (31:2-12).*

### Maintenance of the Temple (31:2-12)

The history of God's people showed that whenever the priesthood was not adequately maintained, the priests and Levites were compelled to support themselves and their families by other means. The result of this neglect is obvious: (a) the worship of the Lord was neglected, and (b) the teaching of His Word was suspended. Hezekiah determined not to allow this state of affairs to continue. He reinstitutes the twenty-four courses of the priests and Levites, so that all will share in the service of the Temple for two weeks every year (cf. I Chronicles 23-24). The *"burnt offerings"* and *"peace offerings"* which they are to offer to the Lord does not mean that these are the only sacrifices they offer up. It is the Chronicler's way of referring to the entire sacrificial system (e.g., as we might say, "from A to Z"; cf. Numbers 28-29).

Hezekiah also gives liberally from his own flocks and herds so that the morning and evening sacrifices are maintained without interruption, and there is no lack of animals to sacrifice when the people celebrate one of their special festivals.

The people also bring their tithes and offerings to the Temple. Portions of these are tokens of their gratitude to God for His numerous blessings and comprise the *"income"* of the priests and Levites (cf. Numbers 18; I Corinthians 9:13-14). As a result, the *"ministry"* is well cared for and the Levites can devote themselves to teaching God's Word throughout all the cities and villages. And so generous are the people that there is an abundance of grain and wine left over. When Hezekiah sees how much food remains, he orders it stored (probably in some of the rooms that had been built on to three sides of the Temple).

This model serves as an encouragement to all of us, for God is no one's debtor. Those who give liberally are liberally rewarded. However, our motives must be pure. God does not reward our selfishness.

### *Distribution of the Tithes (31:13-19)*

After the peoples' gifts have been stored, a fair system is established for their distribution.

*Jehiel, Azaziah, Nahath, Asahel, Jerimoth, Jozabad, Eliel, Ismachiah, Mahath and Benaiah were overseers under the authority of Conaniah and Shimei his brother by the appointment of King Hezekiah, and Azariah was the chief officer of the house of God.   Kore the son of Imnah the Levite, the keeper of the eastern gate, was over the freewill offerings of God, to apportion the contributions for the LORD and the most holy things.   Under his authority were Eden, Miniamin, Jeshua, Shemaiah, Amariah and Shecaniah in the cities of the priests, to distribute faithfully their portions to their brothers by divisions, whether great or small, without regard to their genealogical enrollment, to the males from thirty years old and upward -- everyone who entered the house of the LORD for his daily obligations -- for their work in their duties according to their divisions; as well as the priests who were enrolled genealogically according to their fathers' households, and the Levites from twenty years old and upwards, by their duties and their divisions.  The genealogical enrollment included all their little children, their wives, their sons and their daughters, for the whole assembly, for they consecrated themselves faithfully in holiness.  Also for the sons of Aaron the priests, who were in the pasturelands of their cities, or in each and every city, there were men who were designated by name to distribute portions to every male among the priests and to everyone genealogically enrolled among the Levites.*

As will readily be seen, there were individuals assigned to supervisory positions, and they had people working under them. No one was overburdened with work. And married priests and Levites, while they were serving in the Temple in Jerusalem, received an allowance for their entire family. Even children over the age of three (at which time they were weaned) were included. There is much to be said in favor of a well-supported clergy.

### Commendation of the King (31:20-21)

The Chronicler brings this section of his narrative to a close with some unqualified words of praise for King Hezekiah.

*Thus Hezekiah did throughout all Judah; and he did what was good, right and true before the LORD his God. Every work that he began in the service of the house of God in law and in commandment, seeking his God, he did with all his heart and prospered.*

In his love for the Lord and desire to serve Him with singleness of purpose, Hezekiah sets each of us an important example. And God blessed him because of his unsullied devotion.

### WHAT HAVE WE LEARNED, AND WHAT DIFFERENCE DOES IT MAKE?

The Old and New Testaments use different words for worship. When their meanings are grouped together, it is evident that true worship involves both attitudes and actions. Both have been demonstrated in these chapters. There is the subjective experience and the objective activity. The past history of the Christian church has demonstrated all that to clearly that worship is not a dull formal procedure, nor is it an excess of emotion. It must be balanced. And it involves, first of all, the renewing of our minds, then the purifying of our emotions and finally the motivation of our wills so that we are moved to do what is right in God's sight (Romans 12:1-2).

When the Lord Jesus spoke to the woman and the well He told her that true worship must be *"in spirit"* (the subjective side) and *"in truth"* (the objective side). The challenge is to maintain the balance between the two. And how is this achieved? There must be an objective standard outside of ourselves or the beliefs of our denomination or church fellowship. And that standard can only be Word of God (cf. Paul's statement about his teaching in Acts 20:27). Anything less is to run the risk of developing a dictatorship or lapsing into formalism (cf. II Timothy 3:5). Only the objective truth can provide a secure basis for an appropriate subjective experience of worship.

As we survey the teaching of Scripture on the subject of worship, we find that what keeps it in balance is a reverential awe of God. This involves both love and fear. We must see God as Isaiah did, *"high and lifted up"* with the heavenly creatures singing His praises (Isaiah 6:1-6), and we must see ourselves as sinful creatures (or, to use Isaiah's confession, a person *"of unclean lips"* who *"dwells among people of unclean lips")*. From such knowledge comes godly fear. Then, with forgiveness and cleansing, we respond to Him with love and gratitude. And this becomes the basis of our transformation.

People who worship God in spirit and in truth are transformed by the experience.

The change comes from within. It is wrought by the Spirit of God. Paul wrote:

> *Therefore I urge you, brethren, by the mercies of God, to present your bodies a living and holy sacrifice, acceptable to God, which is your spiritual service of worship. And do not be conformed to this world, but be **transformed** by the renewing of your mind, so that you may prove what the will of God is, that which is good and acceptable and perfect (Romans 12:1-2, emphasis added).*

Two possibilities exist for the believer. The one is to allow the world (as Dr. J. B. Phillips put it) "to squeeze us into its mold" and the other is to allow the Holy Spirit to remake us so that our minds are transformed.[10]

This process involves a decisive act whereby we give ourselves entirely to Christ.

But in contrast to Old Testament sacrifices, Paul likens us to a *"living sacrifice;"* and because we are human, we may need to daily reaffirm our dedication (I Corinthians 15:31). As we do so we are gradually *transformed* into His image from one degree of glory to another by the Spirit of the Lord (II Corinthians 3:18).

It is a fundamental fact that we become like the thing or things we worship (cf. Psalm 115:8). As we see the true God (as Isaiah did) and continue in reverential awe of Him, we are transformed so that we gradually become more like Him. But He must always remain at the center of our lives or else we will become consumed with our own

---

[10] J. B. Phillips, *The New Testament in Modern English* (New York: Macmillan, 1958), 341.

growth and end up with a false (and often extreme) form of holiness.

The greatest danger facing the church today is that people do not know how to worship. All sorts of substitutes are used, but the transformation that results in positive action is missing. It is easy for Christians to assume they have worshipped God simply because they have been to church. But if worship has not changed us, it has not been real worship.

# Chapter Sixteen

# UNEXPECTED OPPOSITION

## II Chronicles 32:1-33

The reality of a person's faith is tested by adversity. There are some individuals within the Christian church, however, who teach that if a person lives his or her life according to God's Word, he or she will be exempt from the trials and difficulties that face the rest of us. They also affirm that such a person will prosper (i.e., God will heap riches on them), that they will enjoy unfailing good health, and that any experience to the contrary is proof of unconfessed sin.[1] This view of life would be great if it were true, for then everybody would want to be become a Christian so as to benefit from God's largesse. Apparently the example of Christ (Matthew 8:20) and the counsel of the apostle Paul (Philippians 4:11-12; I Timothy 6:8; cf. also Hebrews 13:5) are set aside, so that this health and wealth "gospel" can be maintained.

---

[1] Cf. B. Barton, *The Health and Wealth Gospel* (Downers Grove, IL: InterVarsity, 1986), 204pp., and J. Barnett, *Wealth and Wisdom* (Colorado Springs, CO: NavPress, 1987), 326 pp. All of this is surprising, for the Lord Jesus taught that "in the world you have tribulation, but take courage; I have overcome the world" (John 16:33).

All who have accepted Christ as their Savior face adversity (John 16:33; see also Acts 14:22). This is the plain teaching of Scripture. It is true that prosperity can be a blessing, but we learn much more from adversity; and in the end adversity proves to be the greater blessing. Because trials are a part of everyone's life, this chapter about good King Hezekiah contains some important truths that we do well to learn.

The Chronicler has summarized Hezekiah's reign in 31:20-21. There he wrote: *"Hezekiah did what ... was good, right and true before the LORD his God. Every work which he began in the service of the house of God in law and in commandment, seeking his God, he did with all his heart and prospered."* Wow! What an epitaph!

But if he was such a good king, why did God allow the Assyrians to invade the land? Note the words of 32:2, ***"After these acts of faithfulness*** *Sennacherib king of Assyria came and invaded Judah and besieged the fortified cities, and thought to break into them for himself"* (emphasis added).

The attack of Sennacherib took place in 701 B.C. It is told at length in Isaiah 36:1-38:2 as well as II Kings 18:13-19:37. Up to this point, the writer appears anxious to give prominence to Hezekiah's reforms and holds him up as an example. Now, lest his readers conclude that evil things cannot happen to those who walk uprightly, he reminds them that God has made days of prosperity as well as days of adversity, and He does not explain to us the reason for His actions (see Ecclesiastes 7:14). The fact that a good man like Hezekiah had to face adversity was designed to reassure the returned exiles (and us) that their present hardships were not necessarily an indication of God's displeasure.

As we place these events in the context of the Chronicler's times, we realize that news of what had taken place in Jerusalem eventually reached Sennacherib, the king of Assyria. Egypt and Assyria were vying for supremacy, and at this juncture in Near Eastern affairs, Assyria held the upper hand. Having Judah as a loyal vassal was of the utmost importance to the Assyrian monarch, and so, fearing that Hezekiah might lead his people to independence, he chose to attack Judah and subdue the Jews. It was a logical step in order to nip in the bud any possible rebellion. If we use the language of Drs. Robert R. Carkhuff and Bernard G. Berenson, two respected professors of psychology in the State University of New York at Buffalo, Sennacherib knew that he could only *maintain his control over Judah by neutralizing and rendering powerless the one whom he perceived to be powerful.* They wrote:

> "Society, in turn, whatever its origin and whatever service it originally provided man, functions in its advanced stages for its own protection, preservation, and perpetuation. It has functional autonomy. Its institutions are created to serve its end; they flourish or deteriorate with or without support in accordance with the needs of the social system. Its members are shaped in a similar manner to meet society's ends. Now it functions to control man's destructive impulses; now it functions to unleash them; always seeking its own survival and equilibrium.

> "Society is organized most often to fix responsibility for those actions that threaten the continuation of society **in its present form.** This is not to say that society does not change. It does.

However, it changes only through the efforts of those who live independently of society, those who sometimes run against the mainstream of society, and those who live always on or beyond the very tenuous and lonely margin by moving over to incorporate the strong words and actions of this marginal man. However, it does so only when the marginal man is potent, when he has somehow withstood the attempts to be neutralized, and has survived the attempts to destroy him. Society changes in order to neutralize the full effects of the potent man's words and actions. It does so in order to render the potent less potent.

"Society is not organized to free man's creative potential but rather to maintain or render man impotent or maintain him with minimal potency. It frees man's little finger only.... Man cannot construct with his "pinky." In its rules and regulations and in the role models that it presents for emulation, society replaces the individual experience with a collective experience.[2]

Put in simple terms, Sennacherib believed that Hezekiah might prove to be a strong leader, and he wanted to neutralize him lest he cause a shift in the balance of power and disrupt the status quo.

The following outline will help us follow the biblical narrative:

---

[2] R. R. Carkhuff and B. G. Berenson, *Beyond Counseling and Therapy* (New York: Holt, Rinehart and Winston, 1968), 218-19.

## OUTLINE

THE REIGN OF HEZEKIAH (29:1-32:33)

The Importance of His Reforms (29:1-31:21)

The Events of His Reign (32:1-33)

The Defeat of the Assyrians (32:1-23)

The Prosperity of the King (32:24-33)

We dealt with the importance of Hezekiah's reforms in our last chapter, and now we will take a look at some of the events of his reign.

### *The Events of His Reign (32:1-33)*

**The Defeat of the Assyrians (32:1-23).** The Assyrian invasion is met by Hezekiah with his characteristic resourcefulness. Verses 1-8 describe his preparations:

> *After these acts of faithfulness Sennacherib king of Assyria came and invaded Judah and besieged the fortified cities, and thought to break into them for himself. Now when Hezekiah saw that Sennacherib had come and that he intended to make war on Jerusalem, he decided with his officers and his warriors to cut off the supply of water from the springs which were outside the city, and they helped him. So many people assembled and stopped up all the springs and the stream that flowed through the region, saying, "Why should the kings of Assyria come and find abundant water?" And he took courage and*

*rebuilt all the wall that had been broken down and*
*erected towers on it, and built another outside*
*wall and strengthened the Millo in the city of*
*David, and made weapons and shields in great*
*number.  He appointed military officers over the*
*people and gathered them to him in the square at*
*the city gate, and spoke encouragingly to them,*
*saying, "Be strong and courageous, do not fear or*
*be dismayed because of the king of Assyria nor*
*because of all the horde that is with him; for the*
*One with us is greater than the one with him.*
*With him is only an arm of flesh, but with us is the*
*LORD our God to help us and to fight our*
*battles." And the people relied on the words of*
*Hezekiah king of Judah.*

As Hezekiah faces this severe crisis, he is proactive.
To prevent the Assyrians from gaining access to Jerusalem,
he and the people of Judah heap earth over the springs of
water, repair the city's walls,[3] and reorganize and re-equip
the army.  It seems likely that Hezekiah's tunnel, dug
through the solid rock to bring water from the Gihon Spring
into Jerusalem, had been completed.[4]  If this is so, then the
residents of Jerusalem will be assured of a continuous

---

[3] A part of the western wall of Jerusalem which could have
been erected under Hezekiah's supervision is over 20 feet thick.  It
could easily have withstood Sennacherib's powerful battering rams.

[4] Cf. N. Avigad, *Israel Exploration Journal* 20 (1970), 129-
40; A. Mazar, *Archaeology of the Land of the Bible* (New York:
Doubleday, 1990), 420.  For a description of the discovery and a
translation of the text of the "Siloam Inscription," see D. W. Thomas'
*Documents from Old Testament Times* London:  Nelson, 1958), 68,
204, 209-11.  See also G. A. Smith, *Jerusalem*, 2 vols. (New York:
Armstrong, 1908), I:94-97.

supply of water, even if they are faced with a prolonged siege.

We are probably intended to understand the mention of *"kings"* (32:4) as referring to those monarchs of lesser kingdoms who owed their allegiance to Sennacherib and were compelled by oath to support him in battle.

The word *"Millo"* (32:5) has caused interpreters endless trouble. The general view is that it indicates the "supporting terraces" in the lower part of the city. It could also mean a special fortress built into the wall of Jerusalem.

Hezekiah prepares for the invasion of the Assyrians by encouraging the military commanders. He challenges them not to be afraid but to place their trust in God (cf. Isaiah 22:8-11). He knows that submission to God's sovereignty is the only effective antidote to fear. He also knows that only when his officers are confident of God's help can they encourage those under their command.

It is much the same with us. We need constant reminders of the fact that the arm of the flesh (i.e., human strength and resources) is nothing when compared to the fact that our *"God is a very present help in time of trouble"* (Psalm 46:1).

Hezekiah's faith is contagious. The leaders are encouraged by his words, and so are the people. A sense of unity prevails. And with this confidence, they await the siege they know will come.

According to Sennacherib's annals, he boasted of having conquered forty-six of Hezekiah's walled cities.[5]

---

[5] *Ancient Near Eastern Texts*, 288; D. D. Luckenbill, *Ancient Records of Assyria and Babylonia*, 2 vols. (New York: Greenwood, 1968), II:119-21 (#240).

This may be an exaggeration, for he spent most of his time attacking Lachish.[6]  It was during the siege of Lachish that Sennacherib sent some of his generals and a small portion of his army to lay siege to Jerusalem.  Their mission was not to attack the Holy City but to try and instill fear in the hearts of those within the city so that they would surrender the city as the only means of avoiding annihilation.

> *After this Sennacherib king of Assyria sent his servants to Jerusalem (while he was besieging Lachish with all his forces with him) against Hezekiah king of Judah and against all Judah who were at Jerusalem, saying,  "Thus says Sennacherib king of Assyria, 'On what are you trusting that you are remaining in Jerusalem under siege?  Is not Hezekiah misleading you to give yourselves over to die by hunger and by thirst, saying, "The LORD our God will deliver us from the hand of the king of Assyria?"  Has not the same Hezekiah taken away His high places and His altars, and said to Judah and Jerusalem, "You shall worship before one altar, and on it you shall burn incense?"  Do you not know what I and my fathers have done to all the peoples of the lands?  Were the gods of the nations of the lands able at all to deliver their land from my hand?[7] Who was there among all the gods of those nations that my fathers utterly destroyed who could deliver his people out of my hand, that your*

---

[6] *Macmillan Bible Atlas*, 154.

[7] *Ancient Near Eastern Texts*, 287-88.

*God should be able to deliver you from my hand?*
*Now therefore, do not let Hezekiah deceive you or*
*mislead you like this, and do not believe him, for*
*no god of any nation or kingdom was able to*
*deliver his people from my hand or from the hand*
*of my fathers. How much less will your God*
*deliver you from my hand?"*

> *His servants spoke further against the*
> *LORD God and against His servant Hezekiah. He*
> *also wrote letters to insult the LORD God of*
> *Israel, and to speak against Him, saying, "As the*
> *gods of the nations of the lands have not delivered*
> *their people from my hand, so the God of*
> *Hezekiah will not deliver His people from my*
> *hand." They called this out with a loud voice in*
> *the language of Judah to the people of Jerusalem*
> *who were on the wall, to frighten and terrify them,*
> *so that they might take the city. They spoke of the*
> *God of Jerusalem as of the gods of the peoples of*
> *the earth, the work of men's hands.*

In these verses, we have an example of ancient
psychological warfare. In a masterful way, the Chronicler
has pieced together several addresses (cf. II Kings 18:10-
25, 27-35; 19:9-13). The speakers are identified in the
Book of Kings as Tartan, Rab-saris and Rabshakeh. They
launch a verbal barrage against those in Jerusalem. They
hope to undermine their confidence so that they may be
able to persuade them to surrender the city without a fight.
Their strategy was two-fold: (1) they claimed that
Hezekiah had angered Judah's God by destroying His altars
and breaking down His high places, and so could not
expect any help from Him; and (2) they point to the fact
that the gods of the nations they had conquered had not

been able to protect those who trusted in them. So, based upon this precedent, they believe that Judah's God will not be able to turn back an Assyrian attack. But where did they get the information for (1) above? Were there traitors within Jerusalem?

The belief expressed in (2) above is based upon the idea that each nation had a local deity. Sennacherib's officers had no more idea of the reality of Yahweh's power than skeptics have today. The Assyrians were to learn that (to use terminology current at the present time) "religious pluralism is bankrupt in the presence of biblical faith."

Not to be overlooked is the fact that in all of the diatribes used by Sennacherib's generals, they mistakenly place Yahweh on a par with the pagan gods, and challenge Him to show Himself and demonstrate whether He is able to deliver His people.

Hezekiah and Isaiah place these matters before the Lord, for they are men of prayer.

> *But King Hezekiah and Isaiah the prophet, the son of Amoz, prayed about this and cried out to heaven. And the LORD sent an angel who destroyed every mighty warrior, commander and officer in the camp of the king of Assyria. So he returned in shame to his own land. And when he had entered the temple of his god, some of his own children killed him there with the sword.*
>
> *So the LORD saved Hezekiah and the inhabitants of Jerusalem from the hand of Sennacherib the king of Assyria and from the hand of all others, and guided them on every side (32:20-22).*

The brevity of the account and the speed of God's answer leave us expecting more. A longer account is given in the Book of Kings and in the prophecy of Isaiah. The Chronicler simply wants to demonstrate for his readers the fact that the Lord was perfectly able to give the victory to His people. All Assyria's mightiest men died in a single night, and a greatly humbled Sennacherib went back to his palace a defeated man. He did not die until 681 B.C., but when he did it was in accordance with the word of the Lord.[8]

The Chronicler has concentrated attention on the link between prayer and its answer. He concludes this section by mentioning the fact that numerous kings of small kingdoms surrounding Judah sent gifts to Hezekiah. *"And many were bringing gifts to the LORD at Jerusalem and choice presents to Hezekiah king of Judah, so that he was exalted in the sight of all nations thereafter" (32:23).* These kings probably desired to ingratiate themselves into his favor and intimated by their gifts their desire for an alliance. As a part of His blessing on Hezekiah the Lord gave Hezekiah *"rest"* (i.e., peace) on every side.

**The Prosperity of the King (32:24-33).** The remaining high points of Hezekiah's reign are described in four paragraphs. We have had an instance of Hezekiah's prayer when Jerusalem was under siege (32:20). Now we have two further examples illustrating the ways in which the Lord answered his prayers. The first concerns Hezekiah's life-threatening illness, and the second has to do with his prayer for forgiveness.

---

[8] Only one son is mentioned in the Babylonian and Assyrian inscriptions as the assassin of Sennacherib (though his brothers probably collaborated with him). See *Ancient Near Eastern Texts*, 289.

*In those days Hezekiah became mortally ill; and he prayed to the LORD, and the LORD spoke to him and gave him a sign. But Hezekiah gave no return for the benefit he received, because his heart was proud; therefore wrath came on him and on Judah and Jerusalem. However, Hezekiah humbled the pride of his heart, both he and the inhabitants of Jerusalem, so that the wrath of the LORD did not come on them in the days of Hezekiah (32:24-26).*

Though it is not at first apparent, the moment we turn to the next chapter we are confronted with a problem, for Hezekiah's son, Manasseh, is said to have been enthroned at the age of twelve. This implies that if Hezekiah had died from his illness he would have left no heir to sit on David's throne (contrary to II Samuel 7:13*b*,16). God's promise would have become null and void.[9] In grappling with this issue some competent Bible scholars have dated the events of verses 24-26 early in Hezekiah's reign and before the events of verses 1-23. Another view is to look upon Manasseh sharing the throne as co-regent with his father. His ascension, therefore, would have taken place before the Assyrian invasion.[10] This latter view avoids the dubious expedient of rearranging the biblical text and follows a commonly accepted practice of a co-regency.

---

[9] It is assumed by those who hold this view that Manasseh was born in the years that the Lord added to Hezekiah's life. They, therefore, date Manasseh's enthronement before Sennacherib's invasion (cf. Dillard, *2 Chronicles*, 259).

[10] Thiele, *Mysterious Numbers of the Hebrew Kings* (1983), 34-37, 64, 174-76.

Hezekiah's miraculous healing is a rare case recovery. Very few were restored to health in this manner. The Chronicler does not tell us of the nature of the affliction (though the narrative in II Kings identifies it as *"a boil"*). It was as unexpected as it was life threatening. In answer to Hezekiah's prayers, the Lord healed him and lengthened his life by fifteen years (II Kings 20:11). He also gave Hezekiah a sign. Contrary to all established laws, and to confirm His word, the Lord caused the shadow of the sun to go back ten degrees as the sun set. How He arranged this is unknown. Critics, of course, claim that this is scientifically impossible and that for such an event to take place the earth would have had to suddenly reverse its rotation with catastrophic results. That it happened is attested by the embassy from Babylon (32:31).[11]

God who created the earth out of nothing and upholds all things by the word of His power (Hebrews 1:3) could certainly perform a miracle that is contrary to nature without disrupting or destroying that which He had created.

Verse 25 has given faultfinders license to belittle Hezekiah. They are quick to emphasize his pride and apparent ingratitude. What they overlook is his speedy repentance and God's forgiveness. In Hezekiah's defense, we must remember that he was as human as we are and may have looked upon the blessings he received as his just reward for a life of righteousness. He knew the fickleness of Judah's leaders, and quite possibly sensed that the religious enthusiasm of the people had waned. And the

---

[11] They came to Jerusalem ostensibly to congratulate Hezekiah on his recovery (as well as his defeat of the Assyrians); to enlist his aid against the Assyrians, and to inquire how the reversal of the sun's descent was accomplished.

invasion of Sennacherib had left the country in a weakened and impoverished condition. When events took a turn for the better, he congratulated himself on what he had accomplished. This is a common failing! He did not know that Israel's Messiah, the Lord Jesus Christ, would later teach that after we have done all we can we are still to think of ourselves as unprofitable servants (Luke 17:10; cf. Matthew 10:24; John 13:16-17; 15:20-21).

Hezekiah's vanity produced feelings of guilt, and these served a beneficial purpose. Acknowledging his slide into pride, he confessed his sin to the Lord. And the Lord forgave him.

The next vignette has to do with God's blessing of Hezekiah.

> *Now Hezekiah had immense riches and honor; and he made for himself treasuries for silver, gold, precious stones, spices, shields and all kinds of valuable articles, storehouses also for the produce of grain, wine and oil, pens for all kinds of cattle and sheepfolds for the flocks. He made cities for himself and acquired flocks and herds in abundance, for God had given him very great wealth. It was Hezekiah who stopped the upper outlet of the waters of Gihon and directed them to the west side of the city of David. And Hezekiah prospered in all that he did (32:27-30).*

In Old Testament times *"riches and honor"* were the visible signs of Lord's favor and blessing. But doesn't this support the "health and wealth" gospel as many have claimed? In the Old Testament, God gave Israel material blessings. In the New Testament, believers have been *"blessed [already] with every spiritual blessing in the heavenly [places] in Christ"* (Ephesians 1:3), and no earthly possessions can possibly compare with what God in Christ has already given us. Furthermore, the Lord Jesus, during His earthly ministry, instructed all His followers not to worry about material things (Matthew 6:25-34) but to store up for themselves treasures in heaven (Matthew 6:19-20).

But there's more. Hezekiah was not without his faults. *"Even in the matter of the envoys from Babylon, whom the rulers sent to him to inquire of the wonder that had happened in the land, God left him alone only to test him, that He might know all that was in his heart"* (32:31). Hezekiah, we are told, showed them all his riches. He may have outwardly given praise to Israel's God, but inwardly he took pride in displaying all that he possessed (cf. Isaiah 39:1-7).

Once again, it is easy for us to criticize him, but if we are honest with ourselves, we would have to admit that we have often done the same kind of thing. Pride is an insidious evil and we often become aware of it only as we look back on our lives and recall our acts of haughtiness, vanity and self-aggrandizement.

At Isaiah's rebuke, Hezekiah again repented of his folly and prayed for forgiveness.

The final paragraph sums up Hezekiah's life and death. It also refers to the sources where individuals, living at the time of the Chronicler, could find additional information.

> *Now the rest of the acts of Hezekiah and his deeds of devotion, behold, they are written in the vision of Isaiah the prophet, the son of Amoz, in the Book of the Kings of Judah and Israel. So*

*Hezekiah slept with his fathers, and they buried*
*him in the upper section of the tombs of the sons of*
*David; and all Judah and the inhabitants of*
*Jerusalem honored him at his death. And his son*
*Manasseh became king in his place (32:32-33).*

In reflecting on Hezekiah's life the Chronicler did
not want him to be remembered for his failings, but spoke
of Hezekiah's *"acts of devotion."* He may have done so to
encourage the returned exiles with the prospect of living a
godly life in spite of occasional lapses. And he concluded
with the way they honored him at the time of his death.

Hezekiah was a great man. He led his people in a
notable spiritual revival, engaged in engineering feats
unheard of in his day, and was a good leader of the nation.
Most notable of all, *he was a man of prayer, and as we*
*study his life it is comforting for us to know that God listens*
*to and answers the prayers of those who trust in Him*

## WHAT IF . . .?

We live in a hi-tech world. Imagine praying and
hearing something like this:

"Thank you for calling My Father's House. Please
select one of the following options:

"For requests, press 1.

"For giving thanks, press 2.

"For complaints, press 3.

"For all other inquiries, press 4."

And what if you heard the familiar excuse,

"I'm sorry, all of our angels are busy helping other sinners right now. However, your prayer is important to us and will be answered in the order it was received, so please stay on the line."

Or, "If you wish to speak to Gabriel, press 1, now.

"If you wish to speak to Michael, press 2, now.

"For a directory of other angels, press 3, now.

"If you would like to hear King David sing one of his psalms while you hold, press 4, now.

"To find out if a loved one has been assigned to heaven, press 5, now. Enter his or her social security number, then press the pound key. If you receive a negative response, try area code 666.

"For reservations at My Father's House, enter JOHN followed by 3:16

"For answers to nagging questions about dinosaurs, the age of the earth, Genesis 6, and where Noah's Ark is, please wait until you get here."

And what would be your response if you heard a recorded message of a heavenly operator saying, "Our computers show that you have already prayed once today. Please hang up and try again tomorrow. However, this office is closed on weekends to observe a religious holiday. Please pray again on Monday after 9:30 A.M. If you need emergency assistance when this office is closed, contact your local pastor."

It is comforting to know that our God is omniscient, omnipresent and omnipotent. He doesn't sleep (Psalm 121:4*b*) and His ears are always open to hear our prayers (Psalm 34:15).

# Chapter Seventeen

## TOO LITTLE, TOO LATE

II Chronicles 33:1-20

We do not often hear of remarkable conversions, but one that is worth remembering is of a man named John. John Newton to be precise. On his gravestone are carved the words:

> "John Newton, clerk, once an infidel and libertine, a servant of slaves in Africa, was, by the rich mercy of our Lord and Saviour Jesus Christ, preserved, restored, pardoned, and appointed to preach the faith he had long labored to destroy."

Though John had a godly mother he turned away from Christ after reading Lord Shaftesbury's *Characteristics* and became a profligate, a drunkard and an infidel. It was his desire to enjoy to the fullest whatever pleasures life had to offer.

After his mother died, he began to take voyages with his father, and thought he would spend the rest of his life at sea. Later, on leaving his father's ship, he signed on with another vessel, but he was so badly treated he jumped ship. When he was captured, he was brought back to Plymouth, England, in chains. As a felon, he was kept in irons, degraded from his office as midshipman and publicly whipped. But sin and severe punishment only hardened his heart. To gain his release, he signed on with the crew of another ship and sailed abroad. After a while, he obtained permission to transfer to a vessel bound for the African coast. His purpose, as he afterwards declared, was to be free to sin. He left the ship and lived on an island where he descended to the lowest depths of depravity. Before long he became the slave of an African woman.

In despair, he wrote his father who made arrangements for him to return to England. The voyage homeward was tedious, and from sheer boredom he read *The Imitation of Christ* by Thomas A. Kempis. As he did so, the thought flashed through his mind, "What if these things should be true?" That very night, a terrible storm buffeted the ship and it was in danger of being broken up. It was then, as he says, "I began to pray. I could not utter the prayer of faith; I could not draw near to be reconciled to God, and call him Father. My prayer was like the cry of the ravens, and the Lord did not disdain to hear me."

After the storm had subsided, the crew faced an even greater danger: death by starvation. The New Testament now became Newton's constant study. He was particularly impressed by the parable of the prodigal son, and could see very clearly its similarity to his own case. "I continued in much prayer," he wrote, "[and] saw that the Lord had interfered so far to save me.... I saw by the way pointed out in the Gospel that God might declare not his mercy only, but his justice also, in the pardon of sin on account of the obedience and sufferings of Jesus Christ."

John Newton reached home in safety, and the change in his life proved to be both real and permanent. He attempted to preach, but without much success. While working as a tide surveyor, he studied for the ministry, gaining a mastery of both Greek and Hebrew. At the age of thirty-nine, he officially entered the ministry and for the next 43 years of his life faithfully preached the gospel. At 82, Newton said, "My memory is nearly gone, but I remember two things, that I am a great sinner, and that Christ is a great Saviour." Today John Newton is best known for the hundred or more hymns that he wrote, the most famous of which is *Amazing Grace*.

Parallel Lives, Parallel Kingdoms

The story of Newton's life is most interesting, but someone will ask, "What does it have to do with II Chronicles, chapter 33?"

That is a good question. King Manasseh of Judah, like John Newton, could easily be regarded as *"the chief of sinners"* of his day. He had a godly father, but chose to follow the way of evil. His reign parallels that of Charles II who undid all the good done by his predecessors. What the historian and literary scholar, T. B. Macaulay wrote of King Charles could easily have been written of Manasseh: "Then came days never to be recalled without a blush, the days of servitude without loyalty, of sensuality without love, of dwarfish talents and gigantic vices, the paradise of cold hearts and narrow minds, the golden age of the coward, the bigot and the slave."

OUTLINE

MANASSEH, KING OF JUDAH, 33:1-20

Introduction (33:1-2)

A. Relapse Into Idolatry (33:3-9)

B. Rebuke of the Prophets (33:10)

C. Reproof of the Lord (33:11)

D. Repentance of the King (33:12-13)

E. Restoration of the City (33:14-18)

Conclusion (33:19-20)

As we study this chapter, we will take note of the ways in which sin blinds our eyes, causes us to become insensitive to the truth and involves others in the consequences of our wrong doing. We will also take note of the ways in which God reproves and willingly forgives sin when repentance and humility are real. Lastly, we note His blessing upon those who obey Him.

Though there *appear* to be contradictions between II Chronicles and II Kings, the differences are slight and can be explained by taking into consideration the perspective of each writer. The compiler of II Kings carefully selected his material and presented it so as to emphasize the righteousness of God in judging His people and bringing about the captivity. The Chronicler likewise selected his material and included what would be of encouragement to the returned exiles. He laid stress on the faithfulness of God. Key to his thinking is the promise of II Chronicles 7:12-16. There is, therefore, no contradiction between the two accounts. They are complimentary. The Chronicler does not gloss over the sins that caused the exile but instead supplements the history of the Book of Kings.

What is worth noting is the fact that God's door stands open so that all who humble themselves and acknowledge His right to rule over them benefit from His offer of salvation (cf. Luke 14:11; 18:14).

Introduction (33:1-2)

> *Manasseh was twelve years old when he became king, and he reigned fifty-five years in Jerusalem.  He did evil in the sight of the LORD[1] according to the abominations of the nations whom the LORD dispossessed before the sons of Israel (33:1-2).*

Manasseh reigned from 695-642 B.C.[2]—longer than any other monarch,[3] and probably shared the throne with

---

[1] We do well to take note of the brief summary of Manasseh's evils in II Kings 21:10-16: "Now the LORD spoke through His servants the prophets, saying, 'Because Manasseh king of Judah has done these abominations, having done wickedly more than all the Amorites did who were before him, and has also made Judah sin with his idols; therefore thus says the LORD, the God of Israel, "behold, I am bringing such calamity on Jerusalem and Judah, that whoever hears of it, both his ears will tingle.  I will stretch over Jerusalem the line of Samaria and the plummet of the house of Ahab, and I will wipe Jerusalem as one wipes a dish, wiping it and turning it upside down.  I will abandon the remnant of My inheritance and deliver them into the hand of their enemies, and they will become as plunder and spoil to all their enemies; because they have done evil in My sight, and have been provoking Me to anger since the day their fathers came from Egypt, even to this day."  Moreover, Manasseh shed very much innocent blood until he had filled Jerusalem from one end to another; besides his sin with which he made Judah sin, in doing evil in the sight of the LORD.'"

[2] Remember that for the purpose of reckoning time, the Hebrews counted a part of a year as a whole year.

his father for a time.  Because he was very young and highly impressionable there may have been some among his counselors who subtly and slyly suggested to him that the surest way to win the favor of the people would be to relax some of the strict religious policies of Hezekiah.   As soon as Hezekiah passed from the scene of his earthly labors, these advisors probably began to introduce Manasseh to the religious rites of the nations surrounding Judah.  Each of these systems of belief promised untold happiness and prosperity to the practitioner(s).

What Manasseh was led to practice was a form of *religious pluralism*, not unlike the pluralism of our own day.

The primary powers in the ancient Near East at that time were Babylonia, Assyria, and Egypt,[4] with Israel in the middle.  We are not surprised to note, therefore, that Israel was regarded as a land of strategic importance; and in the quest for power, each of the larger nations wanted to control her.

### Relapse Into Idolatry (33:3-9)

What exactly did Manasseh do wrong?

---

[3] From this point onwards the name of each king's mother has been omitted by the Chronicler.

[4] Rich sources of information may be gleaned from the treaties entered into by Esarhaddon and Ashurbanipal (see Myers, *II Chronicles*, 198-99; Dillard, *2 Chronicles*, 264-65; *Ancient Near Eastern Texts*, 291 and 294; and W. M. Schniedewind, Vetus *Testamentum* 41 (1991), 450-61.

*[Manasseh] rebuilt the high places that
Hezekiah his father had broken down; he also
erected altars for the Baals and made Asherim,
and worshipped all the host of heaven and served
them.  He built altars in the house of the LORD of
which the LORD had said, "My name shall be in
Jerusalem forever."  For he built altars for all the
host of heaven in the two courts of the house of the
LORD.  He made his sons pass through the fire in
the valley of Ben-hinnom; and he practiced
witchcraft, used divination, practiced sorcery and
dealt with mediums and spiritists. He did much
evil in the sight of the LORD, provoking Him to
anger.  Then he put the carved image of the idol
which he had made in the house of God, of which
God had said to David and to Solomon his son,
"In this house and in Jerusalem, which I have
chosen from all the tribes of Israel, I will put My
name forever; and I will not again remove the foot
of Israel from the land which I have appointed for
your fathers, if only they will observe to do all that
I have commanded them according to all the law,
the statutes and the ordinances given through
Moses."  Thus Manasseh misled Judah and the
inhabitants of Jerusalem to do more evil than the
nations whom the LORD destroyed before the sons
of Israel.*

Manasseh ignored the history of his people.  A
recounting of the past may even have bored him.  He gave
no thought, therefore, to the fact that the Lord had already
demonstrated His disdain of their practices and had already
allowed the Assyrians to take into captivity the northern
tribes.  Turning a blind eye and a deaf ear, Manasseh
restored the high places that Hezekiah had destroyed.  To

this, he added altars to the Baals and Asherah poles. Most heinous of all was the sacrifice of his sons (most likely to the pagan god Moloch). To these offenses were added all the different forms of spiritism, including sorcery, divination, witchcraft, and necromancy (cf. Deuteronomy 18:9-13). And he dragged the people of Judah down with him. The gods the pagans and the people of Judah worshipped were both sensual and malignant, and the people became like them (cf. Psalm 115:4-8; Jeremiah 10:3b-5, 8b).

Scores of books have been written on the modern manifestations of these ancient cults. As we have noted, Manasseh followed a form of religious pluralism. *Religious pluralism* is the belief that every religion is true and provides a path to, or a genuine encounter with, the Ultimate. One system of belief may be better than another, but all serve a beneficial purpose. This fallacy is possible because *relativism* has been widely taught in our schools and colleges, and people no longer believe that there are any criteria by which they can determine the truth. Consequently, there is present within our society an obsession with different religions, with each person adhering to those facets of different belief systems that have the most appeal to him or her. Such a view is called *inclusivism*.

Those who build their hope for the future on what the Bible teaches are *exclusive*, and view other religions as false. Happily there are many good books that defend every aspect of biblical Christianity. They are generally classified under the topic of "Apologetics" (from the Greek *apologia*, "to offer a defense").[5]

How did God view Manasseh's syncretism? Verses 7-10 contain His indictment. Manasseh had violated the covenant that He had established with David and Solomon. God had put His "Name" (implying the totality of His character, His very essence) in Jerusalem, and he had sanctified the Temple with His presence. With callused disregard for the holiness of the Lord, and of the Shekinah that daily stood over the Temple, Manasseh set up a *"carved image"* which he had made, and worshipped it (cf. Psalm 97:7; 115:4-8; Isaiah 41:29; Jeremiah 11:9-13; 18:13-17).

### Rebuke of the Prophets (33:10)

*"The LORD spoke to Manasseh and his people, but they paid no attention."*

God is gracious. His people had His Word (those portions of Scripture, including the Law of Moses, that had been written thus far) and He sent His messengers to reprove His people and call them back to Him. All His servants were ignored. Obsequious courtiers, all through Israel's history, were notoriously evil counselors. They taught that the gods and cults of the strongest nations were the measure of the oppressor's strength. So it was that when the prophets denounced the sins of the king and his

---

[5] A single source containing an abundance of reliable information is N. L. Geisler's *Baker Encyclopedia of Christian Apologetics* (Grand Rapids: Baker, 1998), 841pp.

people, they were ignored. The hearts of the people had become hardened.[6] They were wedded to their idols.

The apostle Paul warned people living in the New Testament era that in the *"last days"* (and his words are particularly apropos to our time) people would similarly be intent upon doing only those things that pleased them (II Timothy 3:1-5). We see evidence for the truthfulness of Paul's words everywhere we look. He is ignored, however, in the same way as the Old Testament prophets whom the Lord sent to His people.

### Reproof of the Lord (33:11)

Sadly, Manasseh seemed unaware of any danger. He may have felt that inasmuch as he was worshipping the gods of Assyria, Babylonia, Egypt,[7] and the surrounding nations, they would protect him. They could not, and God's judgment, though long delayed, finally came.

> *Therefore the LORD brought the commanders of the army of the king of Assyria against them, and they captured Manasseh with hooks, bound him with bronze chains and took him to Babylon.*

It is interesting to note that Manasseh's fate was not in the hands of the Assyrians. God was sovereignly orchestrating events to achieve His purpose. It is possible that Manasseh had been forced into submission to Assyria

---

[6] Of course, those who stood for what was right, and worshipped the Lord, were martyred (cf. II Kings 21:16).

[7] Manasseh's son, Amon, was named after an Egyptian god.

and compelled to pay a heavy annual tax. In time, when Ashurbanipal's brother, Shamash-shum-ukin, king of Babylon, rebelled against Assyria, Manasseh may have sided with the rebellion. Once Shamash-shum-ukin had been neutralized, Ashurbanipal sent an army to deal with those nations that had sided with his brother. Judah may have been one of these, and Manasseh was captured. A *"hook"* was put through his nose and he was bound with bronze shackles (possibly reserved for royal prisoners) and taken to Babylon.[8] This would have occasioned a great deal of pain and was designed to humiliate a disloyal vassal.

But why was Manasseh taken to Babylon and not to Nineveh? In all probability, Ashurbanipal had moved his court to Babylon to insure that no further uprising took place.

### *Restoration of the City and the People (33:14-18)*

The Chronicler now enlarges on God's grace and forgiveness for, contrary to everyone's expectations, when Manasseh repented of his sins, the Lord brought about his restoration to the throne of Judah. In this respect, his dramatic conversion bears a similarity to that of John Newton who, as a slave, turned to the Lord and was saved.

> *When he [Manasseh] was in distress, he entreated the LORD his God and humbled himself greatly before the God of his fathers. When he*

---

[8] Some scholars believe that this invasion of Judah took place early in the reign of Manasseh and late in the reign of Esarhaddon, and was designed by Esarhaddon to insure the unchallenged ascendance of his son, Ashurbanipal, to the throne of Assyria.

*prayed to Him, He was moved by his entreaty and heard his supplication, and brought him again to Jerusalem to his kingdom. Then Manasseh knew that the LORD was God.*

*Now after this he built the outer wall of the city of David on the west side of Gihon, in the valley, even to the entrance of the Fish Gate; and he encircled the Ophel with it and made it very high. Then he put army commanders in all the fortified cities of Judah.  He also removed the foreign gods and the idol from the house of the LORD, as well as all the altars that he had built on the mountain of the house of the LORD and in Jerusalem, and he threw them outside the city. He set up the altar of the LORD and sacrificed peace offerings and thank offerings on it; and he ordered Judah to serve the LORD God of Israel. Nevertheless the people still sacrificed in the high places, although only to the LORD their God. Now the rest of the acts of Manasseh even his prayer to his God, and the words of the seers who spoke to him in the name of the LORD God of Israel, behold, they are among the records of the kings of Israel.*

In hearing and answering Manasseh's prayer, the Lord showed that He is faithful to His promise (6:21, 24-25; 7:12, 14).  But how did Manasseh meet the conditions that would move God to be gracious to him?  He entreated the Lord.  There was fervency in his prayer.  He also humbled himself (i.e., repented) and confessed his sins. And his prayer moved the hand of God who restored him to his throne.

From a human point of view, Ashurbanipal was probably the one who allowed Manasseh to return to Judah because he wanted to have a loyal vassal looking after his interests in that part of his domain. And this makes it easy for us to overlook the fact that the hand that moved the Assyrian king was the Lord's. He brought Manasseh back. God's graciousness so impressed him that he determined to try and undo all the wrong he had done.

Initially, Manasseh set about rebuilding the wall of Jerusalem that had been broken down.[9] He may have done this at the request of Ashurbanipal who possibly wanted a well-defended city to block any advance by the Egyptians. Manasseh also extended the city so that it offered a better defense to its residents as well as to those who might come into it if a foreign power invaded the land. He also reorganized and strengthened the army. And finally, he sought to purge the land of idols and restored the worship of the Lord in the Temple.

Manasseh's reforms probably took place toward the end of his life. He could command the people of Judah to serve the Lord, but the tentacles of heathenism had become too intimately intertwined in the national psyche to be removed (cf. 14:3; 15:17; 17:6; 20:33). From this time onwards (and allowing for the godly reign of King Josiah [34-35]), it would just be a matter of time before the people of Judah shared in the fate that had overtaken their relatives to the north.

---

[9] See A. Mazar, *Archaeology of the Land of the Bible*, 420-24.

## Conclusion (19-20)

> *His prayer also and how God was
> entreated by him, and all his sin, his unfaithful-
> ness, and the sites on which he built high places
> and erected the Asherim and the carved images,
> before he humbled himself, behold, they are
> written in the records of the seers.  So Manasseh
> slept with his fathers, and they buried him in his
> own house. And Amon his son became king in his
> place.*

This obituary underscores Manasseh's conversion;
reminds readers of his persecution of the prophets; and
records with great brevity his burial.  In spite of
Manasseh's reforms, he was not deemed worthy of a burial
with the other kings, and so was buried in his own house.
Though his prayer is mentioned twice, it is not to be
confused with the composition of some pious Jew in the
inter-testamental period that has been included in the
Apocrypha.[10]

Manasseh was succeeded by his son, Amon.

## AMON, KING OF JUDAH

II Chronicles 33:21-25

---

[10] "The Prayer of Manasseh" was not included in the
Septuagint and is missing from many of the Latin Vulgate editions of
the Apocrypha.  It was included in the Codex Alexandrinus, and is now
found in modern editions of the Apocrypha.  It should not be classified
with the canonical books of the Bible.

Amon's reign (642-640) was very brief.   Though Manasseh tried to undo the evil he had done, his son was a confirmed idolater and gives no evidence of being moved by his father's late conversion.

*Amon was twenty-two years old when he became king, and he reigned two years in Jerusalem.  He did evil in the sight of the LORD as Manasseh his father had done, and Amon sacrificed to all the carved images which his father Manasseh had made, and he served them. Moreover, he did not humble himself before the LORD as his father Manasseh had done, but Amon multiplied guilt.*

*Finally his servants conspired against him and put him to death in his own house.  But the people of the land killed all the conspirators against King Amon, and the people of the land made Josiah his son king in his place.*

Amon was incorrigibly evil and led the people of Judah down a toboggan slide of religious sensuality.[11]   He quickly reversed all of the reforms of his father, and the people of Judah gladly followed him.  Why then did his own staff assassinate him?

The reason is not given us and we are left to speculate about his murder.  We do know that Assyria was beginning to decline as a world power and it is possible that politicians of the pro-Egyptian party did not like Amon's Assyrian loyalties. Wanting to avoid direct conflict with a *"lion"* (*viz.* Assyria) that could still inflict deep and lasting wounds on its victims, it was decided to kill Amon.

---

[11] A. Malamat, *Israel Exploration Journal* 3 (1953), 26-29.

Those who plotted Amon's assassination were themselves killed, and the *"people of the land"* made the young Josiah king in his place.

## TIME FOR REFLECTION

As we have worked our way through this chapter, we have noted several things: The danger of religious pluralism and the accompanying decline of society; the availability of the truth (John 8:28) for all who will seek for it; the failure of generations to learn the lessons of history; and the place of prayer.

One of my duties at Plymouth Church, Whittier, California is to visit the sick in the hospital. One day, I was visiting a ninety-something year-old saint who was very ill. Across the passage from his room was an elderly man who sat on his bed and repeated loudly over and over again "God, I don't want to die. God, I don't want to die."

While I was visiting the member of our church, a nurse came and wheeled him away. When I had finished visiting my elderly friend, I went looking for him. He was nowhere to be found. I was so concerned about him that I went back the next day. This time, I found him sitting as I had seen him before. In much subdued tones, he was repeating over and over, "God, I don't want to die."

I greeted him and asked if I might talk with him. He turned to me with a vacuous expression on his face, then looked away and continued to repeat his mantra. I asked him if he would like me to share with him how he might have peace with God. He dozed off without answering. His sleep was shallow and as soon as he was awake again, I repeated my request. In retrospect, I believe that the hospital staff had heavily sedated him so that he would not disturb the other patients. I tried repeatedly to talk with him, but each time he turned in my direction, he looked at me with the same empty stare. In very simple terms, I explained to him the gospel story. He dozed off again. Each time he awakened, he would go back to repeating the words, "God, I don't want to die," and I would share with him how he could be saved.

Ultimately, I had to leave him. I do not know what belief-system he had followed throughout his life, but most certainly it was insufficient when time came for him to meet his Maker. Following a plurality of beliefs may enable one to excuse their excesses and indulge the flesh, but when death comes, they do not have the hope of eternal life that is available only in and through Christ.

One of the problems of pluralism is that when people are in a crowd and "everyone is doing it," they feel safe. What they fail to realize is that death is a personal experience that each of us must face alone.

Why is there this obsession with a variety of religious beliefs? Our society has cut itself off from the truth and from the lessons of history. Truth, we are told, "is relative and that there's no such thing as absolute truth." And the fact is that other cultures that have thrown off a belief in the Bible have descended into anarchy, a study of the Scriptures has been dropped from their schools and college curricula to make room for courses in Islam, Zen Buddhism, and other popular religions. And so our young people grow up ignorant of the truths that undergird Western civilization.

Of course, in times of adversity, people do tend to turn to God, but which "god" will they believe in? Their theology is confused. Happily some will seek out a theologically conservative, evangelical church or hear the gospel preached on radio or television. Those who respond find that God is gracious (cf. Psalm 145:8-21)! He will hear their prayer and forgive their sin. Blessed are those who follow the Lord with true devotion and make up for lost time by daily studying His Word.

Chapter Eighteen

# AN ATTEMPT TO REVITALIZE THE NATION, Part 1

## II Chronicles 34:1-33

The king was dead. Murdered. No one had liked Amon, and none mourned his sudden demise (33:21-25). Now, however, the nation was in chaos. Was anarchy inevitable or could something be done to insure some semblance of stability?

Once again the people set aside the theocracy[1] and selected a king to sit on the throne. Their choice was Josiah. In this they retained the Davidic succession. Josiah, however, was only eight years old when he became king. Questions in the minds of many were, "What kind of a leader will he be?" "Who will be the real power behind the throne?" "Are the Assyrians likely to install a satrap or governor who will be the *de facto* ruler in Judah?" "If Assyria does not take any overt action, will the influential leaders of the people who appointed Josiah mold him according to their will?" And, "If so, will he be better than his father?"

---

[1] The root idea of the theocracy is God ruling over His creation through His chosen representative who speaks and acts on His behalf.

Under the reigns of Manasseh and Amon, the worship of idols had assumed a prominence never before attained in Judah. These false gods promised prosperity, but this had proved to be an illusive dream (cf. Psalm 115:3-8). Instead of enjoying the freedom these deities promised, the people of Judah had become the vassals of the Assyrians. And now, after two generations of pagan religious practices, many of them did not know right from wrong. All they knew was that they were tired of the sacrificing of their children to the gods and the wholesale murder of anyone who might speak out against the current state of affairs (II Kings 21:16).

Was change possible? What could bring peace and stability to their lives? In the hearts of many, the prospect of a better future seemed little more than a "waking dream."[2]

## OUTLINE

## THE REIGN OF JOSIAH (34:1-33)

*Introduction*: Taking Democratic Action (33:25-34:2)

The Administration of Justice (33:25)

The Choice of a Successor (34:1-2)

---

[2] This was how Aristotle expressed hope for something better. Sophocles once said, "It is hope that maintains most of mankind." See also (I Corinthians 13:13).

### *The Awakening of a Soul (34:3-7)*

> Seeking the Lord (34:3a)
>
> Purging the Land (34:3b-7)

### *Discovering the Book of the Law (34:8-28)*

> Repairing the Temple (34:8-13)
>
> Finding the Scroll (34:14-18)
>
> Recognition of God's Judgment (34:19-28)

### *Renewing the Covenant (34:29-32)*

### *Conclusion (34:33)*

Two chapters are devoted to the life of Josiah. They are dissimilar in content and so will be treated separately. The former has to do with the young king's reforms whereas the latter draws attention to his celebration of the Passover. This was followed by thirteen years of peace.

One of the keys to understanding Josiah's character is to be found in the Chronicler's description of him. From his earliest years, he set his heart to seek the Lord (34:3, 21, 26). In time, he developed a fixed attitude of right and wrong, and as soon as he could, he set about doing what was right in the sight of the Lord.

The Chronicler makes it easy for us to follow Josiah's spiritual growth by tying each new development to his age or the length of his reign (cf. 34:1, 3 [twice], 8).

What is significant is that the Lord was the center of his life.

AN ATTEMPT TO REVITALIZE THE NATION (34:1-33)

## *Introduction (33:25-34:2)*

**The Administration of Justice (33:25)**. The Chronicler precedes his discussion of Josiah's reforms with a brief statement about his father, Amon. He had been a wicked king, and after only two years on the throne he had been assassinated by members of his own staff. The leaders of the people then took matters into their own hands and killed the assassins.

**The Choice of a Successor (34:1-2)**. Amon had given no thought to a successor. In his own mind he probably believed that he had plenty of time to groom one of his sons to take his place. Such an assumption proved to be incorrect (cf. Luke 12:20*a*). He was killed without any warning. Ideally, because Israel was a theocracy, the appointment of a new king should have come at the Lord's direction. Though the leaders of the people may have acted out of the best of motives, the fact that they did not seek the Lord's guidance shows how far they had drifted from His lordship (cf. Daniel 9:6, 10).

Josiah, however, turned out to be a good king. We read:

> *Josiah was eight years old when he became king and he reigned thirty-one years in Jerusalem. He did right in the sight of the LORD, and walked in the ways of his father David and did not turn aside to the right or to the left.*

Verses 1 and 2 form a summary statement. They inform us of the length of his reign (640-609 B.C.) and also bring to the forefront of our thinking the fact that from the very beginning Josiah determined to walk in the Lord's ways. Initially he must have been under the authority of regents who administered affairs of state for him. As he grew older, his relationship with God became the focal point of his life. And though some may have attributed his desire for reform to youthful idealism, the young king never allowed criticism or opposition to turn him from his commitment to the Lord. It is to his credit that he never deviated from what he believed to be right.

Politicians, who specialize in the art of compromise, may have expected that the youthful king would fear antagonizing powerful forces that did not share his desires. But compromise was not in Josiah's vocabulary. He did what was right by adhering unalterably to God's precepts.

### The Awakening of a Soul (34:3-7).

The regent or regents who governed Judah until Josiah was sixteen would have taught the young king the essentials of statecraft. High on their priority list would have been the relationship of Judah to Assyria. They had to pay dearly for Assyria's "protection" and the annual tax left them impoverished.

As we parallel the histories of Assyria and Judah, we find that several years before Josiah's ascension the power of the Assyrian Empire had begun to decline. News did not travel very quickly in those days, and what may have been rumored in the marketplace may not have been reliable. It may have been many months or even years before those in Jerusalem knew that Assyria was gradually

losing its grip on world affairs. But even before the end
came, the Assyrians remained a powerful force in the
ancient Near East. Then, just before Josiah's sixteenth
birthday, Ashurbanipal, the last of Assyria's great leaders,
died (633 B.C.).[3] Ashurbanipal's successors made a show
of strength, but in reality they were weak and a period of
instability followed. Although Josiah was unaware of this,
the weakened state of Assyria gave him the opportunity to
carry out his reforms without Assyrian interference.[4] The
Chronicler writes:

> *In the eighth year of his reign while he was
> still a youth, Josiah began to seek the God of his
> father David; and in the twelfth year he began to
> purge Judah and Jerusalem of the high places, the
> Asherim, the carved images and the molten
> images. They tore down the altars of the Baals in
> his presence, and the incense altars that were high
> above them he chopped down; also the Asherim,
> the carved images and the molten images he broke
> in pieces and ground to powder and scattered it
> on the graves of those who had sacrificed to them.
> Then he burned the bones of the priests on their
> altars and purged Judah and Jerusalem. In the
> cities of Manasseh, Ephraim, Simeon, even as far
> as Naphtali, in their surrounding ruins, he also
> tore down the altars and beat the Asherim and the
> carved images into powder, and chopped down all*

---

[3] Ashurbanipal was followed by a succession of weaker kings,
and in the end, in 612 B.C., Nineveh was overthrown.

[4] F. M. Cross and D. N. Freedman, *Journal of Near Eastern
Studies* 12 (1953), 56-58.

*the incense altars throughout the land of Israel.*
*Then he returned to Jerusalem.*

The full responsibilities of kingship were probably given to Josiah when he turned sixteen, and the weight of the nation resting on his shoulders may have caused him to begin seeking the Lord.  Then when he was twenty, he personally began to supervise the purging of Judah and Jerusalem of all symbols of idolatry.  He destroyed the high places that had been used in pagan worship, tore down the sacrificial altars, smashed the altars of incense, chopped down the groves, hacked in pieces the carved images to the goddess Astarte and ground every idol to dust.  Then before returning to Jerusalem, he exhumed the bones of the pagan priests and burned them on their own altars (34:7; cf. II Kings 23:19-20),[5] and scattered their ashes on the graves of those who had worshipped these false gods.

Such was Josiah's zeal that he extended his purge into the Northern Kingdom and proceeded as far north as Naphtali.[6]  The Chronicler speaks of the *"surrounding ruins,"* and these may refer to the villages of Asher and Dan left desolate after the Assyrians had carried the people into captivity.  The gods of these tribes shared the same fate as those found in Judah.

### Discovering the Book of the Law (34:8-28)

**Repairing the Temple (34:8-13).**  By the time Josiah was twenty-six, his reform movement had been completed except for the repairing of the Temple (622

---

[5] I. Seeligmann, *Vetus Testamentum* 11 (1961), 202.

[6] G. Ogden, *Australian Biblical Review* 26 (1978), 26-34.

B.C.).  As with those before him who had renovated the
House of the Lord, Josiah sought to restore the Temple to
its original beauty and usefulness.

> *Now in the eighteenth year of his reign,*
> *when he had purged the land and the house, he*
> *sent Shaphan the son of Azaliah, and Maaseiah an*
> *official of the city, and Joah the son of Joahaz the*
> *recorder, to repair the house of the LORD his*
> *God.*

> *They came to Hilkiah the high priest and*
> *delivered the money that was brought into the*
> *house of God, which the Levites, the doorkeepers,*
> *had collected from Manasseh and Ephraim, and*
> *from all the remnant of Israel, and from all Judah*
> *and Benjamin and the inhabitants of Jerusalem.*
> *Then they gave it into the hands of the workmen*
> *who had the oversight of the house of the LORD,*
> *and the workmen who were working in the house*
> *of the LORD used it to restore and repair the*
> *house.   They in turn gave it to the carpenters and*
> *to the builders to buy quarried stone and timber*
> *for couplings and to make beams for the houses,*
> *which the kings of Judah had let go to ruin.   The*
> *men did the work faithfully with foremen over*
> *them to supervise: Jahath and Obadiah, the*
> *Levites of the sons of Merari, Zechariah and*
> *Meshullam of the sons of the Kohathites, and the*
> *Levites, all who were skillful with musical*
> *instruments.   They were also over the burden*
> *bearers, and supervised all the workmen from job*
> *to job; and some of the Levites were scribes and*
> *officials and gatekeepers.*

Because of the decadence of the priesthood, Josiah had assumed responsibility for the religious affairs of the nation. He raised money by inviting contributions, and as the funds came in, they were given to workmen who worked faithfully at their assigned duties. And the Levites, who were invariably more righteous than the priests, gave adequate leadership to everything that was being done. They exhibited diversity of spiritual gifts from administrative oversight to record keeping, and from singing the Lord's praises to teaching the people. And they were even involved in the protection of the city.

**Finding the Scroll (34:14-18).** The renovation of the Temple proceeded on schedule for all the craftsmen worked diligently. Then one momentous day, someone found a copy of the Book of the Law. It may have lain in a corner covered with debris from the time of Manasseh, or perhaps it was uncovered when a mason was repairing a section of the wall. This latter option should not surprise us. Whenever there was the threat of an invasion the Jews would hide sacred vessels used in Temple worship or genealogies of their past or sacred documents wherever they thought they would be safe. In such an event, if Jerusalem were sacked, that which was essential to the life of God's people would be preserved. The Chronicler now describes what happened:

> *When they were bringing out the money, which had been brought into the house of the LORD, Hilkiah the priest found the Book of the Law of the LORD given by Moses. Hilkiah responded and said to Shaphan the scribe, "I have found the Book of the Law in the house of the LORD." And Hilkiah gave the book to Shaphan. Then Shaphan brought the book to the king and*

*reported further word to the king, saying,*
*"Everything that was entrusted to your servants*
*they are doing. They have also emptied out the*
*money which was found in the house of the LORD,*
*and have delivered it into the hands of the*
*supervisors and the workmen." Moreover,*
*Shaphan the scribe told the king saying, "Hilkiah*
*the priest gave me a book." And Shaphan read*
*from it in the presence of the king.*

How long the Book of the Law had been "lost" is
not known. What is obvious is the fact that it had been
completely forgotten. On its discovery the scroll was
handed to Hilkiah who in turn gave it to Shaphan, one of
the scribes. This papyrus was recognized as *"The Book of
the Law"* (34:14-15, later referred to as *"The Book of the
Covenant,"* 34:30, and it has traditionally been identified as
the Book of Deuteronomy[7]).

What is surprising is the fact that the religious
hierarchy was more concerned with the progress of the
repairs than with the last written work to come from the
hand of Moses.

Shaphan went to see Josiah to report on progress of
the work. Then, in what seems to us to be an incidental
way, he told the king of the discovery of the scroll. It was
then read in the king's presence. As Josiah listened to the
rehearsal of the blessings and the curses (cf. Deuteronomy
29:20-21, 27), he immediately accepted what he heard as
the Word of the Lord through Moses (34:14). Apparently
the religious leaders remained indifferent, and this is a sad

---

[7] I have discussed the prevailing liberal views in my
commentary on II Kings.

indictment of their spiritual commitments and priorities. On hearing the words of the book, Josiah immediately recognized the danger facing him and his people. In this we see once again an important characteristic of Scripture: Spiritually-minded people immediately recognize as God-given what has been inspired by the Holy Spirit (note II Peter 1:21-2:1; II Timothy 3:16).

### Recognition of God's Judgment (34:19-28).

Josiah was so filled with awe at what he heard (cf. Deuteronomy 30:15-20), that he burst into tears and tore his clothes as a sign of his deep grief. When he recovered his composure, his first thought was how to avert the disaster that threatened his people. He was aware of the history of the kings and knew of other times when the nation had entered into a solemn covenant with the Lord (cf. 29:10; 30:8; 32:26; 33:13). The repentance of the people had been accompanied by a postponement of the judgment, and Josiah hoped that God would do the same again. What happened next is described with commendable brevity.

> *Then the king commanded Hilkiah, Ahikam the son of Shaphan, Abdon the son of Micah, Shaphan the scribe, and Asaiah the king's servant, saying, "Go, inquire of the LORD for me and for those who are left in Israel and in Judah, concerning the words of the book which has been found; for great is the wrath of the LORD which is poured out on us because our fathers have not observed the word of the LORD, to do according to all that is written in this book."*

> *So Hilkiah and those whom the king had told went to Huldah the prophetess, the wife of Shallum, the son of Tokhath, the son of Hasrah, the keeper of the wardrobe (now she lived in*

*Jerusalem in the Second Quarter); and they spoke
to her regarding this.*

*She said to them, "Thus says the LORD,
the God of Israel, 'Tell the man who sent you to
Me, thus says the LORD, "Behold, I am bringing
evil on this place and on its inhabitants, even all
the curses written in the book which they have
read in the presence of the king of Judah.
Because they have forsaken Me and have burned
incense to other gods, that they might provoke Me
to anger with all the works of their hands;
therefore My wrath will be poured out on this
place and it shall not be quenched."'"*

*"But to the king of Judah who sent you to
inquire of the LORD, thus you will say to him,
'Thus says the LORD God of Israel regarding the
words which you have heard, because your heart
was tender and you humbled yourself before God
when you heard His words against this place and
against its inhabitants, and because you humbled
yourself before Me, tore your clothes and wept
before Me, I truly have heard you,' declares the
LORD. 'Behold, I will gather you to your fathers
and you shall be gathered to your grave in peace,
so your eyes will not see all the evil which I will
bring on this place and on its inhabitants.'"*

*And they brought back word to the king.*

Josiah sends a delegation to the *"second quarter"*
where Huldah the prophetess lived.  Their mission is to
inquire of her if the threatened judgment might be delayed
or averted.  Huldah kept the wardrobe (probably containing
the priestly garments that would need to be washed or

replaced due to the blood of the sacrificial animals that would bespatter them). In addition to her regular duties, she has a ministry to the women in Jerusalem, teaching them the Scriptures and leading them in singing (like Miriam, the sister of Moses, and Deborah and Anna).[8]

Huldah's response to the delegation carries the full weight of divine authority. Her words to Josiah's inquiry are two-fold: (1) the captivity of the people is certain, and (2) because the king has humbled himself and wept before the Lord and torn his clothes in anguish, God's punishment will not come during his lifetime.

### Renewing the Covenant (34:29-32).

Josiah believes in God's faithfulness to His Word (cf. 7:14), and as a godly leader who is concerned for his people, he wants to delay his people's punishment for as long as possible. He determines to enter a covenant with the Lord.[9]

*Then the king sent and gathered all the elders of Judah and Jerusalem. The king went up*

---

[8] Unfortunately there have been other supposed prophetesses who, throughout history, have opposed God's Word and sought to thwart His will (cf. Nehemiah 6:14; Revelation 2:20). They took the office upon themselves, and though they gained a certain notoriety, they misled the people.

[9] Many Bible scholars attribute Jeremiah chs. 1-11 to the reign of Josiah. It seems evident that Josiah's purging of the land of idolatry caused the worship of these pagan deities to go underground. Any repentance on the part of the people was superficial and the majority of the people either conformed to Josiah's reforms or were superficial in their beliefs and quickly returned to the old, familiar ways.

*to the house of the LORD and all the men of*
*Judah, the inhabitants of Jerusalem, the priests,*
*the Levites and all the people, from the greatest to*
*the least; and he read in their hearing all the*
*words of the book of the covenant which was*
*found in the house of the LORD.   Then the king*
*stood in his place and made a covenant before the*
*LORD to walk after the LORD, and to keep His*
*commandments and His testimonies and His*
*statutes with all his heart and with all his soul, to*
*perform the words of the covenant written in this*
*book.   Moreover, he made all who were present in*
*Jerusalem and Benjamin to stand with him. So the*
*inhabitants of Jerusalem did according to the*
*covenant of God, the God of their fathers.*

Josiah is not a religious fanatic. He invites to
Jerusalem all the elders and leading men of Judah, together
with the priests and Levites, and all the people (from the
greatest to the least), to attend a solemn assembly so that
they might hear the words of the Law.  Before entering into
a covenant with the God of their fathers, he wanted
everyone to know why this was necessary.  But the people
were unaccustomed to hearing the Word of the Lord.
Being ignorant of its teaching, they do not see the need to
live under its authority.  Jeremiah the prophet, who lived in
Anathoth north of Jerusalem and prophesied during the
reign of Josiah, sensed the people's apathy and indicted
them for their failure to seek the Lord with all their heart.[10]

Certain words indicate that Josiah desired to renew
the covenant God made with His people at Mount Sinai

---

[10] Cf. Jeremiah 3:6-10; 4:22; 5:2, 7*b*-8, 31; 6:10, 13-14; 8:5-6,
9*b*, 12*a*; 9:3, 13, 23-24; et cetera.

(34:31). In leading the people in this act of renewal, the king shows clearly that God's Word is for everyone, not just religious leaders. This is something we tend to forget. Many of us are content to leave the study of Scripture to our pastor or Bible group leader, and seldom study it for ourselves.

The immediate response of the people when they hear the "Book of the Covenant" read to them is a willingness to enter into a covenant with the Lord. Josiah, as a good leader, sets the example, and the people stand indicating their acceptance of the conditions of the covenant.

### Conclusion (34:33)

*Josiah removed all the abominations from all the lands belonging to the sons of Israel, and made all who were present in Israel to serve the LORD their God. Throughout his lifetime they did not turn from following the LORD God of their fathers.*

This verse summarizes Josiah's reform in Judah and in all the lands of the Northern Kingdom. It also indicates that from the time the Book of the Law was discovered (622 B.C.) until his death (609 B.C.), the people conformed outwardly to the teaching of God's Word.[11]

### THE IMPACT OF GOD'S WORD

Though the reading and the study of the Bible are largely neglected today, the story of Josiah—initially

---

[11] J. A. Thompson, *1, 2 Chronicles*, 380.

intended by the Chronicler to encourage the returned exiles—is designed to reveal some important facts.

The ancient roll of Deuteronomy had lain hidden in the rubble that had again, since Hezekiah's cleansing, collected in the holy place. Thus it is that man amid the clutter of his worldliness loses the Word of God. Its provisions nonetheless abide, and *". . . by the Law is the Knowledge of Sin."* Youth found the Law that age had lost. If the book had vanished—discredited, neglected, no longer read and dishonored in the defilement of the holy place—the principal cause, if one man is to be blamed, is that of Manasseh for all his vain seeking, after a misspent half-century, to restore the broken religion. It might well be the prayer of older men and women today, tardily aware of the accelerating rush of a Gadarene society, that youth should recover *"the Law,"* the discipline of faith, the old moralities, the forgotten Savior.[12]

Such is the power of God's Word (cf. Hebrew 4:12) that when it is received with an open mind, it immediately convinces us of our unworthiness, and this is designed to lead us to confess our sins to the Lord and amend our ways. As we turn to God from our sin and pledge in all humility to honor and serve Him, He begins to bless us and fills our hearts with joy and peace that are beyond our ability to describe (I Peter 1:8-9).

The message of the Bible offers hope to all in spite of the work of terrorists and the threat of war. And God's Word is the only reliable source of information giving us His plan of eternal life.

---

[12] Blaiklock, *Today's Handbook of Bible Characters*, 250-51.

## Chapter Nineteen

# AN ATTEMPT TO REVITALIZE THE NATION, Part 2

### II Chronicles 35:1-36:1

What kind of quality support do you think Josiah received from the religious leaders of his day? Do you think they cooperated with him out of necessity or were their actions the result of their convictions? We have good reason to ask about the religious leaders of that day, for whether we like it or not, we lead by example.

It must be admitted that from a material point of view, the priests had long since ceased to derive support from the Temple. Because their homes were some distance from Jerusalem, they sought other means of sustaining their families (e.g. farming). But what of the Levites? Over and over again, we are told that they were more righteous than the priests. Why? Fortunately for the people, the Levites taught them the Word of the Lord and quite possibly derived a slender living in this way. It is likely that, for their own physical welfare, they conducted their ministry in the towns and hamlets far from Jerusalem for, in this way, they escaped the persecutions under Manasseh and Amon. The righteous who remained in Jerusalem were martyred. And perhaps it was the Levites' constant reading and teaching of God's Word that had a purifying effect on their lives.

All this changed when Josiah came to the throne. Though young, Josiah was able to motivate the people and together they purged the entire nation (including the Northern Kingdom) of idols and idolatrous worship. After this, Josiah convened an assembly at which time everyone, both small and great, listened to the Word of the Lord as it was read to them. He then led them in a solemn pledge of themselves to the Lord. But how could he consolidate the gains of the past few weeks? Josiah determined to unite the people with the Lord by celebrating the Passover.

## OUTLINE

We continue our study of the life of Josiah with the closing events of his life.

### THE REIGN OF JOSIAH CONTINUED (35:1-36:1)

#### *The Celebration of the Passover (35:1-19)*

    1.  Preparation (35:1-6)

    2.  Provision (35:7-9)

    3.  Procedure (35:10-15)

Summary (35:16-19)

#### *Invasion of the Land (35:20-25)*

    1.  Warning from a Pagan King (35:20-21)

    2.  Death of King Josiah (35:22-24)

    3.  Lament of Jeremiah (35:25)

Conclusion (35:26-36:1)


## AN ATTEMPT TO REVITALIZE THE NATION, Part 2


### *Celebration of the Passover (35:1-19)*

**Preparation (35:1-6)**.  There were many feasts in Israel.  They began with the Feast of Passover and were held at regular intervals—on the seventh day, the seventh month, the seventh year and the year of Jubilee.  The Passover began the year for God's ancient people.  It had been instituted on the night the Lord delivered them from the might of Pharaoh of Egypt, and it concluded on the day the Lord Jesus was crucified.  His blood took the place of the lamb that had been slaughtered, and it is His blood that to this day covers and protects those who trust in Him.

Other major feasts included Unleavened Bread, First Fruits, Pentecost, Trumpets and the Feast of Tabernacles (or Booths).  Every day began and ended with a lamb being offered up to the Lord.  Other occasions when God's chosen people offered sacrifices to Him were at the new moon, the Day of Atonement, and the Year of Jubilee (to name a few).  We read:

> *Then Josiah celebrated the Passover to the LORD in Jerusalem, and they slaughtered the Passover animals on the fourteenth day of the first month.  He set the priests in their offices and encouraged them in the service of the house of the LORD.  He also said to the Levites **who taught all Israel** and who were holy to the LORD, 'Put the holy Ark in the house which Solomon the son of*

*David king of Israel built; it will be a burden on
your shoulders no longer. Now serve the LORD
your God and His people Israel. Prepare
yourselves by your fathers' households in your
divisions, according to the writing of David king
of Israel and according to the writing of his son
Solomon. Moreover, stand in the holy place
according to the sections of the fathers' households of your brethren the lay people, and
according to the Levites, by division of a father's
household. Now slaughter the Passover animals,
sanctify yourselves and prepare for your brethren
to do according to the word of the LORD by
Moses"* (emphasis added).

Josiah was meticulous in his planning. He followed
to the letter the teaching of Moses, David and Solomon.
The priests and Levites had been exhorted to sanctify
themselves, and everyone stood in his assigned place. Each
person also knew what he was to do. In all his
preparations, we see in Josiah the marks of a good leader.

**Provision (35:7-9).** When all was ready the people
came to offer their sacrifices.

*Josiah contributed to the lay people, to all
who were present, flocks of lambs and young
goats, all for the Passover offerings, numbering
30,000 plus 3,000 bulls; these were from the
king's possessions. His officers also contributed
a freewill offering to the people, the priests and
the Levites. Hilkiah and Zechariah and Jehiel,
the officials of the house of God, gave to the priests
for the Passover offerings 2,600 from the flocks
and 300 bulls. Conaniah also, and Shemaiah and
Nethanel, his brothers, and Hashabiah and Jeiel*

*and Jozabad, the officers of the Levites,*
*contributed to the Levites for the Passover*
*offerings 5,000 from the flocks and 500 bulls.*

Because part of the ceremony required that the people eat the Passover lamb, Josiah insured that no one go hungry. From his own flocks and herds, he set aside 30,000 sheep and 300 bulls; and his officials followed his example by giving the people 2,600 sheep and 300 bulls. The Levites augmented the gifts by providing an additional 5,000 sheep and 500 bulls. Such liberality on the part of the religious and secular leaders occasioned joy in the hearts of the givers, and this spirit of goodwill spread to the people. So many attended the Passover that it continued for an entire week and merged with the Feast of Unleavened Bread (35:17).

**Procedure (35:10-17)**. The Chronicler's use of *"so"* indicates that he is now moving toward a conclusion.

*"So the service was prepared, and the*
*priests stood at their stations and the Levites by*
*their divisions according to the king's command.*
*They slaughtered the Passover animals, and while*
*the priests sprinkled the blood received from their*
*hand, the Levites skinned them. Then they*
*removed the burnt offerings that they might give*
*them to the sections of the fathers' households of*
*the lay people to present to the LORD, as it is*
*written in the book of Moses. They did this also*
*with the bulls. So they roasted the Passover*
*animals on the fire according to the ordinance,*
*and they boiled the holy things in pots, in kettles,*
*in pans, and carried them speedily to all the lay*
*people. Afterwards they prepared for themselves*
*and for the priests, because the priests, the sons of*

*Aaron, were offering the burnt offerings and the
fat until night; therefore the Levites prepared for
themselves and for the priests, the sons of Aaron.
The singers, the sons of Asaph, were also at their
stations according to the command of David,
Asaph, Heman, and Jeduthun the king's seer; and
the gatekeepers at each gate did not have to
depart from their service, because the Levites their
brethren prepared for them.  So all the service of
the LORD was prepared on that day to celebrate
the Passover, and to offer burnt offerings on the
altar of the LORD according to the command of
King Josiah.  Thus the sons of Israel who were
present celebrated the Passover at that time, and
the Feast of Unleavened Bread seven days."*

Because the priests had been tardy in setting
themselves apart for this notable work, the Levites were
pressed into taking over some of their duties, though they
did not sprinkle the blood on the altar.  Dr. J. A. Thompson
describes the situation for us: "For a time the streaming of
celebrants to receive the animals for the ceremony, the
process of slaying and skinning the animals, and the
removal of the portions used as burnt offerings turned the
temple into a vast hive of activity.  All these actions were
dictated by the centralized nature of the celebration.... The
offerings probably included fellowship offerings, the fat
portions of which were burned on the altar (Lev. 3:6-16)."[1]

**Conclusion (35:17-19)**.  Once again, the Chronicler
summarizes for his readers the events of this important
convocation in Jerusalem.

---

[1] Thompson, *1, 2 Chronicles*, 383.

> *"Thus the sons of Israel who were present*
> *celebrated the Passover at that time, and the Feast*
> *of Unleavened Bread seven days.  There had not*
> *been celebrated a Passover like it in Israel since*
> *the days of Samuel the prophet; nor had any of the*
> *kings of Israel celebrated such a Passover as*
> *Josiah did with the priests, the Levites, all Judah*
> *and Israel who were present, and the inhabitants*
> *of Jerusalem.  In the eighteenth year of Josiah's*
> *reign this Passover was celebrated."*

It was a magnificent restoration of the ancient tradition that had been neglected for two entire generations. Not even in Hezekiah's time had so many animals been sacrificed at one time.  The Passover in Josiah's eighteenth year (622 B.C.) was truly a momentous event.

### Invasion of the Land (35:20-24)

For the next thirteen years, God's people enjoy peace and prosperity.  However, as Matthew Henry has observed, these years are passed over in silence because *"the people were not turned from their love of their sins, nor God from the fierceness of His anger."*[2]  Though this may seem like a harsh judgment, it is borne out by Jeremiah in his book (cf. Jeremiah 11:6-13).

**Warning of a Pagan King (35:20-21).** After all that Josiah has done for the Lord and His Temple, there is

---

[2] M. Henry, *Commentary on the Whole Bible*, II:790.

an unexpected invasion of their land.[3]  The Chronicler describes the events for us.

> *Necho king of Egypt came up to make war at Carchemish on the Euphrates, and Josiah went out to engage him.  But Necho sent messengers to him, saying, "What have we to do with each other, O King of Judah?  I am not coming against you today but against the house with which I am at war, and God has ordered me to hurry.  Stop for your own sake from interfering with God who is with me, so that He will not destroy you."*

Some writers believe that Pharaoh Necho transported his men in ships up the Palestinian coast, disembarking south of Mount Carmel.  Whatever he did, Josiah interpreted his actions as hostile and moved to intercept him on the Plain of Megiddo.[4]

For this he is resoundingly condemned.  His critics quote Necho's own words that "God" (or god) had sent him on a mission, and that the king of Judah was not to consider his actions hostile.  But why should Josiah believe the Egyptian monarch?  Trust is based upon a relationship, and there is no evidence that Josiah and Necho had such a relationship.

---

[3] B. Couroyer, *Journal of Near Eastern Studies* 12 (1953), 56-58.

[4] C. Begg, *Vetus Testamentum* 37 (1987), 1-8; S. Frost, *Journal of Biblical Literature* 87 (1968), 369-82; A. Malamat, *Journal of the Ancient Near Eastern Society of Columbia University* 5 (1973), 274; M. Rowton, *Journal of Near Eastern Studies*, 10 (1951), 128-30; H. Williamson, *Vetus Testamentum* 32 (1982), 242-48; idem, *Vetus Testamentum*, 37 (1987), 9-15.

We have no credible evidence that Necho believed in Judah's God or that the true God had revealed Himself to him. Josiah, therefore, was correct in being cautious. Rabshakeh, Sennacherib's spokesman, had claimed that his king was acting on orders from Israel's God, but his words proved as false then as Necho's words lack conviction now. What Josiah's critics overlook is Necho's explanation of how God communicated with him. In ancient Near Eastern literature, pagans were fond of telling how the gods communicated with them (e.g. necromancy, a dream or a vision in the night). Such an explanation carried considerable weight.

It should also be noted that Necho did not ask for permission to pass through the land. The only explanation he offered was when he learned that Josiah was preparing to intercept him. And his words, *"I am not coming against you today . . ."* leave the impression that he may well have planned to invade Judah in the future.

Josiah cannot escape from his detractors. He is rebuked by modern writers for not praying and seeking guidance from the Lord before rushing to the field of battle. This point has some validity. The land, however, belonged to the Lord and an invasion of it required prompt action to repulse those who were trespassing.

Also, the suddenness of the invasion did not give Josiah time to plan his strategy.

When Pharaoh's ambassadors explained to Josiah Necho's intent to aid Assyria against the Chaldeans (or Babylonians), Josiah may have thought this an ideal opportunity to be free of Assyria's suzerainty. If he could prevent the Egyptians from moving northward, the

Assyrians might be defeated and Judah would no longer
have to pay the Assyrians their annual tribute.

**The Death of the King (35:22-24).** Whatever
Josiah's reason(s) for going to war, he gathered his forces
together at the foot of Mount Megiddo. Unfortunately for
him and for Judah, the battle went against them, and in the
clash of forces, Josiah was mortally wounded. He gave his
servants instructions to take him out of the battle. They did
so. Then, placing him in a second chariot, they brought
him to Jerusalem.

All of this brings to mind Huldah's prophecy. She
had assured Josiah that he would be gathered to his people
in peace. There was no mention of him dying a painful
death. Does this imply that God was indifferent to the
suffering of His faithful servant? No. The problem can be
easily resolved. If Josiah, suffering from a loss of blood,
lapsed into a coma, the journey to Jerusalem would have
been painless and he could easily have died without
regaining consciousness. On the other hand, he may have
died on the plain of Megiddo and only been pronounced
dead when his servants arrived in Jerusalem with his body.

Josiah had been a good king, and he was buried
with the utmost respect. In fact, we are told that *"all Judah
and Jerusalem mourned"* for him. It is evident that he was
greatly loved by his people.

### Jeremiah's Lament (35:25)

> *"Then Jeremiah chanted a lament for
> Josiah. And all the male and female singers speak
> about Josiah in their lamentations to this day ...*

*behold, they are also written in the*
*Lamentations."*

Unfortunately, good people are quickly forgotten. Their families remember them for a time, but within a generation or two, the memory of them fades as individuals are caught up in their own pressing concerns. It is comforting for us to know that our God keeps accurate records, and the good we do while we are on earth is not forgotten. It is also important for us to realize that Jeremiah placed his lamentations for Josiah in a book so that they could be used continuously by the choirs of the Jews.

### Conclusion (35:26-36:1)

*"Now the rest of the acts of Josiah and his deeds of devotion as written in the law of the LORD, and his acts, first to last, behold, they are written in the Book of the Kings of Israel and Judah."* The standard by which Josiah governed his life was the Word of God. It was then, and it still is, the one sure source of inspiration and guidance from the cradle to the grave.

*"Then the people of the land took Johoahaz the son of Josiah, and made him king in place of his father in Jerusalem."* They probably did so to insure national stability. As we shall see, Josiah was the only king to be succeeded by three of his own sons and one of his grandsons.

In placing Johoahaz (also known as Shallum, see Jeremiah 22:11) on the throne, the people bypassed his older brothers. The reason for their choice is not mentioned, but they probably expected him to continue

Josiah's political policies (if not his religious ones).  And it may have been a fear of such continuity that caused Pharaoh Necho to remove him from the throne when he returned from Carchemish (36:3).

## GOD'S GRACIOUS INTERVENTION

As an historian, the Chronicler has described Josiah's attempt to revitalize his people.  He has done so with a purpose.  He desired to encourage the people of his day with the evidence of God's blessing that accompanied his reforms.  God was real to Josiah.  The Lord never appeared to him as He had done to others in the past, but from the time Josiah set out to seek the Lord, the Lord became increasingly personal to him.

We do not read of any individual or group who gave Josiah strong support.  It appears as if he had to act alone. However, there may have been many who were glad to see the idols removed, and they may have welcomed a return to God's Word.  Josiah's dedication and perseverance were remarkable, and at no time did he deviate to the right or to the left.   In his death, the people mourned their loss and Jeremiah composed a special eulogy in his honor.

Other writers have similarly composed poetry or music to commemorate the passing of a great person who will be sorely missed.  An example is Longfellow's "A Psalm of Life."

> Tell me not, in mournful numbers,
>
> Life is but an empty dream!—
>
> For the soul is dead that slumbers,
>
> And things are not what they seem.

Life is real!  Life is earnest!
And the grave is not the goal;
Dust thou art, to dust returnest,
Was not spoken of the soul.


Not enjoyment, and not sorrow,
Is our destined end or way;
But to act, that each tomorrow
Finds us farther than today.

....

In the world's broad field of battle,
In the bivouac of Life,
Be not like dumb, driven cattle!
Be a hero in the strife!

....

Lives of great men all remind us
We can make our lives sublime,
And, departing, leave behind us
Footprints on the sands of time.


Footprints, that perhaps another,
Sailing o'er life's solemn main,
A forlorn and shipwrecked brother,
Seeing, shall take heart again.

Let us, then, be up and doing,

With a heart for any fate;

Still achieving, still pursuing,

Learn to labor and to wait.[5]

---

[5] H. W. Longfellow, *The Complete Poetical Works of Longfellow* (Boston: Houghton Mifflin, 1922), 2-3.

Chapter Twenty

# WHEN GOD WITHDRAWS HIS HAND

II Chronicles 36:1-23

The events of September 11, 2001 forever changed our lives. Up to that fateful morning, we in North America prided ourselves on being the most powerful nation in the world. We believed that we were unassailable. While some terrorists might bomb our embassies abroad and blow up a plane or two, we were confident that none would dare to raise a hand against us on our home soil. But we were wrong. When a score of Arabs commandeered four of our airplanes, flew two of them into the twin towers of the World Trade Center, a third into the Pentagon, while a fourth (that was destined for the White House) crashed into a field in Pennsylvania, we suddenly awoke to our vulnerability. And 3,000 innocent civilians and children died.

The premeditated attacks on unsuspecting U.S. citizens were captured on film and flashed into our homes via television. Even then, it took hours for the full horror of what had taken place to sink in. Our leaders promised reprisals, and to the best of their ability, they have fulfilled their word. But the solemn realization each of us must face is, *We are no longer safe*.

The ancient Hebrews labored under a similar illusion. They believed that God would never allow Jerusalem to fall into enemy hands because the Temple was there (Jeremiah 7:4). They might have to strip the Temple of its treasures to buy off an invader, but God was in His Temple[1] and so they were safe. After all, hadn't He delivered His people from the might of Pharaoh (cf. Exodus 12:42; 23:15; Deuteronomy 5:14), decimated the army of Jabin (Judges 4:23-24), slaughtered the Midianites (Judges 8:1-21), and more recently destroyed Sennacherib's army (II Kings 18:13-19:37)? With such a history, the people of Jerusalem felt supremely confident. God would protect them for His Temple's sake.

But they were mistaken. Just as the Tabernacle in Shiloh did not save the city and its people from falling into the hands of the Philistines (Jeremiah 7:12), so now the Temple would not save Jerusalem and those who lived in it from the fierce Babylonians (Jeremiah 7:13-15).

## OUTLINE

Following the tragic death of Josiah, four kings occupy the throne: Joahaz (or as he is better known, Jehoahaz, 609 B.C.), Jehoiakim (609-597 B.C.), Jehoiachin (597 B.C.), and Zedekiah (597-586 B.C.) each reigned over God's people.

In describing each king, the Chronicler's style changes. Though sitting on David's throne, none of them are compared with him. Instead monarchs from other

---

[1] God's presence was evident in the Shekinah and manifested in the pillar of cloud by day and the fire by night.

countries enthrone or dethrone Judah's kings. The right of selecting a new ruler, that had temporarily resided with the people (33:25b; 36:1), is now gone. First Pharaoh Necho, king of Egypt, and then Nebuchadnezzar, king of Babylon, set a member of the royal family on the throne. Gone is Judah's sovereignty. They are now a mere pawn in a game involving the powerful kingdoms of Egypt and Babylon.

### Joahaz (36:1-4)

The death of Josiah must have come as a terrible shock to the people of Judah. He had been a good king, and his people honored him at the time of his burial. Then they appointed Joahaz as his successor. They bypassed Jehoiakim, the heir apparent, and chose instead his younger brother (generally referred to as Jehoahaz). The Chronicler's report is unmistakably brief.

> *"Then the people of the land took Joahaz the son of Josiah, and made him king in place of his father in Jerusalem [609 B.C.]. Joahaz was twenty-three years old when he became king, and he reigned three months in Jerusalem."*

During his brief reign, Pharaoh Necho was engaged in a battle at Carchemish. When he returned, he deposed Joahaz (possibly because he represented the pro-Babylonian party), and made Eliakim his brother king over Judah and Jerusalem, changing his name to Jehoiakim. He also imposed on the people a fine of one hundred talents of silver and one talent of gold. Then he took Joahaz captive to Egypt.

Up till now Judah was still nominally the vassal of Assyria, but there were strong parties in Jerusalem that had begun to favor Egypt while others preferred Babylon.

Jeremiah, who had his finger on the pulse of the people, instructed them not to mourn for Josiah (now dead for only three months), but to mourn for Joahaz, for he would never again see his homeland (Jeremiah 22:10-12).

### *Jehoiakim (36:5-8)*

Jehoiakim was placed on the throne by Pharaoh Necho, and he reigned from 609-597 B.C. The fact that Necho changed his name from Eliakim[2] to Jehoiakim, and imposed a fine on the land, tacitly showed that he had the right (borne of might) to do so.[3]

> *"Jehoiakim was twenty-five years old when he became king, and he reigned eleven years in Jerusalem; and he did evil in the sight of the LORD his God. Nebuchadnezzar king of Babylon came up against him and bound him with bronze chains to take him to Babylon. Nebuchadnezzar also brought some of the articles of the house of the LORD to Babylon and put them in his temple at Babylon. Now the rest of the acts of Jehoiakim and the abominations that he did, and what was*

---

[2] "Eliakim" meant "God will establish." When his name was changed to "Jehoiakim," "Yahweh will establish," the meaning remained essentially the same. Unfortunately he never fulfilled the wishes of his parents.

[3] The silver amounted to 120,000 ounces (3.75 tons or 3.4 metric tons) and the gold to 1,200 ounces (75 pounds or 28 kilograms).

*found against him, behold, they are written in the*
*Book of the Kings of Israel and Judah. And*
*Jehoiachin his son became king in his place."*

For the first few years of his reign, Jehoiakim was
looked upon as the puppet of Egypt. But instead of
building up his nation, he chose to oppress his subjects and
parade his wealth. Recent archaeologists from the Hebrew
University in Jerusalem have uncovered his palace. The
light of history now illumines his malevolent reign. What
appears from these remains is a "Jewish Nero" who
squandered money on himself while his people languished
in poverty.

The prophet Jeremiah denounced Jehoiakim (cf.
Jeremiah 22:13-19) for he used forced labor to build his
palace that was protected by great outer walls, nine to
twelve feet wide, and enclosed a five-acre compound. The
windows of his palace were magnificent. Fragments of
them found among the debris indicate that they were
contained within decorated columns.

Wanting to be rid of servitude to Nebuchadnezzar,
Jehoiakim appealed to Egypt for help, but to no avail.
Egypt promised much, but delivered little. Jeremiah had
warned Jehoiakim of what was going to happen and even
wrote on a papyrus scroll all that the Lord had told him.
Jehoiakim was not amused. He personally destroyed the
Word of the Lord. But the truth could not be dispensed
with so easily. God had Jeremiah rewrite the scroll, and
this time added to it the things that would befall
Jerusalem's king.

In the end, in 605 B.C., Nebuchadnezzar came up
against Jerusalem. He had Jehoiakim killed and his body

dragged through the streets and then thrown outside the city on to the garbage dump (22:19; 36:30).

### Jehoiachin (36:8-10)

No one mourned the death of Jehoiakim. He was given the *"burial of a donkey,"* and Nebuchadnezzar set his son on the throne. *"Jehoiachin was eight[4] years old when he became king, and he reigned three months and ten days in Jerusalem [597 B.C.], and he did evil in the sight of the LORD."*

There must have been rebellion of some sort, for *"at the turn of the year King Nebuchadnezzar sent and brought Jehoiachin to Babylon with the valuable articles of the house of the LORD. And he made his kinsman Zedekiah king over Judah and Jerusalem."* Perhaps the pro-Egyptian party was responsible for bringing to an end Jehoiachin's one hundred-day reign.

Rather than face the same shameful fate as his father, Jehoiachin (called Coniah or Jeconiah by Jeremiah) surrendered to Nebuchadnezzar's representative, and was taken into exile (Jeremiah 22:24-30).

A prophet by the name of Hananiah predicted his soon return (Jeremiah 28:4, 15; cf. 52:31-34), but he was wrong. Hananiah's erroneous prophecy serves to warn us that not everyone who claims to speak in the name of the Lord has been appointed by Him. There are many in our pulpits who claim to be anointed by the Holy Spirit, but are

---

[4] Jehoiachin was probably eighteen at the time of his ascension, a copyist's error being responsible for the discrepancy. It is difficult to imagine an eight-year-old capable of being guilty of the evils attributed to him.

*"false shepherds"* (cf. Matthew 7:15; 24:11; II Peter 2:1; 1 John 4:1). Their ministry should be shunned.

To demonstrate his power, Nebuchadnezzar took treasures from the Temple and placed them in the temple of his god. This was a symbolic act designed to demonstrate the superiority of the deity he worshipped.

### *Zedekiah* (36:11-21)

With the deportation of Jehoiachin, Nebuchadnezzar seated Zedekiah (whose name means "God's righteousness") on the throne. To insure his loyalty, he made him swear by the Lord that he would be a faithful vassal.

> *Zedekiah was twenty-one years old when he became king, and he reigned eleven years in Jerusalem [597-586 B.C.]. He did evil in the sight of the LORD his God; he did not humble himself before Jeremiah the prophet who spoke for the LORD. He also rebelled against King Nebuchadnezzar who had made him swear allegiance by God. But he stiffened his neck and hardened his heart against turning to the LORD God of Israel. Furthermore, all the officials of the priests and the people were very unfaithful following all the abominations of the nations; and they defiled the house of the LORD that He had sanctified in Jerusalem. **The LORD, the God of their fathers, sent word to them again and again by His messengers, because He had compassion on His people and on His dwelling place; but they continually mocked the messengers of God, despised His words and scoffed at His prophets, until the wrath of the LORD arose against His***

*people, until there was no remedy.   Therefore*
*He brought up against them the king of the*
*Chaldeans who slew their young men with the*
*sword in the house of their sanctuary, and had no*
*compassion on young man or virgin, old man or*
*infirm; He gave them all into his hand.   All the*
*articles of the house of God, great and small, and*
*the treasures of the house of the LORD, and the*
*treasures of the king and of his officers, he*
*brought them all to Babylon.   Then they burned*
*the house of God and broke down the wall of*
*Jerusalem, and burned all its fortified buildings*
*with fire and destroyed all its valuable articles.*
*Those who had escaped from the sword he carried*
*away to Babylon; and they were servants to him*
*and to his sons until the rule of the kingdom of*
*Persia, to fulfill the word of the LORD by the*
*mouth of Jeremiah, until the land had enjoyed its*
*sabbaths. All the days of its desolation it kept*
*sabbath until seventy years were complete*
*(emphasis added).*

Zedekiah's attitude is described first (36:12-13),
and then the attitude of the people (36:14-16).  The king is
condemned for his refusal to humble himself before the
Lord and His resistance to the words of Jeremiah.  And the
people are condemned for their increasing unfaithfulness to
the Lord and rejecting the prophets whom He sent to them.
In this, both the king and the people failed to learn from the
past.  They didn't realize that He was giving them one last
chance.

To impress upon Zedekiah and his courtiers the
seriousness of the situation, Nebuchadnezzar made him
take an oath of loyalty in God's name.  Under normal

circumstances, a God-fearing person would realize the weight of responsibility that accompanied such a commitment. Zedekiah did not. Almost immediately, he permitted the reoccupation of the Temple by the abominations that his noble father, Josiah, had expelled. Such was the abandonment of all that was good by the king and the people that Ezekiel, in Babylon, lamented the desecration of the Temple (Ezekiel 8:8-18).

Trust in the gods of the nations and the worship of idols could not save Judah.[5]

Instead of heeding the Lord's messengers, Zedekiah and the people turned a deaf ear to God's messengers preferring to listen to the words of false prophets and to information that came from Edom, Ammon, Moab and Phoenicia urging a coalition with Egypt. Jeremiah warned against rebelling against Nebuchadnezzar, but no one in authority listened. And instead of heeding his warnings, he was accused of treason and thrown into prison.

Interestingly enough, the false prophet Hananiah clothed the conspiracy with lies, and made the actions of the king appear to be in the best interests of the nation. In the course of time, he died (Jeremiah 28:10-17), and two other "prophets" who had similarly lied to the people were burned to death (Jeremiah 29:21-23).

Why were the people so prone to listen to the false prophets and so loathe to listen to the truth? First, they judged those who ministered to them by their appearance, and the false prophets had a more impressive standing than Jeremiah, the much maligned prophet of the Lord. Second,

---

[5] The words of the text remind us of Christ's parable in Mark 12:1-9 (cf. Jeremiah 7:25; 35:14).

they gave attention to those who told them what they wanted to hear. Third, the false prophets had a powerful authority figure backing them up.

> *In the end, in 586 B.C., Nebuchadnezzar attacked Jerusalem, breached the walls and slaughtered the people. The city was then sacked and burned, and everything of value from the Temple and the palace, and the homes of the officials and the people was taken to Babylon as part of the spoils of war (36:17-18).*

Had God forgotten to be gracious? Our society is quick to blame God whenever some misfortune overtakes us. We develop a false confidence in God's goodness that gives us an excuse to continue in our sins, and to forget that God is righteous as well as loving. Centuries before the time of Zedekiah, Moses had acknowledged

> *"The LORD is slow to anger and abundant in lovingkindness, forgiving iniquity and transgression; but He will by no means clear the guilty, visiting the iniquity of the fathers on the children to the third and the fourth generations"* *(Numbers 14:18).*

The people had broken God's laws. Generation after generation (with only a few exceptions) had gone awhoring after other gods (cf. II Kings 24:3). They also turned their backs on His Word. He had said that every seventh year the land was to lie fallow. For 490 years, the people had ignored His command (cf. Leviticus 25:2-4; 25:10-12; 26:34-35). To cure them of their waywardness, the Lord allowed them to be taken to Babylon (cf. Daniel 9:2). But even then, He was gracious to His people. He limited the extent of the exile to seventy years.

## GOD'S GRACIOUS REMEMBRANCE

God is gracious. The Davidic dynasty was still alive. In II Kings 25:27-29, we read that in the thirty-seventh year of the exile of King Jehoiachin, the king of Babylon who had succeeded Nebuchadnezzar released him from prison; and set his throne above the throne of the kings who were with him in Babylon. So Jehoiachin changed his prison clothes and ate his meals in the king's presence for the rest of his life (cf. II Kings 25:27-29).

Second, when Cyrus, king of Persia became king, the Lord moved his heart to set the Jewish people free.

> *"Now in the first year of Cyrus king of Persia—in order to fulfill the word of the LORD by the mouth of Jeremiah—the LORD stirred up the spirit of Cyrus king of Persia, so that he sent a proclamation throughout his kingdom, and also put it in writing, saying, 'Thus says Cyrus king of Persia, The LORD, the God of heaven, has given me all the kingdoms of the earth, and He has appointed me to build Him a house in Jerusalem, which is in Judah. Whoever there is among you of all His people, may the LORD his God be with him, and let him go up!'"*

And so, for those so inclined, the exile came to an end. Whoever wanted to could return to Judah and rebuild the Temple. We know from the book of Ezra that a large number under Zerubbabel did return to Judah.

God is gracious. He punishes sin, but His anger does not last forever. All He desires of us is that we obey His Word and His blessings will be ours.

## THE AUTHOR

Dr. Cyril J. Barber is an associate pastor on the staff of Plymouth Church, Whittier, California. He previously served on the faculties of the Trinity Evangelical Divinity School, Rosemead Graduate School of Psychology, and the Simon Greenleaf University/School of Law (now a part of Trinity International University). Dr. Barber studied at Dallas Seminary (where he crowded four years of graduate study into five), obtained a D.Min. degree from Talbot Theological Seminary/Biola University, and has been awarded two D.Litt. degrees. He has authored more than 30 books and numerous journal articles. Now, semi-retired, he spends his time writing and counseling.